Cylone ~ 632 BCE pg 22

Draco ~ 621 pg 22

Solon 594 pg 22 Aristo - Oligarcy

Pies i

Sons H ? H   Tyranny

A Thenian Constitutional Ref

Politics and Society in Ancient Greece

POLITICS AND SOCIETY IN ANCIENT GREECE

Nicholas F. Jones

Praeger Series on the Ancient World
Bella Vivante, Series Editor

Westport, Connecticut
London

Library of Congress Cataloging-in-Publication Data

Jones, Nicholas F.
  Politics and society in ancient Greece / Nicholas F. Jones.
    p. cm. — (Praeger series on the ancient world, ISSN 1932–1406)
  Includes bibliographical references and index.
    ISBN 978–0–275–98765–7 (alk. paper)
1. Greece—Politics and government—To 146 B.C.   2. Greece—Social conditions—To
146 B.C.   3. Athens (Greece)—Politics and government.   4. Athens (Greece)—Social
conditions.   I. Title.
  JC73.J66 2008
   320.938—dc22   2007040764

British Library Cataloguing in Publication Data is available.

Library of Congress Catalog Card Number: 2007040764
ISBN: 978–0–275–98765–7
ISSN: 1932–1406

First published in 2008

Praeger Publishers, 88 Post Road West, Westport, CT 06881
An imprint of Greenwood Publishing Group, Inc.
www.praeger.com

Printed in the United States of America

The paper used in this book complies with the
Permanent Paper Standard issued by the National
Information Standards Organization (Z39.48–1984).

10 9 8 7 6 5 4 3 2 1

To my twin brother, Chris, with thanks for everything.

Contents

Preface

Ancient Greece is known to the modern world for many things, from the Trojan War, immortalized in Homer's *Iliad,* to the Parthenon on the Acropolis of Athens, to the *Dialogues* of Plato, to the conquests of Alexander the Great. But no such list would be complete without the inclusion of the form of government called democracy, literally "rule by the People." Whether actually the world's first democracy (as popularly believed), we'll never know for sure, but we can trace democracy's creation at Greece's first city, Athens, to a specific historical occasion approximately 2,500 years ago. It is consequently one of the oldest known governments of a major city in human history. Nonetheless, the sheer antiquity of Athens' case is not the only, or even the primary, reason for its interest to us. Among the approximately 1,500 original archaic and classical Greek city-states, it was Athens that dominated through much of antiquity—militarily, economically, and culturally. Thanks to the production (and survival) of abundant source materials (especially written ones), it is Athens that is far and away the best documented and understood. Beyond the Aegean region, Greek civilization occupies a formative position near the origins of the civilization of the West and, indeed—with our increasingly international interconnectedness—of a single unified global civilization. The democracy of Athens without a doubt can make a strong claim on our attention.

Democracy, of course, like any form of government, was a complex, multidimensional institution. The "rule" or "power" built into the word "democracy" (from the ancient Greek *kratos*) is what politics is about, whether one's concern is with meetings of an assembly, trials before popular juries, or campaigning and elections. But a government is also inextricably embedded in a society and is subject to the operation and influence of that society's cultures. Neither one, neither politics nor society, can be studied or understood in isolation from the other. Fortunately, in Athens' case, we are richly blessed with the kinds of explicit and detailed contemporary source materials that make possible a joint investigation of politics and society or, more precisely, politics in its societal setting.

Front and center throughout our investigation will be the basics, the fundamentals—or, to invoke the familiar metaphors, the mechanics, the nuts and bolts. No deeper understanding will be possible unless the reader is first grounded in the particulars of municipal organization, organs of government, processes and procedures, and the actual acts or careers of real flesh-and-blood ancient Greek politicians in their societal settings. To put these same categories in terms of concrete examples: We need to understand the articulation of Athens by town and village; we need to be familiar with the legislature, magistrates, and courts; we need to grasp how decrees were passed, how generals were elected, how trials were conducted; and we need to see all of these institutional arrangements embodied in the lives (private as well as public) of a Theseus, Pericles, or (in faraway Egypt) Queen Cleopatra. Such has been my primary concern in each and every chapter, and in the Appendix I mention some print, digital, and Internet sources to aid my reader in his or her efforts to carry further the investigation of the evidence.

The term "politics," however, above all in this day and age, needs further definition and specification. Chapter 1 among other introductory topics takes up this matter, but, with today's reader in mind, I must mark at the outset a fundamental distinction. Traditionally, we academics have been accustomed to think of politics in terms of the formation and operation of factions and parties, competition for public office, and the wielding of legally sanctioned authority. Such would be a fair characterization of the great preponderance of the existing academic scholarship on ancient Greek and Roman politics, until relatively recently. Yet how many of us who follow current events in today's world would unconditionally endorse such a characterization of "politics"? Isn't politics about paid television ads, sound bytes, photo ops, on-stage appearances with rock stars, eating hot dogs at baseball games, and a full head of hair? That is, isn't politics now predominantly about image-making? About the cultivation of a kind of celebrity status as much as establishing an ideological profile and taking positions on the issues?

Throughout this book, I have kept in mind this distinction—between the politician as ideologically identified power-holder and the politician as celebrity identified by the image created by others or by him- or herself. Theseus, the Founding Father of Athens, helped achieve national hero status by being recast in the image of Hercules and his Twelve Labors. The general Pericles, while studiously underplaying his superficial physical resemblance to the previous century's hated tyrant Pisistratus, incongruously maintained an "Olympian" aristocratic profile despite his sponsorship of a consistently populist agenda. Cleopatra, Macedonian Queen of Egypt, reinvented herself for the occasion as Aphrodite surrounded by Cupids when she floated on a barge up the river Cydnus amid adoring fans—all in a successful effort to humiliate the Roman politician Marc Antony. No doubt about it, the politics so familiar to us in today's world was alive and kicking in ancient Greece more than 2,000 years ago.

No book on ancient Greek politics, least of all one that, like this one, acknowledges its embeddedness in society, can ignore politics and politicians in their dimensions as consciously created images. "Clothes make the man" goes the saying attributed to Mark Twain. If the notion of "clothes" is enlarged so as to embrace the other elements of surface appearance and momentary impression, the saying might, without excessive exaggeration, tell us a lot about what made "the ancient Greek politician." Image can, and does on occasion, become the reality—that is, the thing that makes historical change happen. Perception more often than not trumps the truth. Even when the truth is known (granting that, at the level of significance, it is knowable), it is far from assured that people, in antiquity or today, would prefer it to a wish-fulfilling falsehood. Accordingly, an important part of the ancient historian's task, at least where politics is concerned, is to try to recover the image—as produced by the politicians themselves and, perhaps even more crucially, as received and acted upon by their public.

Images might have the immediate goal of winning an election, promoting a domestic policy, or currying favor abroad, but they also often outlived any such momentary purposes. In the case of Greek antiquity, the *Nachleben* was often the result of deliberate design. From Homer on, Greeks conceptualized "afterlife" (the literal meaning of my German term) as the enduring memory of one's (or a people's) achievements. Besides Homer, the *Histories* of Herodotus are expressly dedicated to rescuing from oblivion the memory of the combatants' achievements in the Persian Wars. Thucydides famously muses that his *History* of the Peloponnesian War will be "a possession for all time," in the phrase's context owing to the cyclical repetition of human events but also reflecting the author's need to preserve the record of what he argues was the greatest of all wars. At Athens in all periods, wealthy politicians who erected inscribed stone monuments commemorating their achievements were obviously, in view of their choice of building materials, thinking long term. The surviving accounts of the life and campaigns of Alexander the Great preserve utterly divergent assessments of the man, among which are clear traces of Alexander's own efforts to create his own "official" (and, of course, favorable) version of his acts. Vanity and a desire to be well thought of by others are impulse that all of us recognize, but with the ancient Greeks there was an additional, deeply running attitudinal factor that sets their case apart from ours. It has long been a commonplace in classical studies to think of the Greeks in terms of a "shame" culture. "Shame" (perhaps not the best word to denote the idea) refers to the need to gain recognition and approval by one's peers (and, as well, by future generations), with the result that prizes and awards, prestige, reputation, and undying fame become the goals of a person's existence. (By contrast, in a "guilt" culture, a sense of one's own inner worth can compensate for the absence of such recognition and approval.) Which is to say, in a "shame" culture, we should expect to find an even more insistent attention to "images"—their creation, dissemination, and enduring popularity.

If enduring popularity was actually something the ancient Greeks wanted, then they succeeded beyond their wildest dreams. By the phrase "classical tradition," however, we mean something more, indeed something much more, than simply the preservation of antiquity in its original form. To suppose that any historical regime could—or should—be permanently frozen as a lifeless museum object is, first of all, to ignore the evolution of traditions within Greek antiquity itself. Literature, architecture, painting and sculpture, films and movies, and not least of all political institutions—all testify to the health of the processes by which Hellenism has reached our own modern world. The processes are healthy because the classical tradition, far from representing a mechanical repetition of the ways of a distant time and place, comprises the acceptance, reworking, and fresh expression of those ways so as to suit, and benefit, our own time and place. Just witness the spate of commercial movies on ancient Greek subjects that helped usher in the American twenty-first century!

Each age, it seems, reinvents the ancient Greeks in the image of itself, in the image of its own needs. This rather hoary platitude bears importantly, finally, on the resolution of the dilemma that besets any such historical investigation. To contextualize or to make relevant? To attempt to understand a Pericles or a Cleopatra solely in terms of their historical settings—geographical, material, technological, societal, cultural, ideological, and so on—is, in the final analysis, to imprison that historical person (or other subject) in its context and to erect a barrier between the past and the investigator's present. To make relevant, however, incurs a quite different danger, since by making Pericles or Cleopatra into a person who can speak to us we may rob our subject of its different-place-and-time authenticity. There is no easy way out of this dilemma. As a classical scholar and historian, I am bound to acknowledge the facts (whether facts about realities or images), but as a teacher I am no less obligated to find educational value in my subject. My reader will doubtless perceive the tension as my discussions tend now toward the one pole, now toward the other, but in the end the deeply running currents of commonality between the ancient Greeks and ourselves will help, I hope, to resolve, or at least mitigate, that tension.

Acknowledgments

Since this book is an introduction to its subject, I have placed considerable emphasis on the fundamentals: definition of terms, matters of method, alternative approaches, and the primary sources of our knowledge. The last mentioned, primary sources, are almost invariably ancient Greek (and occasionally Latin) texts of one kind or another, and within the limits of clear exposition and readability it is on these texts that I have based my discussions. While all translations are my own, I have consulted existing published versions, especially in the Loeb Classical Library and Penguin Classics series, and occasionally have adopted from them without comment an especially felicitous turn of phrase. Where a collection of ancient texts, standard treatment of a particular subject, or widely accepted work of interpretation has achieved the status of primary source, I have cited it by author's name and title either in the body of my discussions or in the Notes or Further Readings. Several of the strands of interpretation that run through the book (such as patronage and rural society and culture) reflect my own research, published in scholarly monographs or books, and these publications, too, I have referenced where appropriate.

One

Politics and Society in Ancient Greece

DEFINING OUR TERMS

The English words "politics" and "society" are already familiar to most of us, so it would be natural for my reader to think that this book is simply about a familiar topic but as applied in the relatively less familiar time and place of ancient Greece. And to a very real extent such an expectation will be borne out in the chapters that follow. After all, it is precisely an interest in our own world, whether the specific subject is politics, society, or something else, that bestows a deeper value and meaning upon the study of a people far removed from us in place and time, as in the case of the ancient Greeks. At the same time, however, it would be a mistake to assume a complete correspondence between today's world and ancient Greece, as the readers of this book will soon realize for themselves. To provide a foundation for the proper appreciation of "politics" and "society" as historians understand them, let us begin by defining our terms.

"Politics," paradoxically, has rather different meanings (or sets of meanings) when applied to ancient Greece and as used today—paradoxically because the origin of the word comes from the ancient Greek. The adjective *politikos* means of or belonging to a *polis,* a city-state, or a *polites,* a citizen of a polis. When that adjective in its plural (and grammatically neuter) form is used as a noun, *ta politika,* the meaning is "the affairs of the polis" (or of its citizens). So, although the Greek phrase was in antiquity sometimes used narrowly, as with the English "politics," with reference to government and governmental activities, it actually possesses a much wider range of references and meanings. An example is the title of the philosopher Aristotle's "The Politics," a comprehensive treatise that treats the business of government, such as elections and the activities of governmental officials, as merely one subject among many (although, to be sure, an important one). Nonetheless, despite the proper root meaning of *ta politika* (and not to mention Aristotle's transcendent authority in such matters), "politics" in this book will refer to more or less the same phenomena in our own experience, namely politicians, campaigns and elections, and official acts, as well as to the less savory and sometimes hidden wheelings and dealings of government.

"Society," by contrast, is derived from the Latin *socius,* meaning something like "associate," "compassion," or "ally," with the abstract collective term *societas* approximating some of the several specific meanings of our "society." In this book, "society" will refer to the sum total of the human population of a polis or city-state in its more or less organized, structured, and often public dimensions. The ancient Greek peoples taken collectively (that is, from all the many city-states) could be termed a nation, but a society is the people, free and unfree, male and female, young and old, of a particular city-state (which, through much of our discussions, will turn out to be Athens, and occasionally Sparta). "Society" may be further defined by contrasting it with a related though fundamentally different term, "culture." Whereas society comprises the organized structure, the classes, groupings, and categories of, say, the people of ancient Athens, it is culture that constitutes the norms, values, or ideals that animate and direct the lives and activities of that society and its components.

"Ancient Greece," finally, needs some attention inasmuch as the meaning of antiquity changes from one part of the world to another, and "Greece" was and is a place of varying extent from one historical period to the next. "Greece," modern Hellas, to take the less complicated, spatial dimension first, now occupies the southern terminus of the Balkan Peninsula, extending east to the Aegean Sea with its northern coast, islands, and in the south the mountainous spine of Crete. But whereas modern Greece is a nation-state, that is, a single sovereign territory occupied by a "nation" of relatively ethnically homogeneous people, ancient "Greece" was actually a collectivity of hundreds of individually sovereign *city*-states united only by a shared past and a common culture (especially language). Ancient Greece did constitute a kind of "nation," but that nation did not correspond to a more or less unified entity until later in antiquity when, first by the Macedonians and then by the Romans, rule was imposed from without. The present nation-state of Hellas did not come into existence until 1829, when independence from the Ottoman Empire was finally achieved after a long struggle. Nor do the territories occupied by the city-states map easily onto the present Aegean region, since, beginning in prehistoric times, the civilization of the homeland base expanded eastward and westwards, from India to Spain, accompanied by penetration into Egypt and along the northern African coast. And later, in the train of the conquests of the Macedonian Alexander the Great, Hellenism was disseminated abroad and worked into the local cultural repertories of much of western Asia.

Chronology, the reckoning of time, is fraught with complexity and controversy, but for present purposes a simplified period-by-period table is fully justified. The one potentially confusing element that cannot be eliminated is that years are counted in reverse throughout antiquity until well into the time of the Roman Empire, when, long after Greece had been incorporated into the Empire as a province, the count begins anew with "A.D. 1." It was to this year that Christians assigned the birth of Jesus, hence *anno domini,* "in the year of the Lord." The designation "B.C." means "before Christ," but modern usage prefers "B.C.E.," "before the common era," while the years from 1 on are designated "C.E.," "common era," in preference to the traditional "A.D." Since, furthermore, no one was recording or calculating years "B.C." until well into the Christian era, it is obvious that many of our dates are the result of equations with numerous previously existing systems of reckoning. Still other dates are the products of estimates by archaeologists and historians in the absence of recorded chronology of any kind and where often the only clues (very crude ones) are provided by largely uncommunicative surviving material remains. And one final refinement: Where a precise year is known, it is often expressed in the form (to take an actual example from the table presented here) 508/7, which means more or less the second half of 508 and the first half of 507 and thus corresponds roughly to our own "fiscal year" (from July 1 to June 30). So much said, here is a table of the periods and approximate or precise years B.C.E. used throughout this book:

Period	Years B.C.E.	Developments/Events
Stone Age	from earliest times	pre-Greek occupants of Greece
Neolithic	6500–3000	agriculture, stock-raising, fixed settlements
Bronze Age	3000–1200	bronze preferred to stone as material
Early Bronze		Greeks enter Greece around 1900 B.C.E.
Middle Bronze		
Late Bronze	1600–1200	Mycenaean era of palaces, Trojan War
	1250–1200	Mycenaean civilization destroyed
Iron Age	1200–end of antiquity	iron preferred to bronze
Dark Age	1100–800	civilization in collapse, no records
	1100	Dorian Greeks enter Greece
	1000	migrations from Greece to Asia Minor
Archaic period	800–500	origins of "classical" Greek civilization
	from 800	city-state develops
	750–500	colonization of Mediterranean seaboard
	632–508/7	government evolves at Athens
Classical period	500–300	highest development of Greek civilization
	508/7	democracy installed at Athens
	490, 480	Persian invasions repulsed by Greeks
	478–404	Empire of Athens
	431–404	Peloponnesian War, Athens vs. Sparta
	404	Athens defeated by Sparta
	404–338	hegemonies of Sparta, Thebes, Macedon
	377–338	second Empire of Athens
	338–323	Alexander the Great's conquests of East
	322	Athens falls to Macedon

Hellenistic period	323–31	dissemination of Greek civilization to East
	323–272	kingdoms of Egypt, Syria, Macedon
	about 200	Rome intervenes in Greece
	146–30	Greece and Macedon fall to Rome
	86	Athens sacked by Roman Sulla

This book, while occasionally looking backward or forward to earlier or later phases of Greek antiquity, will concentrate on the classical period, approximately 500 to 300 B.C.E. There are multiple reasons for such a concentration. Historically, these were the centuries of Greece's greatest expansion and military dominance. The classical age was ushered in by the triumphant defense of Greece against two invasions by the Persians, whose aim was to extend their empire westward, incorporating Greek lands as a tribute-paying province. The subject of the Greek historian Herodotus's *Histories,* this glorious "defense of the West" is believed by some scholars to have invigorated the Greeks, convinced them of their own self-worth, and thereby to have helped lay the groundwork for the great achievements that were to follow. Not to be overlooked or discounted, either, is the presence of favorable material conditions. A mild climate, the presence of good farmland and natural resources (such as silver, marble, and clay), and ready access to the sea all were necessary conditions for the achievements of ancient Greece.

Where Athens is concerned, additional conditions contributed to its classical Golden Age. The fifth-century Empire (precise dates 478–404 B.C.E.) provided the city with the wealth, leisure, and dominant position among Greeks that made for its cultural as well as political, military, and hegemonial ascendancy. No less important is the form of government in place at Athens at this crucially formative time—democracy. Whether the Athenian *dēmokratia* was actually, as often claimed, "the world's first democracy" we will never know for sure, but it is certain that "rule by the People" did serve to set the Athenians free from the culturally as well as politically repressive forms of government that had preceded it. The exact year was 508/7, just two decades in advance of the invasions from Persia and at the outset of the great cultural outpourings we call "classicism." Perhaps, then, it was democracy, over and above the necessary conditions of climate, natural resources, and location, that provided the crucial sufficient condition that allowed for the release and full expression at Athens of the ancient Greek genius.

So the sheer greatness of this one city-state, Athens, is one good reason to make it the focus of our attention. But it is important to keep in mind the many, many other city-states that were to occupy Greek lands throughout antiquity. The recent *Inventory of Archaic and Classical Poleis Greek Poleis*[1] catalogues a grand total of 1,035 city-states—about two-thirds of the estimated actual total of 1,500. By the present author's own conservative estimate, the surviving records of approximately 1,000 (or more!) of the 1,035 city-states in the *Inventory* could not support the kinds of discussions the reader will find in the following chapters. And, of the remainder, only a dozen or so—such as the well-known Sparta, Argos, and Corinth—have ever been the subjects of stand-alone academic studies of "politics and society." Another rough index, again based upon the author's own work, is provided by his study of the internal administrative segmentations (corresponding to counties, townships, boroughs, and the like) of the individual city-states. A thorough search of surviving documents (and other written sources) from all of ancient Greece yielded traces for about 200 city-states. Thus, for only 20 percent or so of the 1,035 known city-states could anything at all be found in surviving written sources regarding this important feature of the "politics and society" of ancient Greece—and in most cases the indications are very fragmentary. Indeed, the record of Athens on this topic far surpasses in quantity and quality of detail that of *all the remaining city-states combined!*

This is but one illustration of the institutions of ancient Athens and of the wealth of information we have about them, in contrast to the scarcity or total absence of such information for all but a few of the other city-states. But, obviously, if we're going to study politics and society in an informed way, we need to have lots of detailed data. We need to know about the organs of government (legislature, magisterial boards, and courts) and the procedures characteristic of their operation. On the politics side, we need to know about public offices, elective or otherwise, and in the case of elective offices something about candidacy, campaigns, and elections. On the society side, we need to know about the family, voluntary associations, career paths for men and women, and occupations, as well as cultural norms of behavior both public and private.

Nor can we rest content with mere institutions, as though an awareness of the actual living people who operated within those institutions were not indispensable to a deeper appreciation of our subject. The ancient Athenians, fortunately, are known to us in considerable number and richness of detail. Another rough index will be helpful. At the beginning of the twentieth century, an exhaustive register of all known Athenian citizens (that is, Athenians who were both male and of adult age) reached about 15,500 individuals. A century later, as I write, a Canadian scholar, John Traill, is nearing the completion of his *Persons of Ancient Athens.*[2] This register comprises people of all conditions—male and female, citizen and noncitizen, free and nonfree—linked significantly to the city from the earliest to Byzantine time. Once completed, the register is projected to reach a grand total of about 100,000 "persons." Many are just names to us, but quite a few are known just as well or better than living practitioners in the politics and society of our own contemporary world. To see how this could be so, and in support of the entire foregoing discussion, let us now turn to an overview of the primary source materials for the politics and society of ancient Athens.

ANCIENT SOURCES

The primary source materials are written, pictorial, or material (i.e., archaeological). For a subject such as "politics and society," which by the definitions of its very terms necessarily involves the perception of much precise detail, intricate processes, and abstract ideas, it is of course the written, textual evidence that occupies our attention. Occasionally, a painted vase or ruinous public building (in both cases, once identified by texts of one kind or another!) provides illustration, example, time and place, or the like. Also, as by now will already be clear to the reader, the written evidence itself embodies limitations owing to multiple factors. Among the 1,035 catalogued city-states, for example, how many ever created in antiquity a significant written record of their "politics and society"? Decrees and laws? Inscriptions of all kinds? Local histories? And, if such a record was created, how much of it has reached us? And is the surviving material sufficiently rich in detail and meanings as to provide answers to the questions posed by this book?

Well, let us begin with the histories, from local (say, the foundation story of one's own city) to universal (say, a comprehensive narrative covering all of Greece from the earliest times to the author's own present), and everything in between. Besides the intact histories to be briefly discussed in a moment, a major publication of the "fragments" of the Greek historians (executed singlehandedly by a single scholar, Felix Jacoby) had reached several large volumes of text, commentary, and notes by the time of the editor's death. The sections encompassing "authors on individual cities and lands" include just over 300 writers, of whom just over 50 wrote on Athens (amounting to about 200 pages, or more than 25 percent of the whole). And these are just the "fragments" (actually, quotations, excerpts, and paraphrases) and do not, of course, include the intact histories of Herodotus, Thucydides, or Xenophon, whose subjects are Athens in very large part. And, as we'll see in just a moment, a similar trend is in evidence when we look at the great surviving fund of inscriptions on stone.

Why, then, the dominance of this one city? Athens was a democracy, while many, many other city-states continued to retain the more restrictive systems (such as aristocracy or oligarchy) inherited from earlier times. And it is precisely the nature of a democracy to record and publish its acts in order to make those acts accessible to large, universally enfranchised citizen-bodies. Athens, too, had from an early date cultivated and produced various genres of literature, including but of course not limited to historiography—a specifically Athenian "national" trait that probably bears some organic relationship to democratic ideology and institutions. Freedom to express oneself politically, that is, seems to contribute to other kinds of expression, including literature; and to the benefit of all subsequent human civilizations, that literature, once committed to writing, has reached us in very substantial part.

Historians

Historiography, the "writing of history," has its origins in the oral poetic traditions that eventually reached their triumphant expression in the *Iliad* and *Odyssey*, ascribed to Homer, the blind bard from the Greek island of

Chios. The story of the Trojan War, and its antecedents and aftermath, is a kind of history, a legend originating in a core of reality and expanded, elaborated, and embellished over the half-millennium between the time of the War itself and the time of Homer's activity. But history, strictly defined, initially, and thereafter down to the classical period and even beyond, represented itself as an antidote to poetry, not so much denying a factual core to the legends as stripping them of fanciful poetic accretions. Thus, the earliest known prose writer (the Greek term is *logographos,* "writer of narratives"), Hecataeus of Miletus (a major city-state on the Greek coast of Asia Minor), is recorded to have written that "I write what seems to me to be true; for the Greeks have many stories which, it appears to me, are absurd"—thereby voicing a skepticism entirely foreign to the poetic impulse and its expression. Several of these prose writers, who flourished in the sixth century B.C.E., are known to us by quotations from their published writings. They concerned themselves with such quotidian matters as travel itineraries (resembling a modern Blue Guide or Fodor), local history (the story of my hometown!), chronology based on lists of priests or kings (much like an American history organized around the terms of the presidents), and the codification and systematization of myths into a form resembling a narrative prehistory. For our purposes, the group of early prose writers we need to know something about is the Atthidographers, "writers about Athens."

Atthidographers

The "writers about Athens" were local historians of the city who were active in the later classical period, from the end of the fifth and into the fourth and third centuries B.C.E. Hellanicus and Cleidemus are regarded as the founders of "Atthidography," and the later practitioners include Androtion, Phanodemus, Demon, and (the most celebrated and best preserved) Philochorus. Favorite subjects included religious cults and festivals, geography, ethnography, and (importantly for our subject) the origins of political institutions. Necessarily, since the overriding goal was to reconstruct the early history of Athens, reliance on mythical traditions could not be avoided, but as the narrative approached the author's own present day, evidence became more factual. Organization, following the example of the early prose writers just discussed, was chronological according to the sequence of kings, later of the chiefs of the boards of executives (the so-called archons eponymous) who served one at a time for a single year and whose name (not a number, as 1492 or 1776 in American history) designated that year for historical purposes. Within a given year, the arrangement was also ruthlessly chronological. Obviously, given such a plan of attack and execution, the larger sweeping themes of modern historical writing could not have been handled successfully. The texts run to more than 130 big pages of Greek in Jacoby's "Fragments." The second edition, now under way, besides an improved text, will add an English translation and updated commentary. (And, incidentally, the author of this book has been entrusted with six of the Atthidographers, including the important Androtion and Philochorus, among a total of 37 writers on the city of Athens allotted to him.)

Herodotus

Herodotus is the author of the intact major narrative in nine books, the *Histories.* Its subject is conventionally "The Persian Wars," that is, the two great invasions of Greece by the Persians in 490 and 480–479 B.C.E., but a more accurate (though clumsy) title might be "The Rise and Fall of Persian Imperialism." Understood in terms of this larger historical process, the two assaults on Greece recounted in the latter books (namely 6–9) represent the "Fall"—a major failed effort at expansion and the consequent retraction of imperial ambitions. Importantly (and with Thucydides in mind), Herodotus neither participated in nor witnessed the events he narrates (he may not even have been born when the battle at Marathon occurred, in 490 B.C.E.) and, following the oral methods embodied in the works of Homer and other poets, he seems to rely on word-of-mouth traditions, what we moderns would call "oral history." Also importantly for this book, Herodotus was not an Athenian; indeed, he never says or implies that he ever visited Athens, though it is quite likely that he did. Rather, the author indicates that he is from Halicarnassus (on the western seaboard of Asia Minor, not far from Homer's island home of Chios), making understandable his evident sympathies with the neighboring Persians (though not with their sacrilegious imperialist ambitions!) and generally cosmopolitan outlook and values. While warfare is his proper subject, Herodotus along the way tells us much about the "politics and society" of Greece, above all in two priceless digressions on Sparta and on Athens under the tyranny of Pisistratus and his sons.

Thucydides

Arguably the greatest of the ancient Greek (and Roman) historians, Thucydides, the author of the intact (though never finished) *Peloponnesian War,* was in important respects the opposite of Herodotus. Thucydides was an Athenian citizen and so far as we know remained so, despite spending his mature years in exile from Athens. Thucydides lived during the times that are his subject, witnessed the War (or at least its more important effects), and, indeed, as he himself informs his reader, actually participated in one of its crucial campaigns. Telling us that he was aware of the War's future significance at the time of its outbreak (in 431 B.C.E.), by 424, seven years in, he had been elected general and in that capacity was placed in charge of a squadron assigned to protect the northern Aegean city Amphipolis. By virtue of its strategic position and access to important war materiel (such as tall timber and precious metals), Amphipolis was of vital importance to Athens in the struggle against Sparta. But, according to the historian's own narrative, the city was captured by the brilliant and innovative Spartan general Brasidas in a surprise raid on a snowy midwinter night (see his biography in chapter 8). Thucydides was recalled to Athens, put on trial, found guilty, and sentenced to exile. For the remainder of the War, he remained abroad but in contact with both sides, thereby (and paralleling Herodotus' access to both Greek and Persian viewpoints by reason of his birth in Asia Minor) acquiring a balanced and objective perspective on his two-sided subject. Again unlike Herodotus, however, Thucydides evidences an interest that is rather narrowly political, strategic, and military, whereas his predecessor had seen his "Persian Wars" in a more broadly cultural setting. But narrowness of coverage is more than made up for in depth of analysis, since Thucydides, by re-creating the public speeches of the Peloponnesian War's principal actors and by providing taut and penetrating reflections of his own on human nature, brings our understanding of "politics and society" (Spartan as well as Athenian) to Greek antiquity's greatest heights.

Xenophon

Xenophon, too, was a citizen of Athens, probably having been born in town during the first year of the Peloponnesian War, hence younger than Thucydides by a generation. As a result of his various involvements in oligarchic antidemocratic politics (among which must be included his close association with the philosopher Socrates), Xenophon went into exile with the successful return of the democracy in the years immediately following the loss of the War to Sparta. Settled on an estate in the Peloponnesus by grateful Spartans, he remained there until Sparta's own fall from international prominence, in 371 B.C.E. Relocating to Corinth, he was eventually pardoned by the Athenians and returned to the city of his birth for the final decade of his life. Among his substantial surviving writings, the *Hellenica* resumes classical Greek history from Thucydides' breaking-off point in 411 B.C.E. Several single-subject monographs record observations or impressions of "politics and society," Athenian and otherwise, from multiple perspectives.

The Philosophers Socrates, Plato, and Aristotle

Socrates, an Athenian citizen, was tried and executed by the Athenians at age 70, in the year 399 B.C.E., on charges of impiety and corrupting the youth of Athens. Although no writing in the name of Socrates survives (and, in any event, conversation seems to have been his preferred mode of communication), Socrates is credited with sustained engagement in the public affairs of Athens. Indeed, it was such engagement that got the philosopher into trouble with his citizen contemporaries—the very contemporaries from whom were to be drawn in part the 500 jurors who years later voted for his condemnation. According to Plato's re-creation of Socrates' speech in his defense at the trial, rather misleadingly called in English the *Apology* (from Greek *apologeisthai*, "to speak in one's defense"), his interlocutors included, besides poets and artisans, the "politicians" (Greek *hoi politikoi*), among them undoubtedly elected officials and other prominent and influential citizens. If we take at face value the words Plato puts in Socrates' mouth, it was the philosopher's regular practice to position himself in the Agora, the public square of the town, and to accost passers-by and cross-examine them with a view to unmasking any false claims to knowledge. Poets, artisans, and the "politicians," it could be granted, did indeed possess specialized knowledge in their respective areas of expertise, but they went wrong, argued Socrates, when on the basis of that genuine specialized knowledge they further supposed knowledge in other matters, especially higher-order matters.

"Politics and society," the subject of this book, were, according to Plato's explicit testimony, certainly one major focus of the philosopher's attention. But it is unlikely that, even if we were fortunate enough to possess actual transcripts of these public, open-air discussions, we would be able to deepen our understanding of either politics or society or their intersection. Socrates was a thoroughgoing skeptic, eager to debunk any pretensions to a deeper understanding of the world. Putting his position in more graphic terms, Socrates says that the god (Apollo) at Delphi told a friend that no person was wiser than Socrates, a typically puzzling "oracle" that the philosopher interpreted as a divine command to confute and expose others' false claims to knowledge. His own knowledge, he concluded, consisted in the realization that he himself at least knew that he knew nothing. This is part of the meaning of Socrates' moral precept that "the unexamined life is not worth living," a principle innocent enough when applied to oneself but apt to give rise to unhappiness, anger, or worse when applied to others. And the fact that Socrates carried out these examinations of others' lives before an audience of onlookers can only have resulted in painful humiliation in this "shame culture," particularly when the victims were persons of high literary, artistic, or political standing in the community.

The famous *Dialogues* of Plato, which have come down to us intact, purport to reproduce the actual conversations between the (by now) elderly Socrates and interlocutors of various ages, statuses, and pursuits. Curiously, Plato never places himself by name in the discussions, thereby giving rise to the unresolvable question whether the ideas expressed by "Socrates" are really the master's or Plato's own. Nor does the Academy, the park-like sanctuary to the north of town and the scene of the scholarch's formal instructional activity, ever provide the setting for a "dialogue," as might be expected. Nonetheless, all the *Dialogues* are placed within a "dramatic" setting of some kind, although some are only scantily sketched and little if any development extends beyond an introductory scene. And these settings, where identifiable, are in every case but one (the last of the *Dialogues*, the voluminous *Laws*), the author's contemporary Athens. Examples are[3]:

1. In and around the Agora: the King's Stoa *(Euthyphro)*, the courtroom of Socrates' trial *(Apology)*, the prison where Socrates was incarcerated and executed *(Crito, Phaedo)*.

2. The house of Agathon, where the celebrated dinner-party of the *Symposium* was held.
3. Exercise or athletic facilities called in Greek *gymnasium* or *palaestra (Gorgias, Laches, Theaetetus, Charmides, Lysis).*

Whatever the specific setting, the general location of all the *Dialogues* is Athens town within the fortification walls. The pattern is consistent with the explicit statement made by "Socrates" in the *Phaedrus* that philosophical activity is by its very nature the business of "the people in the town."[4]

Moreover, complementing these identifiable "real-life" urban venues, which can only have reflected Plato's own (and his Athenian readers') presumable daily experiences, are the biographies of the interlocutors themselves, several of whom are the namesakes of the *Dialogues* in which they participate. Notable examples are:

1. *Alcibiades* (participant in the *Symposium* and eponym of the two spurious *Dialogues* bearing his name). A noble born into wealth, raised in the house of Pericles, a pupil of Socrates, Alcibiades' imperialist political (and military) leadership led eventually to his exile and desertion to Sparta, where his traitorous counsels contributed materially to Athens' defeat. For his biography, see chapter 7.
2. *Charmides.* Uncle of Plato and nephew of Critias (see next entry), this Athenian noble was urged by Socrates to enter politics. Joining Critias and the oligarchs in the revolution that overthrew the democracy in 404 B.C.E., he died in battle the following year when the democrats made their successful return.
3. *Critias.* Born into the noble, propertied family of which Plato was a member, Critias was a friend to Alcibiades (as well as a follower of Socrates). Critias admired the conservative Spartans, and, when Sparta prevailed in the Peloponnesian War, he joined the Thirty Tyrants. With Charmides, he died in the return of the democrats in 403 B.C.E.

Venue and personality combine to suggest something about Plato's take on "politics and society." The symposium with its elevated discourse, the gymnasium or palaestra frequented by the leisured male, the public square with adjacent court and stoa—these were the haunts of an urban elite. And the political profile of that elite as noble, conservative, antidemocratic, and even pro-Spartan is the consistent trend of Plato's choice of philosophical discussants. Now, the content of the *Dialogues* is admittedly rarely addressed explicitly to contemporary ideological debates—much less to actual personalities and events of Plato's Athens—since debate of the issues implies the possibility of departure from the current policies of one's own city. At the most, Plato gives us a utopia, which by its very nature presupposes wholesale dissatisfaction with life as author and reader live and understand it. "Utopia" is a modern Greek-looking word constructed from *ou* (the classical Greek "not" or "no") and *topos* (the classical Greek "place"), hence No Place—an imagined ideal polity. The two best-known major examples are the *Republic* and the *Laws*, but several lesser utopias, such as the famous description of the lost civilization of Atlantis, are embedded in *Dialogues* on nonutopian subjects. Thus, Plato's contributions to the subject-matter of this book are abstract and idealizing. "Politics," for example, is represented by the rule by philosopher-kings in the Fair City of the *Republic* and "society" by that same dialogue's abolition of private property and the conjugal family in favor of the communism of the State. For comment upon the real-world "politics and society" of his classical Athens, we must be content with his characteristically disparaging references to the urban "rabble," to manual laborers, to the port town and its inhabitants—in short, to the principal components of the contemporary democratic regime.

The intellectual dynasty founded by Socrates and continued by Plato reached a third generation in the person of Aristotle, the most distinguished of Plato's disciples. Aristotle, however, unlike his two predecessors, was not an Athenian citizen. A native of Stagira to the north in Macedonia, Aristotle came to Athens at age 17 when he entered Plato's Academy as a student, staying until the master's death 20 years later. Returning again in 335 (after the assassination of King Philip II of Macedon), he remained based in Athens until his own death, in 322 B.C.E. Continuing the tradition of Plato's Academy, Aristotle founded a school of his own, called the Lyceum, which in essentials resembled its predecessor: a sanctuary on the periphery of town, an all-purpose space used for a variety of recreational and educational purposes, and frequented by, among others, leisured Athenians from privileged circumstances. (Still another such "school" was to be founded by the Cynics at the sanctuary of Heracles at Kynosarges.) Perhaps best known as the teacher of King Philip's son, Alexander the Great, Aristotle was extraordinarily productive. Under his name, major path-breaking writings have reached us covering virtually every branch of learning in existence in his day. *Philosophia* means in ancient Greek simply "love of wisdom" and had not yet acquired its far narrower present academic disciplinary meaning. In fact, another Greek word, *polymathia*, "much learning," might better describe the scholarch's unprecedented breadth, perspicacity, and mastery across the intellectual disciplines. Relevant to the present book's concerns are:

1. The *Constitutions*. Aristotle is credited by ancient authority with the production of 158 "Constitutions" (Greek *politeiai*) of the city-states, but only one, the Athenian, has reached us relatively intact (owing to the lucky preservation of a papyrus text first published in 1890). The work falls into two main parts; the first traces the history of the constitution of Athens from the earliest times, and the second describes in detail the arrangements in force during Aristotle's own day.

2. The *Politics*. A general work called *ta politika* would be expected to bear some organic relationship to the same author's *politeiai*, but in fact the *Politics* does not read as an overview, summary, or analysis based on the 158 particular "constitutions." Nor, despite Aristotle's lengthy periods of residence and academic activity in Athens, does the work particularly remind us of that city, even though we have virtually intact the *Constitution of Athens* with which to compare it. Be that as it may, the *Politics* follows a topical plan without significant recognition of geography, much less the individual polis, as a principle of organization. Three preliminary, foundational books concern the family (book 1), the best constitution (2); and the nature of the state (3); the next three, based on real-world politics, treat existing constitutions (4); revolutions (5); and democracy and oligarchy with a supplement on governmental magistracies (6); and the final two books

concern the "best" constitution with respect to environmental conditions (7); and education (8).

3. Ethical writings. The *Nicomachean Ethics* and *Eudaemian Ethics,* as well as other writings, are in whole or part concerned with the nature and especially the goal of "happiness" (Greek *eudaimonia*). Inevitably, these writings impinge upon "politics" in its wider sense and "society" to the extent that any organization of the state and of its people can only reflect judgments on happiness.

Biography and Plutarch's Parallel Lives

Ancient Greek (and Roman) historical narratives normally embody more or less sustained attention to individuals, especially those individuals identified as playing pivotal or decisive roles in the unfolding of events. The classical historians introduced earlier, Herodotus, Thucydides, and Xenophon, all provide good examples, and Xenophon in particular has given us rounded appreciations of Agesilaus (monograph under that name), Cyrus the Great (*Cyropaedia,* "the education of Cyrus"), and Socrates *(Memorabilia).*

Half a millennium later, the scholarly Greek writer Plutarch (about 50–120 C.E.) penned, among other voluminous surviving works, the celebrated *Parallel Lives,* which juxtapose and compare in pairs a selection of famous Greeks and Romans. We have today 23 pairs, 19 with the author's comparison appended. Each life follows a set sequence of topics: family background, upbringing, entrance into public life, greatest achievements, reversals of fortune, twilight of career, and death. Plutarch's purpose is consistently ethical. Rather than concentrating on places, events, or dates, this popular essayist's overriding goal is to isolate the virtues animating the lives of great men. Determining what made an Alexander the Great or a Julius Caesar tick is the objective of this literary genre. True, as a result of Plutarch's far remove from his subjects and his complete lack of personal or firsthand knowledge, the accuracy of his claims has long been contested by scholars. But the overriding moral purpose of the *Parallel Lives*—and a moral purpose worked out in a positive and edifying style—has, from the Renaissance on, bestowed a special importance upon these readable appreciations of our classical forebears. In keeping with this long-standing tradition, it is one of the purposes of the present book to help restore biography to its former place in the business of history by examining the lives of some eminent classical Greek men (and women)—not a few of them Plutarch's subjects—in chapters 7 and 8.

Inscriptions

Writings, the proper subjects of classical philology ("the love of words"), have always, are now, and will always be the primary—and ultimate—sources of the meanings that inform us of the ancient Greek world. Where the present book is concerned, narratives (such as the war chronicles of Herodotus and Thucydides) and biographies (such as the "lives" of a

Xenophon or Plutarch) naturally command center stage. But other types of writing survive, and most important among these are inscriptions on stone. And why "most important"? Most "literary" texts reach us through centuries of hand-copying of manuscripts and, as a result of the inevitable scribal errors, are often only imperfect records of what the authors actually wrote. Papyri, writings on plant material approximating our own modern "paper," owe their survival to the dry climates of the Middle East, but even the earliest are sometimes centuries removed from the original and, again, reveal some of the same errors characteristic of European manuscripts. But inscriptions are originals, or at least only one remove from the original if they are understood to be official copies of a papyrus document. Inscriptions, unless they have been moved (as is usually the case) from their original site to a museum or other location (for use, say, as building material), emanate from the community that produced them. Inscriptions, indeed, were physically produced (the stone cut, the letters incised) by the very people to whom their texts refer or apply. And, yes, stone masons can (and sometimes do) commit errors, but any such errors are original, ancient errors—as opposed to the errors committed centuries later by enthusiastic but ill-informed ancient scholars or by monks, toiling in a Christian monastery and utterly lacking in classical experience or learning.

Inscriptions survive from nearly all corners of the ancient Greek world. Once engraving texts on stone had become established practice, in the late archaic and early classical periods, the production of inscriptions continued unabated down into the later Roman empire and the end of antiquity. Sparta stands out as an exception, for, as is discussed in chapter 3, at an early date the authorities in that city-state reorganized society around militarism and discarded as superfluous distractions such luxuries as fine food, drink, and clothing; the arts in all their forms; and even literacy! Thus, one of the most powerful and successful of all the 1,500 city-states, after the fitful abandoned attempt at conventional Hellenism, produced virtually no inscriptions, public or private, until long after the demise of the bizarre regime so familiar to us from our classical sources. But Sparta, of course, was the exception to the rule. Greek cities of all descriptions produced an epigraphic record, just as all Greek cities produced pottery and other distinctively Mediterranean artifacts. Athens, in particular, is abundantly represented by many, many thousands of texts, but this is a result, as we have already seen, of the workings of an extreme democratic ideology that demanded the publication of the acts of the People. Yet even the most oligarchic of states engraved at least some of their acts on stone slabs as well and placed them in public, accessible locations for all who cared (and were literate) to view and read.

Nearly every imaginable thing that can be committed to writing is represented by a stone inscription somewhere or at some time during Greek antiquity. Poetic epigrams, philosophical creeds, mile markers, and casual graffiti ("John loves Mary") exemplify the extreme range of subject-matter of preserved epigraphic texts. And what use do inscriptions have for our purposes? While almost anything could be made relevant one way or another to "politics and society," our relatively focused approach limits the types that lie behind and inform our discussions of the topic. These are (with Athenian examples as a basis):

Decrees. The democracy at Athens regularly produced *psēphismata* ("decrees") by a two-house "bicameral" procedure not unlike that followed by a modern parliamentary legislature. The lower house, the Council of 500, composed bills on the proposals and votes of its members; and the upper house, the Assembly of the People, acted upon them by voting to accept, accept with modifications, or reject. The official text of the resulting decree was committed to writing on papyrus sheets, and these, under the developed constitution, were deposited in an official archive. Technically, the papyrus original may have been available to visitors to the archive, but the People made accessibility more realistic by normally calling for the decree (or other text) to be inscribed on a stone *stēlē* (Greek for "slab"), which was then usually erected in some public place (such as the Athenian Acropolis). It is these stone stelae, not the perishable papyri, that have survived in large quantity, with the decrees of the Council and Assembly numbering several hundred. All manner of public business was subject to decree, and collectively the decrees constitute the single most important primary contemporary source for the activities of Athenian politicians.

Lists of archons, lesser magistrates, victors in public competitions, and so on. Ordered lists of persons and things were regularly compiled, inscribed, and displayed, often with a purpose relevant to our concerns. Perhaps most important were the registers of annual chief magistrates at Athens called the archons (Greek singular *archōn*, plural *archontes*). The head archon, termed the eponymous, named the year of his service, and, in the absence of a numerical system such as ours that counts forward to (B.C.E.) or backwards from (C.E.) a fixed point (year) in the past, the lists of eponymous archons in order of service provided a system of chronology for the dating of events. Thus, the historian Thucydides used the eponymous archons to date each year of the Peloponnesian War. The recovery of fragments of the list and the partial (though sometimes hotly contested) reassembly of the original sequence have resulted in a valuable tool for our understanding of the chronology, relative and absolute, of Athenian (and Greek) antiquity. Not all lists, however, were chronological. Many were merely honorific or ceremonial, such as the registers of members in the Council of 500, panels of various magistracies, victors in the dramatic competitions in the Dionysian festivals, and so on. All have played vital roles in amplifying and adding specificity to our appreciation of politics and society, especially at Athens.

Calendars. Public life at Athens, as in our own society, featured numerous events or holidays of a cultural, patriotic, and often religious nature. Examples include the Dionysian dramatic competitions just mentioned, the Greater and Lesser Panathenaia festivals honoring the patron goddess Athena, and countless statewide and local village cultic gatherings such as animal sacrifices, ritual feasts, and coming-of-age celebrations. All these events were nominally "religious" in that they were conducted under the auspices of some divinity or divinities that enjoyed official recognition. Calendars, regularly engraved on stone, recorded the schedules, identified personnel and specified their duties, and presented the outlays of public monies to be expended. To the extent that religion, in contrast to our own experience and expectations, was part and parcel of public life, these calendars play a significant role in our understanding of Athens in both its political and, more broadly, its social dimensions.

Honorary monuments and dedications. Ancient Greece never ceased to be a "shame" culture in which honor, reputation, and recognition of one's achievements far outweighed any internal sense of one's identity and goodness (as is true in a "guilt" culture). Accordingly, it was a natural, expected, and not immodest thing for a citizen to advertise his accomplishments in the form of an inscribed stone monument. Accomplishments might include the meritorious holding of an elective political office, distinction in warfare, or victory in the tragedies or comedies at the festival of Dionsyus. When such an honorary monument took the outward form of an act of piety toward a god, it is conventionally called a dedication. Surviving in the hundreds, these texts provide us with welcome information regarding the doings of both the famous and the influential and more ordinary and otherwise unknown folk.

Sepulchral monuments. Gravestones marked the place of burial of people of both genders and all classes, and normally the stone bore an inscription recording a few vital facts about the deceased, such as name, father or husband's name, village of origin or affiliation, and occasionally a bit of personal biography. Besides the accretion to our rosters of citizens and others, the monuments provide vital demographic evidence. For example, when the find-spot of the headstone (hence of residence at time of death) does not agree (as expected) with the village affiliation (the so-called demotic) of the deceased, this is usually taken as an indication of permanent relocation from the village of origin to the place of burial, movement from rural districts to the town being the most common pattern. Demographics of this kind obviously play an important role in any attempt to grasp the politics and society of a city in its spatial, as well as temporal, dimension.

PROSOPOGRAPHY: THE PEOPLE OF ANCIENT GREECE

From the inscriptions, the historians, and other textual sources we learn the names of many thousands of persons at Athens alone, not to mention at the other ancient Greek city-states. Many are just that, names, persons about whom we know nothing other than what an isolated mention can tell us. But quite a few, when all the vast store of material is brought together, emerge as substantial biographies and, in combination with everything else that we know, do much to flesh out what would otherwise be a bare skeleton. "Prosopography" (literally, "the recording of faces") is the technical scholarly term for the study of individual persons in a classical

Greek (or Roman) setting such as represented by ancient Greek politics and society. Prosopographies of ancient Greeks from all regions and city-states have long been available to scholars, and, as it happens, major registers of Athenians are as of this writing approaching final publication (or significant revision).

Athenian Propertied Families, 600–300 b.c., by John K. Davies (Oxford University Press 1971). A new, expanded edition has been announced. By "propertied" is meant membership in the so-called liturgical class, composed of the families known to have produced at least one citizen member eligible to contribute the mandatory public service at one's personal expense called, in Greek, *leitourgia,* "liturgy." The liturgical class was made up of the wealthy or rich of classical Athens. The liturgies themselves are discussed in chapter 2.

Persons of Ancient Athens, by John S. Traill. Replacing a bare catalogue compiled by a German scholar and published around the turn of the twentieth century, Traill's *Persons,* now nearing completion, will in some 20 volumes record thumbnail biographies of all the persons significantly associated with Athens from the earliest through Byzantine times. Including not only citizens (as in most prosopographies) but also women, noncitizen foreigners, slaves, and others, a total of about 100,000 individuals is projected. Besides the name and source references, each entry will add data regarding place of residence, occupation, public offices held or other identifier, relatives, and so on. Marking a qualitative departure from previous registers, *Persons* is online and searchable, with hard-copy volumes accompanying the release of each new installment. Its exhaustive coverage, in combination with its searchability (and other digital features), gives promise that, when it is completed, a new generation of definitive studies of old topics and of studies not yet imagined or feasible on the basis of print materials will eventually follow.

PICTORIALS, ARCHITECTURE, AND SITES

Nontextual sources often illustrate or help us to appreciate better the persons, events, institutions, processes, and ideas that the written word, and only the written word, can and does provide us.

Pictorials embrace painted pottery, sculpture, and architectural decoration. For sources, online and hard copy, the reader may consult the Appendix.

Architecture includes the structures that played various roles in the politics and society of ancient Greece. Examples include, on the "politics" side, the buildings that housed the organs of the democratic government at Athens; and, on the "society" side, the numerous sanctuaries, temples, and altars that were the scenes of the practice of religion. Again, the reader may consult the Appendix for guides to the visual and other sources.

Sites represent, in archaeological terminology, places of settlement or occupation. Where Athens is concerned, sites significantly include some of the 139 villages (as well as the remains of monumental architecture in Athens town itself). Very little remains of the village sites, but some accessible

Internet and print sources, as well as links to some rural landscape images, are given in the Appendix.

CHAPTER PREVIEW

The introduction, chapter 1, has just provided the preliminaries to the study of ancient Greek politics and society. These subjects have value and interest in their own right, but they are preliminary in the sense that they are necessary for understanding "politics and society" on the ground in ancient Greek terms rather than as mere extrapolations from our modern world experience of those phenomena.

Chapter 2, "Politics and the Constitution," looks at Athens both diachronically and synchronically (thereby following the lead of Aristotle's *Constitution of the Athenians,* mentioned earlier in this chapter). Diachronically, we reconstruct the centuries-long transformation from monarchy (the rule by king in the Bronze Age) to the democracy that governed the city during the "classical" era, from about 500 to 300 B.C.E. Synchronically, the democratic constitution is examined with respect to components, operation, and dominant characteristics, with special attention to how the ancient Athenian version of democracy agreed or contrasted with democracies of the modern world, especially the American.

Chapter 3 focuses on Sparta, and here we see how this land-locked Peloponnesian settlement differed in nearly every imaginable way from Athens, and especially over much of the ground covered by "politics and society." Following an introductory acknowledgment of the "mystery" shrouding the city, we trace Sparta's rise to power; examine and attempt to characterize the hybrid classical government; and overview economy, social organization, and educational system. Against this broad historical and institutional background we can then spotlight, by means of citation of the ancient sources, the unconventional, even bizarre, career paths of Spartan men and women.

Next, chapter 4, "Conflict, Trials, and Ostracism," departs from the archaic poet Hesiod's *Works and Days* as an exemplar of conflict and takes up, stage by stage, the process of conflict resolution in classical Athens, culminating in the democracy's highly developed system of courts. The courts themselves are examined with respect to the pool of jurors and juror selection, the trial and its procedures, and differences between Athenian courts and our own. Our findings are then applied to the most celebrated (and notorious) judicial episode in ancient Greek history, the trial of the philosopher Socrates. Ostracism, a uniquely Athenian procedure for exiling Athenians and not, strictly speaking, judicial in nature, rounds out our discussion of conflict resolution.

Chapter 5, "The World of Men," is the first of four chapters designed to show the workings of ancient Greek politics and society in terms of actual people. The lives of all Athenian citizen males observed certain constitutionally or socially mandated "rites of passage," including recognition of legitimate birth, entry into various groups and associations, and assumption of civic obligations such as military service. However, our discussion departs from standard accounts of the subject by drawing attention throughout to the important differences that distinguished life in rural and in urban settings.

Chapter 6, "The World of Women," opens with a comment on the thorny methodological problems peculiar to the study of females in a patriarchal society. We then take up, in parallel with chapter 5, the life course of women of the Athenian citizen class. Discussion of marriage, children, and questions of legitimacy and citizenship sets the stage for an alternately anecdotal and speculative look at "public roles." "Fantasy or reality?" is the question underlying our gallop through Aristophanes' "women" comedies, including the still widely performed "sex-strike" antiwar play *Lysistrata*. The life story of Aspasia, former brothel madam and the extramarital lover of Pericles, Athens' most powerful and celebrated politician, suggests conclusions regarding the fate of the city's more conventional ladies of the citizen class.

Chapters 7, "Some Ancient Greek Politicians," and 8, "Some More Ancient Greek Politicians," continue, with generous excerpts from the ancient primary sources, our examination of the lives of eminent Athenians, Spartans, and other Greek politicians. Inspired, as well as informed, by Plutarch's *Parallel Lives*, perhaps the most widely read and most influential ancient book about the Greeks and Romans in modern times, we place considerable emphasis on moral character as a force in history and draw attention to the difference made by the individual Great Man or Great Woman in the unfolding of classical Greek antiquity.

An Appendix, as already noted, lays out, for use in your library or at your computer, some informative and fascinating archival, reference, and visual resources that will help to flesh out and bring to life "politics and society in ancient Greece."

Two

Politics and the Constitution

Politics in its radical sense of the "affairs of the polis" was by definition concerned with various aspects of the city-state's functioning. The English word "politics" is not nearly so broad in reference (we might use instead an expression such as "civic" or "public affairs"), but even so we recognize many different kinds of "politics" beyond the limited and well-defined matters of running for office, campaigning, elections, and so on. "Academic politics," "office politics," "sexual politics"—the list could be extended indefinitely to include nearly every species of competitive or merely social human endeavor or activity. But in our own experience, it is elections and the political party that seem to be at the core of politics, while the political dimensions of the others are merely derivative, figurative, or metaphorical. So, while keeping in mind this preliminary observation, let us try to get a handle on the "politics" of the classical Greek city-state.

TRANSFORMATION OF THE CONSTITUTION
FROM ARISTOCRACY TO DEMOCRACY

As mentioned in chapter 1, a recent encyclopedia compiled by a team of ancient historians lists a total of just over 1,000 ancient Greek city-states (of an original approximate total of 1,500). But many of these were small settlements no larger than a village or town at best, and, small or large, again, only concerning a tiny percentage of the 1,000 do we have enough information to allow us to reconstruct a phenomenon as complex as "politics." Nor are we alone in our ignorance, for it is questionable whether the ancient Greeks themselves knew much of anything about cities other than their own or a select group of neighbors, allies, or enemies with which they were in significant contact. Take, as an indication of the state of ancient knowledge (or ignorance), the report that the philosopher Aristotle (a citizen of Stagira, in Macedonia, who resided in Athens and headed the school called the Lyceum) compiled a dossier of 158 *Politeiai* or city-state constitutions. Prior to the publication of this compilation, inferentially, little about the subject was known by most ordinary Greeks. At all events, nearly all the 158 have failed to survive for us to read, but from the fragments and one nearly intact example, it is possible to get an impression of the sorts of things Aristotle for one understood as belonging to a "constitution." By a lucky accident, the intact example is Athens, the one city-state that ancient historians are most concerned to learn more about, especially if the source is an authentic writing of the classical period by the hand of a contemporary witness (and resident) such as Aristotle. So, since, in addition to all the other plentiful sources of information about Athens that we have to work with, Aristotle's *Constitution of the Athenians* has reached us, it would be a good idea to look first at politics at Athens in the classical period and especially late in that period, in the time of the great scholarch of the philosophical school in the Lyceum.

When Aristotle (or other member or members) of the Lyceum wrote the Athenian *Constitution*, the government had already undergone three centuries of development. Abstractly put, that development amounted to a steady enlarging of the circle of the enfranchised—of those qualified to participate in constitutional processes. Aristocracy (rule by the *aristoi*, or "best") was followed by oligarchy (rule by the *oligoi*, or few) or timocracy (rule by the wealthy, from *timē* "price" or "value"), followed next by tyranny (rule by a single autocratic *tyrannos*), with tyranny eventually giving way at Athens to democracy (rule by the *dēmos*, or People). This sequence occurs with variations across much of the Greek homeland during the Archaic period, but only at Athens can we flesh out the process in any detail:

Aristocracy

The *aristoi*, locally known at Athens as the Eupatridai ("high born," literally "with good fathers"), ruled in the place of the monarchy of the Mycenaean palace-state. The defining quality of high birth reflects the preeminence of the rule of descent—the fundamental principle that important characteristics are inherited from one's ancestors—which will continue to be recognized even with the rise of democracy centuries later. Institutionally, the aristocrats controlled affairs through domination of the board of archons (who had divvied up the powers of the king) and of a council of elders known as the Areopagus after its meeting place on a low hill near the Acropolis called the "Hill of Ares." The assembly of free Athenians—the adult males of Athens' army—probably voted on matters of war and peace, but the almighty archons (who, upon completion of their term of office, passed into the council of elders for life) were probably drawn exclusively from the Eupatridai.

Oligarchy or Timocracy

The transition from aristocracy to democracy was far from uneventful—indeed, on more than one occasion an outright revolution was attempted or at least in the offing. The first such occasion was the abortive coup d'état in 632 B.C.E. masterminded by Cylon, an Athenian aristocrat. Scoring a victory in the Olympic Games (the event is reported to have been the so-called *diaulos,* an out-and-back sprint equivalent to our 200 meters or 220 yards), our sprinter affords the earliest example in the Western tradition of a person attempting to convert athletic success into political influence. At some point, Cylon also married the daughter of the tyrant of Megara (a nearby city-state on the road to the Peloponnese), thereby providing a similarly early example of a political dynastic marriage. Two Olympiads (or eight years) after his own victory, the Eupatrid, with his father-in-law's army in tow, marched on Athens and seized the Acropolis. However, while Cylon had expected a popular uprising in support of his attempt, instead the people poured in from the countryside and bottled up the rebels on the citadel. The leader (and his brother) luckily managed to escape, and the remaining revolutionaries were lured down by promise of a fair trial. But the Athenian authorities reneged on the agreement, and the Cylonians were put to death as they descended.

Failed though the coup was, it nonetheless illustrates the nonideological and even personal dynamics of the political culture and experience in review throughout this book. A decade or so later, perhaps in 621 B.C.E., another stage in the march toward democracy occurred when Draco, an Athenian of unknown class membership, brought about the first codification and publication of the city's traditional laws. Because the laws before Draco were (compared to later standards) unnaturally harsh and because the codification and publication did nothing to ameliorate their harshness, "draconian" soon became synonymous with cruel (indeed, Draco was reported by ancients to have written his laws in blood). But Draco's work was indisputably progressive in that publication of the laws for the first time did much to remove legal authority from the capricious and arbitrary edicts of aristocrats by fixing the laws in writing and making them potentially accessible to all Athenians.

About a generation still later (the exact date is 594 B.C.E.), substantial and enduring change did finally come about when Solon, the eponymous archon of the year, took decisive action in the face of a serious economic crisis. The immediate and most pressing problem concerned indebtedness. Farmers had fallen behind in paying off their loans and, in a desperate effort to ward off foreclosure on the crop lands, actually took out new loans using themselves, that is, their personal freedom, as collateral. The crisis point was reached when, the farmers having defaulted on these new loans, creditors were selling the debtors—free Athenians just like themselves—into slavery for use outside Athens. Solon, acting as arbiter with dictatorial powers, confronted this intolerable situation by instituting the Shaking Off of Burdens (Greek *seisachtheia*), whereby enslaved Athenians were redeemed at public expense and borrowing on the person of the borrower was made illegal.

The Shaking Off of Burdens was a serious blow to the propertied lenders at Athens, but a more fundamental assault was launched by Solon on the very ideology of the aristocracy. The lawgiver substituted, in place of high birth, annual income as the criterion for eligibility for participation in political processes and offices. Thus, rule by the "best" (aristocracy) was replaced by rule by the "few" (oligarchy) where the few were defined by wealth (timocracy). The four categories of citizens according to annual income (expressed in agricultural produce) were as follows:

Pentakosiomedimnoi ("500 Bushel Men")	500 bushels and up
Hippeis ("Knights" or "Horsemen")	300 bushels and up
Zeugitai ("Two Oxen Men"?)	200 bushels and up
Thetes (landless laborers)	under 200 bushels

Actual examples of the application of the new classifications from this early period are few, but we do know that the Pentakosiomedimnoi were eligible for election to the archonship. This meant that an Athenian who was merely rich but lacking a distinguished family pedigree could challenge the aristocrats' erstwhile monopoly on the board of chief executives. At the other end of the spectrum, and negatively, we know that Thetes were ineligible for all offices. Wealth (measured in terms of annual income), not birth, now reigned supreme as the dominant criterion for determining which classes of Athenians could or could not engage in political life.

Tyranny

Solon's work had addressed the city's problems on a broad front: relief for the indebted, reform of the judicial system (to be discussed in chapter 4), and attention to some underlying economic issues—and it is undeniable that he left Athens in better condition than he had found it. But the classification of citizens by wealth, and the favoring of the more over the less prosperous, had simply replaced rule by one elite with rule by another elite, and for all we know the 500 Bushel Men may have been dominated by the same blue-blood aristocratic families as before. So, while the New Rich (translating French "nouveaux riches") had benefited by gaining access to higher office for the first time, the plight of the far more numerous poorer citizens had failed to be addressed. That they were citizens, as opposed to resident aliens or slaves, probably exacerbated their frustrations, since their in-group status nominally qualified them for privileges not accessible to outsiders. Part of the problem was that Solon's new system ranked Athenians by income—the greater the income, the greater the privileges. But there was another, perhaps equally serious, complication for many of the poor: the geographic situation of their residences and properties (such as they were) in the countryside of Attica, far from the urban power bases of many of the aristocrats and New Rich and from the seat of government in and around the Agora. Thus, it should come as no surprise that the next stage of the power struggles was marked by the emergence of regional factions—or that they were characterized by distinct *political* orientations.

Three such factions are identified in our sources. The People from Beyond the Hills hailed from remotest eastern Attica, where they were not only isolated from the affairs of the town but also suffered from the general impoverishment of the soil of the region. Aristotle called them the "most populist" of the factions, and indeed the fundamental plank of their revolutionary platform was a call for the confiscation and redistribution of Attica's farmlands.

The People of the Shore, who took a more moderate position, were led by a renegade aristocratic clan, the Alcmeonidae, which had been and would continue to be at odds with the dominant blue-blood families. The "shore" in question was the coastal strip south and east of the town, but the Alcmeonidae were well represented in the urban center, as well. While alienated from others of their class, they did not favor the radical agenda of the People from Beyond the Hills either, so Aristotle typified them as moderates.

The People of the Plain, the aforementioned blue bloods, occupied the prime cereal croplands that were the source of their earlier and continuing social and political ascendancy. Having suffered financially in Solon's cancellation of debts, these conservative aristocrats favored a return to conditions that had prevailed prior to the lawgiver's reforms.

Geography is destiny, one might say, since each region seems to have generated a distinctive ideology. At the same time, however, there was a fundamental likeness shared by the factions in that each group was organized around a prominent leader, and the goal of that leader, however different his ideology might have been from that of his rivals, was to establish a personal ascendancy over all of Attica. The situation was not unlike that which prevailed a few centuries later in ancient Rome, where the leaders of the liberal *populares* were no less aristocratic, no less elitist in attitude, no less bent on personal domination than their conservative *optimates* opponents. Not until the emergence of the "new politicians" under the developed democracy will we see anything like grassroots politicians, true "men of the people," and even they will be wealthy, if not old-fashioned, aristocrats. Before that time, politics at the state level meant rivalry between fundamentally similar dynamic and charismatic men of ambition who differed chiefly with respect to the contrasting goals of their followers.

The struggle for ascendancy among these three factions filled a full half-century, beginning with an assault—the first of three—on Athens by the People from Beyond the Hills under the leadership of Pisistratus. According to Herodotus, Pisistratus fooled the Athenians by wounding himself and then, claiming that his enemies had attacked him, requesting a bodyguard from the Assembly. Pisistratus proceeded to use this armed force to seize the Acropolis. But, only a short time later, Pisistratus was expelled by a coalition of the Alcmeonid Megacles of the Shore and Lycurgus of the Plain. Then, when Megacles fell out with Lycurgus, the former cemented a new alliance with Pisistratus by marrying off his daughter to him, with the promise that he would return him to power. The two found a tall country woman, dressed her in armor to look like Athena, put her on a chariot with Pisistratus by her side, and, with a messenger leading the way and announcing that the goddess was bringing Pisistratus back to Athens, succeeded in reestablishing the tyranny! But the second tyranny came to an end when Pisistratus refused to engage in normal sexual relations with his wife, daughter of Megacles. And why? Well, Pisistratus already had grown sons of his own and presumably would have had no desire for a new child (and a grandson of his former rival, no less) with whom they would have had eventually to share power (and inheritance). The production of children was implicit in any ancient Greek marriage, but in a dynastic arrangement like this one a son or daughter would have served to confirm and preserve the political alliance that the marriage had created. Again forced to withdraw from Athens, this time Pisistratus resorted to seeking alliances with non-Athenians both within and outside Greece, and in 546 B.C.E. he invaded Attica and defeated the Athenian force that came out to meet him. From this moment until the year 510, when an alliance of Athenians and Spartans finally expelled the last of Pisistratus's sons, Athens was ruled by a single, unopposed extraconstitutional leader that the Greeks called by the Asian word *tyrannos*—hence our English word "tyrant."

Before we comment on this (to us) derogatory term, what are we to make of the bizarre machinations used by Pisistratus prior to his more conventional (and decisive) resorting to blunt-force military means? What do these machinations have to do with politics? Perhaps the bit about the bodyguard is not so bizarre after all, for it does recall many a palace intrigue such as the coups d'état set in motion more than once at Rome by the Praetorian Guard. Marriage alliances may be outside our own personal experiences, but they were very much a part of politics at all levels of society throughout antiquity. The dynastic marriage is but one manifestation of the essentially personal nature of politics that will be in evidence throughout the succeeding chapters of this book. If such a marriage seems strange to us, it is only because we moderns have sundered the public from the private, placing politics in one and marriage in the other. And Pisistratus's famous chariot ride with "Athena"? Students of Greek mythology might think of the many epiphanies by divinities, often female; in particular, Athena's role as adviser to Odysseus in Homer will have been known to every Greek. So the ruse, even if not persuasive in the case of every educated urban sophisticate, at least had familiar and accepted cultural precedents and could be taken seriously by many people—and thus was far more than the modern "publicity stunt" designed merely to get the public's attention. And it hardly needs pointing out that the modern Western notion that matters of religion should be left out of politics would have struck Athenians of the sixth century B.C.E. as very peculiar indeed.

Tyrannos is a non-Greek title introduced from Lydia, in western Asia Minor. When this loan word first came into currency in order to denote something that previously had not existed in Greece and for which accordingly no Greek word was available, it was at least neutral in connotation, if not universally complimentary. And, in fact, at Athens the "third tyranny" of Pisistratus and his sons proved, until near its end, to be a very popular regime, however autocratic or undemocratic its nature. Constitutionally, little had changed. Existing laws were not disturbed, although the tyrants are reported to have made sure to have at least one of their friends or family members serving in the higher magistracies. In apparent response to the regional fragmentation that had given rise to the factional combat out of which Pisistratus himself had emerged victorious only after years of conflict, the tyrant sought to unify Attica by various means. Monumental temples dedicated to the pan-Greek (as well as pan-Athenian) Zeus and Athena were constructed on the Acropolis, and the great festivals in honor of Dionysus (such as the Rural and City Dionysia) and of Athena (especially the Greater and Lesser Panathenaia), celebrated on a grand scale and open to all Athenians, were instituted or expanded.

At the same time, these efforts at unifying the land and people of Attica were countered by measures to decentralize by bringing about an effective segregation of town and country. Thus, judges were dispatched from the urban center to outlying villages in order to administer justice on the spot and thereby remove the necessity for a trip to the Agora. In this and other matters, Aristotle is explicit on the tyrant's purpose: to prevent country folk from getting involved in the affairs of the town. The virtual detachment of the countryside (whether by deliberate act of urban politicians or not) is a phenomenon in evidence across many aspects of Athenian public life. And why? Again, we are brought back to the corrosive regional fragmentation of the decades that preceded Pisistratus's rise to power. While fragmentation might be temporarily relieved by the corporate acts of the entire Athenian citizen-body—decrees of the Assembly, elections of the higher magistrates, court decisions by large mass juries, and so on—the deep-seated fundamental differences that separated urban from rural, urbane from rustic, were not to be so easily glossed over. Even under the fully developed democracy, as we shall soon see, the walls defining the line between intramural and extramural marked a boundary of fundamental political, social, and cultural significance.

Despite the use of violence (and foreign intervention) to seize power, and despite the maintenance of power through extraconstitutional means (namely the control of military and financial resources), Pisistratus and his sons looked to the greater good of Athens and its people and, presumably on that basis, won their reported wide-ranging popularity. But, if it was so popular, why was the tyranny expelled in favor of *dēmokratia*? Historians have found evidence in reversals of foreign policy, but the immediate cause was domestic, even personal. The story was told in antiquity by Thucydides, later by Aristotle. Following the death of Pisistratus, in 527 B.C.E., rule passed to his sons (the so-called Pisistratidae), among them Hippias, the eldest, and the younger Hipparchus. Much later, in 514, Hipparchus, the story goes, made a sexual approach to another Athenian man, Harmodius, whose own lover at the time was Aristogeiton. (Tyrants, the later hostile tradition reports, customarily extracted sexual favors from their unwilling subjects.) Harmodius rejected Hipparchus's attentions, and the angered Hipparchus responded by publicly insulting Harmodius's sister. In retaliation, Harmodius and Aristogeiton plotted to overthrow the tyranny, selecting as the occasion for the attempt the Panathenaia festival, when the tyrants would be in public view and accessible. But Hippias was tipped off, and the conspirators had to settle for killing Hipparchus. Surviving, Hippias captured and tortured to death the two assassins, then inaugurated a reign of terror that was to last until 510 B.C.E., when the tyrants were finally driven out of Athens.

That final episode resumes the essentially personal nature of this epoch-making power struggle. The Alcmeonidae, led by Clisthenes, now in exile, used their wealth to rebuild the Temple of Apollo at Delphi; in exchange for their generosity, the oracle agreed to say in response to any and all questions that the Spartans should free Athens from tyranny. Accordingly, in short order, the tyrants found themselves trapped on the Acropolis by overwhelming numbers of Athenian revolutionaries and their Lacedaemonian allies. Under most circumstances, however, such a siege was likely to fail if, as was probably the case, adequate provisions and especially fresh water were available to the besieged. But when the tyrants attempted to sneak their children out through the lines, they were captured and held hostage. At last, the Pisistratidae agree to depart from Athens, thus bringing nonconstitutional one-man rule to an end and setting the stage for the next, and climactic, stage in the evolution of the Athenian constitution.

The resulting vacuum of power soon gave way to a final struggle pitting against each other two Athenian aristocrats, the moderate renegade Clisthenes and the archconservative Isagoras. When neither side could be budged, then and only then did Clisthenes, in the words of the historian Herodotus, "take the *dēmos* into his faction"—that is, he enlisted as allies the great mass of non-elite Athenians. Emerging victorious, Clisthenes then had no choice but to enfranchise the supporters who had brought him to power, hence the name of the new regime, *dēmokratia*, "rule by the Demos." Thus, the West's reputed first democracy arose not out of an ideological debate or expression of popular will but out of the taking of hostages and, at the very end, one person's act of desperation to secure his own political survival.

THE DEMOCRATIC CONSTITUTION: COMPONENTS AND OPERATION

Dēmokratia means "rule by the Demos," but how were the purposes implicit in this grand notion to be implemented? In a constitutional environment, ruling means decision making, so what we're in search of are the various processes whereby, with the full institution of the democracy, the People rendered the decisions that were to guide Athens through the next two centuries of free government. To this end, it will be best to break our subject down into three main categories: legislative and deliberative bodies, magistracies, and the courts.

Legislative and Deliberative Bodies

The Athenian democratic legislature was bicameral, that is, it consisted of two houses, the Assembly of the People and the Council of 500. Although both houses had important additional functions, the two cooperated in the formulation and passage of decrees of the People (the English terms "legislature," "legislation," and so on refer, taken literally, not to decrees but to laws, but we can overlooks this distinction for the moment). The Council of 500 created what we would call "bills," which then moved on to the Assembly of the People for passage, modification, or rejection. When passed, the decrees (the Greek term is *psēphismata*, from *psēphoi*, the pebbles once used in voting), abstractly put, directed the magistrates to carry out the People's will as expressed in their texts. (The court system, the third branch of government, served to arbitrate disputes regarding the accumulated laws and decrees that together governed Athens.)

The Assembly of the People

Let us begin with the Assembly. In Greek *ekklēsia,* or "calling out," the Assembly comprised, strictly speaking, all adult Athenian citizens, but in actual practice the all-inclusiveness of the body was only a technicality. The reason for this rather undemocratic observation is simply that the assembly place itself, the sloping surface of a rocky hill near the Agora called the Pnyx, was capable of accommodating only about 6,000 people—a number that by no accident corresponds to the quorum, that is, the minimum number of citizens required in order to do business. But the total citizen-body at all times for which we have information always exceeded 6,000 by far and in fact is never known to have stood at fewer than 21,000 Athenians. A widely accepted estimate for the fifth century prior to the outbreak of the Peloponnesian War is 30,000. Since, further, the Pnyx, like the known venues of all the other organs of democratic government, was situated in the urban center within the relatively small but densely populated space inside the fortification walls, it is highly probable that the minority of Athenians who made up a quorum of 6,000 on any given assembly day was always more or less the same disproportionately urban minority. As in other ways, democratic government and the politics characteristic of its operation were largely the business of the town—a theme to which we shall return again and again.

In the time of Aristotle (late in the fourth century B.C.E.), the Assembly met four times per *prytany,* or 40 times per year. No single meeting exceeded one day in length, and meetings of one-half day were the norm. The agenda of topics might vary considerably, but Aristotle records that specific meetings were designated for the consideration of certain topics (usually of strategic importance, such as the grain supply), which under penalty of law had to be discussed. More than 600 decrees, either quoted in historical texts or inscribed on stone, have reached us in their entirety or in substantial fragments. Of these 600, about half are honorary in nature, about a third deal with military matters or foreign policy, and the remainder are concerned with finances, festivals and cults, judicial matters, and the Assembly's own procedures. Also known are some details of the administration of an Assembly meeting. As the opening of the session neared, officials dragged a rope saturated with red paint through the Agora, so that any citizen it touched might be detected by the telltale color and fined for nonattendance (this procedure is recorded only in a late and not entirely trustworthy source, however, and is in conflict with the otherwise mostly voluntary participation characteristic of the democracy). Barriers were erected behind which non-citizen spectators could view the proceedings. These proceedings consisted largely of speeches, which, since any citizen in attendance was eligible, must occasionally have been very amateurish, although the speakers recorded on inscriptions as speakers are disproportionately citizens known to have been politically active. The presiding official, called the *epistatēs* or foreman, had been selected by lottery from the entire citizen body to serve that one day and that day only; again, this amateur's efforts to manage so enormous and potentially disorderly a gathering must also have generated considerable interest—or amusement! Once a motion had been made, voting was by the casting of voting tokens (the "pebbles" mentioned earlier) or, later, by show of hands. The majority ruled. The specific wording of a carried motion was recorded on papyrus by a secretary, and this, the official original text, was in the later democracy deposited in the public archive, called the Metroon, in the Agora. Eventually, the official text was copied onto a stone stele by a mason, and this formal inscribed monument was erected in or around the civic center. Upon completion of the meeting, the citizens received a substantial payment for their participation as they descended from the Pnyx.

The Council of 500

The Assembly, as we've seen, was a literal "calling out" of the entire citizen body, however severe its de facto seating limitations or bias toward the town. But with the Council we see at least the appearance of an effort to ensure the geographical representation of all of Attica. The membership was constituted by lottery from all 139 demes (the technical constitutional term for Attica's many villages) on the basis of quotas—quotas reflecting the size of the citizen population of each deme at the time of the creation of democracy's deme-system back in the late 500s (nearly two centuries before Aristotle's *Constitution*). The preserved quotas (that is, the number of seats on the Council assigned to individual demes) range between one and at least 16, with a heavy numerical imbalance (since 139 units had to be apportioned over only 500 seats) of tiny demes with only one or two members each. What's more, a new panel of 500 was installed at the beginning of each civil year, while only one (nonconsecutive) repeated tenure was permitted in a person's lifetime. Given an estimated population of 30,000, it is a demographic certainty that a large majority of Athenians sat on the Council at least once. The same trend is exemplified in the body's presiding magistrate—the very *epistatēs* or foreman that we just met presiding over the Assembly; if both the Assembly and Council happened to meet on his day, he was King for a Day at both meetings. In short, the Council was a radically democratic body. Every deme, however tiny, remote or insignificant, was guaranteed at least one seat; the nonrepeat rules necessitated that a large majority of the citizens served once or twice during their lifetimes; and of these, a fair number must have served as foreman for a day, since that position too was subject to a strict nonrepeat restriction.

The bill-making function of the Council was called *probouleusis,* or "advance deliberation," and the bill a *probouleuma.* But while this legislative function is arguably the most consequential aspect of the body's work, there were other important duties, as well. Oversight of financial administration and monitoring of the boards of magistrates are notable among these. Furthermore, since the Council was charged with the official welcome of envoys from abroad, it played a vital role in the conduct of foreign policy. But, when all is said and done, however pivotal and weighty its duties, the Council remained subordinate to the sovereign Assembly of the People.

The Council of the Areopagus

A remnant of the powerful predemocratic council of elders, after the democracy was installed the Areopagus enjoyed largely ceremonial privileges while operating in the shadow of the legislature and courts. The membership continued to consist of former archons, who entered the body upon expiration of their terms and remained Areopagites for life.

Magistracies

The Athenian magistrates (*archai,* plural of *archē,* "rule") were citizens charged with the implementation of the decisions of the People both at home and overseas. In keeping with the classical democracy's opposition to one-man rule in any form, magisterial functions were meted out to boards of 10 (one from each *phyle* or tenth part of the citizen body) or, occasionally, five (one from each of five pairs of *phylai*). No single magistrate unchecked by a colleague existed anywhere in the government; the enforcement of the doctrine of collegiality was absolute. The roles of the boards corresponded, roughly speaking, to the various competencies of the legislature: military, financial, domestic, judicial, and cultic. Not surprisingly, not a few boards were required in order to cover so much ground. Between 40 and 50 can be counted (that is, between 400 and 500 magistrates), to which must be added the *archai* engaged in imperial administration overseas (hence Aristotle's grant total of 700)—quite a large segment of the citizen body when the citizen population is unlikely to have exceeded 30,000 or so. Since the minimum age was set at 30, thereby eliminating the numerous "20-something" Athenians, the percentage of 30-or-older citizens serving at any given time must have been substantial; since a nonrepeat rule was enforced, it is again a demographic certainty that just about every adult male Athenian sat on a board at some time in his life.

Among the many boards were two that deserve special mention. We met the nine archons earlier. Enjoying unrivaled executive power before Clisthenes, the nine continued to be elected (that is, not selected by lottery) under the early democracy, and, since their appointment rested at least in part on qualifications, they remained for a while the dominant magistrates. But, in the epochal year 487 B.C.E., a reform changed the mode of selection to sortition (or, in more familiar terms, a lottery). From this time on, no recorded archon is known to have been an Athenian of distinguished ability or achievement, and their erstwhile leadership position was now filled by another, quite different board that was still subject to election after 487, the 10 generals. Thus, throughout all but the opening decades of its existence, the classical Athenian democracy operated under the leadership of its chief military officials. Since, however, a *stratēgos* had to be elected each year, he was first a politician and only secondly an (amateur) military commander. Furthermore, since alone in the case of the generals, reelection, and consecutive reelection at that, was permitted, it was possible for a popular figure to sustain his leadership position over a lengthy stretch of time. Pericles, perhaps the most charismatic and dynamic *dēmagōgos* Athens was ever to see, owed his ascendancy, institutionally speaking, to his repeated election to the generalship over more than two decades, including 15 annual tenures in consecutive sequence. True, at any given time Pericles was but one of a board of 10, but his political leadership as a speaker in the Assembly and in other essentially political roles went virtually unchallenged.

Courts

Technically *archai*, "magistrates," the jurors who sat on the panels dispensed justice under the classical democracy. For Aristotle, the judiciary, inasmuch as the courts issued final, binding decisions in the name of the People, did much to render the Athenian government as a whole democratic in character. Because the courts, for this reason, played vitally important roles in the city's political life—roles that are moreover extensively documented by authentic texts left by actual litigants—they will be taken up in the next chapter as a subject in their own right.

Elections and Lotteries

With these categories of organs of the democratic government in mind, it will be well to comment on the procedures by which decisions were reached, whether in a vote of the assembly or council, or election, or trial. Simply put, the procedures in use in classical Athens were two: show of hands and balloting. Show of hands (as in our experience, when voters raise a hand and someone tallies or estimates the outcome) was the normal method in the deliberative and legislative bodies. Balloting, with the potential for keeping one's vote secret, was the method normally used in the courts (see chapter 4 for the details of procedure). But the selection of magistrates was perhaps the most problematic—and consequential—of the three kinds of decision making, and it is here that we should concentrate our attention for the moment.

Election, by show of hands of the citizens in Assembly, was the earlier and less egalitarian procedure—less egalitarian because it allowed for the evaluation of candidates on the basis of personal characteristics such as merit, experience, platform, and political influence. At one time, all or most officers of the state were elected, but over time election came to be used only in cases where performance in office was inextricably tied to a candidate's personal abilities or attainments, such as in the case of the higher financial and military posts. Success in an election required an appropriate popularity, and such popularity could in classical Athens, as today, be achieved by any manner of means, such as exemplary experience or track record, effective public speaking, or the enduring respect accorded aristocrats even under the domination of democratic ideology. Two additional factors, however, are receiving emphasis in the present book. Candidates for office could achieve celebrity status by making public appearances in elaborate and expensive clothing, jewelry, fancy hair-dos, and perfume, by scoring victories in the Olympic Games (especially if horses, as with the chariot races, were involved), by hooking a trophy wife (or husband) for one's son or daughter accompanied by widely publicized big dowry and spectacular ceremonies, or simply by spending lavishly on the voting public as holder of a liturgy. My last example shades into my second factor—the operation of patronage. The well-heeled or -placed "patron" candidate could, and did, cultivate the loyalty of a clientele of potential citizen voters. Spending on the public was one such modus operandi, but any kind of gift or favor would do as long as an appropriate feeling of obligation was instilled in the recipients. At election time, the payback for that gift or favor could be called in in the form of votes in favor of the patron's candidacy.

Procedure in elections suited the operation of patronage in more than one way. When voters raised their hands, they could be observed by others keeping check on their loyalty. And the presiding officials themselves might, of course, act in the interests of a more powerful patron. Balloting was used concurrently in the courts, and the specific method described in the sources allowed the juror to keep his vote secret if he wished (see chapter 4 for the details on judicial procedure), but this (to our minds) more democratic mode of operation was not applied in elections. It is easy to guess why. Powerful patrons could not afford to give their clienteles the freedom to accept their largess, then have them turn around and use a secret ballot to vote for some other candidate in an election.

Show of hands and balloting are methods for determining outcomes of votes that represent the will of individual citizens expressing their preferences. But, in the case of the magistracies, a competing mode of selection, reflecting a completely different ideology, was in use from early in the democracy. This was the lottery (or, to cite its Latinate synonym, sortition), whereby, after a number of candidates had been assembled, the winner was selected by some random procedure (such as our drawing straws or pulling tokens from a hat). The underlying assumption seems to be that *all* Athenians were deemed to be qualified for holding the very numerous less-sensitive magisterial positions. The vast majority of the boards of 10 (and five) mentioned earlier were filled by use of the lottery. Because, again, the minimum age for magistrates (among which was the Council of 500, also subject to sortition) was 30 and because (except for the Council) a nonrepeat rule obtained, a large percentage of older Athenians must have found their way into governmental positions by the luck of the draw. What remains unknown is how the lists of candidates were assembled and whether political factors might have operated at this preliminary stage, but even if merit or experience or influence were not entirely eliminated, the sheer numbers of officeholders involved over the whole system ensured the essentially impartial, egalitarian nature of the corps of magistrates in office at any given time.

Besides these variations in the methods and principles underlying selection of decision makers, still another complication requiring comment is place of residence. It is no exaggeration to say that on this imponderable factor depends the very character (and, we moderns might say, legitimacy) of Athens' democratic government. Every citizen had an official deme affiliation, which was indicated by an adjectival modifier called the *dēmotikon*, added to his citizen name. Examples are Alkibiades son of Kleinias of Skambonidai, Kimon son of Miltiades of Lakiadai, and Perikles son of Xanthippos of Kholargos. Since the *dēmotikon* is recorded for thousands of Athenians, it would seem at first glance that we could make some definitive judgments about the geographical representation of the organs of the democratic government. For example, the Council of 500, with its quota system based on the demes, was a supremely representative body in terms of the territorial affiliations of its members. But the inference appears to be without warrant. The *dēmotikon* was both inheritable (that is, a citizen inherited his citizen father's village affiliation) and portable (that is, when a citizen relocated outside the village of his *dēmotikon,* he took his *dēmotikon* with him). Thus, if (as we are pretty sure we know was the case) there was substantial movement over time from the rural demes to the six (of 139) demes located within the fortifications defining the urban center, the actual places of residence of the 500 Athenians sitting on the Council at any given time may have been disproportionately urban. Similar doubts arise concerning the residences of the many boards of 10, including, above all, the 10 generals. The 10 members of a board regularly represented the 10 territorial divisions of Attica (called in Greek *phylai* or "tribes"), but no known rule precluded the possibility that all 10 actually resided in or near the urban center. Was the democracy in fact, as seems to have been the case, therefore dominated by the town?

Whatever procedure of selection was employed, the new magistrate was subjected to a preliminary examination and, upon entry into office, took an oath binding him to act in accordance with the laws. With the completion of his term of office, the magistrate was subjected to an audit as a protection against graft of public monies or other malfeasance. Vigilance was clearly a necessity. After all, most of these citizens were pure amateurs, and, even assuming their essential honesty, the likelihood of an irregularity of some kind must have been very real. Later on, under the democracy, expertise came to be more highly valued, but, as the modern experience illustrates all too clearly, even experts can make mistakes—and even experts are subject to the temptations of influence peddling.

DOMINANT CHARACTERISTICS OF THE DEMOCRACY

We have just described the Athenian democracy—the organs of government, some of the more important procedures, with hints of a typical citizen's participation during the course of a year and over a lifetime. We now need to get an idea of the character, the flavor, of the Athenian *dēmokratia*, especially in contrast with our experience of democracy in the twenty-first century.

Does the Democracy Treat Us All as Equals?
Or Does It Favor Some People over Others?

Egalitarianism, the ideology that (as the American Declaration of Independence puts it) we are all "created equal," is very much a part of the contemporary political experience. Only a few minimal qualifications have to be met for any American citizen to vote, serve as a juror in the courts, or run for elective office. Age, registration for voting, absence of felony conviction, and (in the case of the presidency) birth in the United States are among the more familiar of these. What about ancient Athens?

As we have already seen, only adult male Athenians who were the legitimate offspring of lawfully married Athenian parents were eligible for citizenship. And on possession of the citizenship depended all facets of participation in democratic processes, from voting in the Assembly, to sitting on a judicial panel, to appointment by lottery to a magisterial board, to seeking election to a higher military or political office such as the generalship. Thereby were excluded all women, minors under the age of 20 or so (the age at which most Athenians were admitted to the citizen body), foreigners (whether or not registered as resident aliens), and slaves. Exact numbers and percentages elude us, but it is likely that no more than 25 percent of the entire adult population of Attica enjoyed the franchise. This seems like a rather small fraction for a form of government going by the name "democracy," but we might compare the reported levels of voter participation in the United States with its universal (adult) eligibility. While absence of qualifications and voluntary nonparticipation are, to be sure, two very different things, we have in the Athenian and American cases two contrasting illustrations of how a democracy may remain stable even when only a small minority is actively engaged in its functioning.

Within the narrow circle of the enfranchised, however, the ancient Athenian commitment to egalitarianism is very much in evidence. Upon entry into the Demos, all were qualified for participation in Assembly and Courts (as well as ostracism). For the Council of 500, the magistrates, and the higher elective offices, a minimum age of 30 was imposed, which by our standards seems high when measured against the much lower life expectancies of antiquity. Why 30?—especially in view of the fact that by eliminating all citizens in their twenties, high-participation bodies (such as the Council and the courts) were unnecessarily deprived of a very large percentage of their pools of potential members? Was it the perception of a need for greater maturity? Greeks certainly held in great esteem the wisdom acquired by experience, but another answer is suggested by thresholds of eligibility that obtained concurrently in the Athenian social organization. Men normally married for the first time at age 30. And it was at age 30 that a citizen might expect to inherit his father's property if the latter, now age 60, died or voluntarily retired from leadership of the household. Thus, the "politics" and "society" of this book's title may have been in close synchronization. Maturity at home, to put the point more concretely, meant that a man was ready to be a mature member of the larger household of the state.

Do I Have to Be Educated in Order to Participate in Government? In Elections?

One of the often stated purposes of mandatory education in the twenty-first century is to prepare citizens for roles in public life, including (but of course not limited to) voting in elections. Campaigning candidates often make important presentations before academic audiences, and television viewers of such presentations are expected not to find unusual or objectionable the implicit link between politics and high learning. The great majority of elected or appointed officeholders in the United States are educated, often with college or professional degrees. But what about Athens? Under the developed democracy, the ability to speak effectively before Assembly, Council, or jury was certainly a valuable asset, and the many texts of such speeches that have come down to us suggest a high level of competence indeed—something more than the intelligent but untutored extemporaneous remarks of a charismatic personality. The skills in question fall under the discipline of rhetoric, the art of persuasive speech, but there is no reason to think that the study of history or of what we would call civics or political science played any role in an aspiring public speaker's preparations. The object was to persuade, to win over, and only secondarily to inform. As for the listeners (and viewers) themselves, the classicist who reads the oratorical texts in the original Greek can hardly escape the conclusion that they too must have needed some formal education in order to fully comprehend these often elaborate, even wordy, rhetorical flights of eloquence.

At a more mundane level, the written word was a conspicuous landmark on the democratic landscape: on the inscribed bronze identification plates carried by citizens, on the frequent notices or announcements painted onto whitewashed boards displayed in public venues, and on the innumerable inscribed monuments and stelae, especially those bearing crucial texts such as the laws of the state or decrees passed by the legislature. Granting that the extent and degree of ancient literacy has long been a topic of scholarly debate, it seems inescapable that appreciable numbers of citizens could read or at least comprehend aurally formally elevated language. Arguing against such an inference is the general absence of the preconditions of mass literacy (such as a compulsory public educational system), of the availability of texts to large numbers of citizens, and, perhaps most important, of generally accepted cultural ideals promoting literacy. There is also some nagging anecdotal material to be accounted for, such as the famous story concerning the politician Aristides the Just told by the late biographer Plutarch. On the occasion of an ostracism procedure in the Agora, the general was approached by a rustic who, failing to recognize the famous man, asked him to inscribe upon the *ostrakon* the name of Aristides. When asked why he wanted to ostracize Aristides, the rustic answered that he was tired of hearing him called "the Just," at which Aristides took the shard and inscribed it as requested. So here we have at least one "unlettered" citizen (to cite Plutarch's adjective), but it is anybody's guess how many others there were.

Do I Have to Be Wealthy or at Least Prosperous?
Or Can a Poor Citizen Participate, Too?

We recall that, according to the system of income classifications instituted by Solon back at the beginning of the sixth century B.C.E., eligibility for participation in political life was linked to one's annual income. But the classifications appear to have gone unenforced in later classical times, and any advantages conferred by wealth—and admittedly there were many—were informal and unofficial.

Am I under Obligation to Participate in Government?
To Run for Office? To Vote?

"Responsibilities of citizenship," "civic duties," and the like are phrases that one often encounters today, but by no means is it self-evident that any such responsibilities or duties were recognized by the ancestral democracy of ancient Athens. From the uncontested fact that *dēmokratia* means that power belongs to the people it does not follow that any particular individual or group or even the government itself at any given time actually promoted participation beyond the few minimal demands placed upon a relatively small citizen population by relatively big democratic organs and institutions. And, in fact, despite the voluminous surviving discussions of political theory, much of it directly or indirectly pertaining to Athens, there is hardly a trace of the notion that getting involved in democratic institutional politics was a good or desirable thing in and of itself. True, politicians running for office urged the assembled to support their candidacy. True, the ambitious or upwardly mobile accepted liturgies even at considerable personal expense in the pursuit of honor or in order to place the recipients of their largess under an obligation to be called in at some future date. And, true, the poor sought allotment to magistracies or selection for a jury panel with a view to receiving what was for them a substantial supplement to their personal income. But, so far as we know, in none of these instances was the party concerned motivated by any democratic ideal of participation.

How Are People Informed about Government and Politicians?

Mass media deliver to us information about politics in unprecedented quantity, variety, and depth. Opportunities to inform oneself about politics abound. The situation in classical Athens is less clear. Notices concerning important matters were regularly posted in the Agora. A handful of surviving prose writings of ideological content or slant have been characterized by modern scholars as "political pamphlets," but it is impossible to judge their frequency, extent of readership, or impact. What is much in evidence is speech-making before the Assembly and Council, the very visible holding of crowd-pleasing liturgies, and the seeking of favorable publicity at athletic contests or on the dramatic stage. A spectacular wedding procession for one's daughter, public appearances in fashionable clothing, the cutting of a fine (nude) figure at the gymnasium before one's aristocratic peers, all enhanced by the multiplier effect of word-of-mouth communication in this smallish town—such were the makings of a politician's "reputation." And this does not even take into account the workings of the old-fashioned patronal influence peddling and the calling in of favors. Ancient Athenian politicians were probably quite well known by the time they stood for election to a major magistracy, but it was a popularity won and maintained by means far more personal—and less obviously "political"—than anything most of us are accustomed to.

Are Elections Controlled or Influenced by Organized Special-Interest Groups?

The key term in the phrase above is "organized." Ancient writers tell of the rich and the poor, of aristocrats and "the mob," of city folk and country people, of farmers or craftspeople or military personnel, and often distinctive political leanings are ascribed to one group or another. But none of these groups was ever organized in the ways that political parties or labor unions or special interest groups (with their lobbyists) are organized today.

Do Obstructions to Participation Exist?

At Athens the most serious obstruction to participation—whether as voter or magistrate or juror—was place of residence. The seat of government was situated within the fortification walls—the tiny portion of Attica's vast expanse that we call the "town." Any citizen who wished could participate, but, given the available arduous modes of transportation, on donkey-back or foot, the spirit might be willing but the body too weak to make the effort. Another impediment was availability of time. As we have seen, government service might require a commitment ranging from a half-day or so on up to a full year's duty as magistrate or member of the Council of 500. Given willingness to serve, the question became one of expenses. Who could afford to take so much time off from farm, urban shop, or other gainful employment? Compensation for service was significant or not significant depending upon one's income bracket. A very poor citizen might find attractive the equivalent of a few dollars for one day's jury service, but a member of the hoplite infantry class probably preferred to keep working at plow or anvil, and a rich aristocrat would not be swayed by so paltry a sum one way or the other. So, given the variations of income and demographics indicated by the sources, a meeting of the Assembly or a particularly large jury panel might combine a large percentage of indigents with a scattering of politically minded wealthy urbanites. And what we might call the "middle class" may have been significantly underrepresented.

Do the Outcomes of Plebiscites and Elections Make Any Difference?

Yes, in classical Athens the outcomes certainly did make a difference. One of the striking characteristics of ancient governments (and Rome, as well as the other Greek states, is relevant here) is that by and large the power-holders, the movers and shakers, were occupants of elective offices. That is to say, the actual power-holders did not come from outside the circle of legitimated civil authority, as is true of the lobbyists, television or radio talk-show hosts, entertainers, editorialists, and bloggers who in the modern world wield such influence in the shaping of events. No ancient Athenian citizen could use as a reason for not running for office or voting the belief that the decisions had already been made by outsiders or that a candidate, once elected, would be powerless to act in the face of opposition from extragovernmental interests.

Three

Sparta

THE MYSTERY OF SPARTA

Sparta was the greatest military land power of classical Greek antiquity before the rise of Macedon under Philip II and his son Alexander the Great. Sparta owned, dominated, or influenced the entire Peloponnese and much of the adjacent Greek mainland to the north and east. Sparta's foot soldiers, the Spartiates, were feared as were no others, and few Greek armies ever dared a face-to-face confrontation on the field of battle. Late in the fifth century (431–404 B.C.E.), Sparta and its Peloponnesian allies engaged in a protracted military struggle against mighty imperial Athens and its subjects and eventually prevailed, thereby inheriting a maritime empire—and, with it, absolute dominance over the entire Greek world. So, of course, it seems logical to assume that an abundance of information about this transcendentally powerful city-state must have reached us and that on its basis we can construct a richly detailed account of its politics and society. Surprisingly, this assumption is wrong. Ancient Greece's most powerful city-state (if only for a time) is at once its least well documented, least understood, most problematic—indeed, its deepest mystery. How can this be?

It is to Sparta itself that we must look first for the answer. As the following chapter makes abundantly clear, Spartans were distrustful of others, even to the point of paranoia, and as a consequence consistently discouraged the creation of a record of their internal activities. No local history of the Spartan polity is known to have been composed prior to the *Constitution of the Lacedaemonians* attributed to the exiled Athenian Laconian sympathizer Xenophon—and none ever by a Spartan. Laws, decrees, and other official acts were not inscribed on durable stone so as to reach later Greeks, much less ourselves. Visits by outsiders—who might return to their own cities to compose accounts of their sojourns—were officially frowned upon or prohibited outright. Nor do we learn of Spartan presence abroad except in a few cases, such as that of the general Pausanias, whose time in Asia Minor ended disastrously for all concerned (see chapter 8 on Pausanias and other

Spartans). *Paranoia* is a Greek word, but another Greek word (and one free of clinical meanings), *xenophobia,* "fear of strangers," perhaps gets at the essence of the Spartan attitude in a more specific and concrete way.

The mystery of Sparta, however, is not simply a matter of the silence of the sources, because there are in fact ancient sources about Sparta—and therein lies the problem. Non-Spartan Greeks (and Romans, too) were just as fascinated with this city-state as we classical historians are, but they didn't let the absence of primary documents halt the production of all manner of written materials—histories, biographies, proverbial sayings, anecdotes, and so on. Speculation, inference, hearsay, gossip, and outright invention are some of the terms that might characterize the great bulk of the reportage. The *Constitution of the Lacedaemonians* was just mentioned, to which may be added (besides the general histories by Thucydides, Herodotus, and Xenophon that necessarily bring Sparta into play) the *Parallel Lives* of Plutarch (famously used by Shakespeare and Dryden) and various belletristic essays by the same author (traditionally collectively labeled the *Moralia*). But what could Plutarch, not himself a Spartan and living a half-millennium after the Peloponnesian War, have known, especially since he was no political or military man but a private scholar and popularizer utterly dependent upon his own library of (now mostly lost) classical writings? Answers differ, but some would say he actually knew very little. So, we must proceed with caution. Rather than throw the baby out with the bathwater, the present writer's policy is to accept the gist of these ancient traditions but to remain agnostic concerning specific details. Readers conversant with election-year attack ads, anonymous Internet gossip, or supermarket tabloids may find much that is familiar here, but in the end each of us must decide for ourselves, in accordance with our own personal comfort levels for truth and falsity.

But the process of evaluation, finally, cannot in Sparta's case simply end with expressions of skepticism or belief. Truth or falsity, I contend, is not really the issue. Rather, the issue is what impact, if any, the widely disseminated popular perceptions of Sparta and the Spartans had on the course of events in antiquity—that is, their status as actual historical causes. Perception might easily trump reality in a case such as Sparta's. Given Sparta's reputation for military invincibility, to take the crucial example, how many Greek city-states would ever seriously consider confronting the Spartan army on the field of battle? The "mystery" that seems to have been the product of simply a lack of information may well have worked to Sparta's advantage in ways that went well beyond immediate concerns about the threat of espionage. When dealing with other Greeks, and even with their own subject populations, the ancient Spartans were always preceded by their reputation.

SPARTA'S RISE TO POWER AND ITS CONSEQUENCES

In the beginning, Sparta, or rather the ancestors of the people who would eventually become the Spartans of classical antiquity, appears to have differed in no substantial respect from the rest of Greece and its peoples. Scholars of later antiquity, attempting (as we are now) to understand the city's meteoric rise to power, wrote of the so-called Return of the Heraclidae, with reference to the myth of the "sons" of Heracles. After murdering his wife and their children, the hero, as an act of penance, was assigned to perform the famous Twelve Labors under the taskmaster Eurystheus, who, as an additional penalty, also drove these "sons" out of the Peloponnese. The eventual "return" of the sons (or rather their descendants) supposedly marked the (re)entry into the Peloponnese of Sparta's ultimate founders. Archaeology adds little, but it is significant that no trace has been found of material culture at variance with that of other prehistoric settlements. The same goes for Homer. The *Iliad* and the *Odyssey* purport to tell a tale of the late prehistoric Bronze Age, but, again, the Spartē of Menelaus and Helen is fundamentally indistinguishable from Mycenae, Argos, Pylos, and the other Achaean palace strongholds. Shrouded in myth though they may be, nothing in Sparta's beginnings presages the city's eventual extreme eccentricity.

At all events, the Sparta we know from contemporary literary records of the city's glory days was founded during the Dark Age on the banks of the Eurotas River in the central Peloponnese. By that time, the Dorian branch of the Greek people had swept into the Peloponnese from the north, and from this point on "Spartan" is synonymous with "Dorian"—indeed, the quintessence of the Dorian culture and mindset. Something about the re-foundation of Sparta as a Dorian city-state can be deduced from the disposition of the archaic and classical polity. As we'll see momentarily, the Spartans organized themselves into four (later, five) village quarters, and at no point were these village segments ever consolidated into a unified conurbation surrounded by fortifications on the model seen elsewhere in Greece. Inferentially, this later village organization reflects the pattern of the original Dorian settlement. Maintenance of so primitive an arrangement into classical times is surprising enough in itself, but the really amazing thing is that from so fragile a base the Spartans were able eventually to carry out the conquest of much of the Peloponnese. And herein resides the key element determining Sparta's future eccentricity (as I have termed its anomalous profile throughout antiquity). Conquest of foreign territory presents the victor with two options: either to abandon the conquered land and its peoples or to incorporate them into an enlarged state—and it was the latter option that was taken by the Spartan conquerors. As it worked out, the Spartans were remarkably successful in pursuing the incorporation. Details, as always in this well-named "Dark" period, predictably elude us, but we can distinguish broadly the two principal populations brought under the Spartan heel.

First, the helots. "Helot" means something like captive, and these people (or peoples) were eventually to become the state-owned slaves of classical Sparta that powered the city's agrarian economy. The ethnic identity of the helots is not known, but they could have been remnants of the old pre-Greek populations or even Mycenaeans (and Greeks) who had survived the collapse of the palace centers at the end of the Bronze Age. Their numbers were large, with a ratio of seven or eight helots to every Spartan citizen guaranteed by records of the number of helots assigned to each Spartiate soldier during foreign campaigns. The helots supplied the state's workforce, males toiling on the citizen-owned farms, females staffing the citizen households.

Second, the *perioeci,* or "dwellers around." These were the free and pre-sumably Greek populations of the numerous formerly independent towns of the conquered territories. Formerly autonomous polities, the perioe-cic towns retained their infrastructures, administrative arrangements, and local economies but under Spartan domination lost their independence—economic, military, and political. Henceforth, they would pay tribute or taxes to Sparta, supply large contingents in Lacedaemonian military expedi-tions, and serve as satellites in the unified bloc that was Sparta's powerful land empire. One attractive theory sees the perioeci communities as primar-ily industrial—supplying metal goods (including military weaponry, as well as farming and other implements), ceramics, household utensils, and so on, thereby complementing the agrarian pursuits of the helots.

And what of the Spartans themselves? The name "Spartans" itself is the more familiar rendering of the Greek *Spartiatai,* or Spartiates, by which the citizen elite was technically designated. (They are also called, confusingly, Lacedaemonians, with reference to Lacedaemon, an alternative name for Sparta, and Laconians, with reference to Laconia, the region in which Sparta was located.) Upon the reorganization of the state by Lycurgus, a nominal 9,000 men were assigned 9,000 equal allotments of arable land, each allot-ment to be worked by helot labor. Thereafter, in recognition of this egalitar-ian distribution of real property, the Spartiates were sometimes called the *Homoioi,* or "Equals."

These three populations performed complementary functions that be-stowed upon Sparta its unique and distinctive economy and social orga-nization. Basically, helots and perioeci together supplied the workforce of what would otherwise have been a traditional developed ancient city-state grounded economically in agriculture and industry. Thereby, the Spar-tiate citizen class (adult men and their wives and children), freed from the day-in-day-out drudgery that typically consumed the energies of an an-cient person's life, could devote itself entirely to the business of propagating, training, maintaining, and operating what was eventually to become ancient Greece's premier land-based military machine.

But the important thing to understand now is that this machine's original—and thereafter continuing—reason for existence was primarily to maintain order at home, to hold in check large enslaved or subjugated populations, and to enforce the payment of taxes and involuntary military service. The Spartans had found themselves holding the wolf by the ears. Yes, the prey was in hand, but if you released your grip, you'd be savagely torn to shreds. Once the conquests had been consolidated, the Spartan citizen ruling class seems to have realized that it had no choice but to reorganize as a police state. And only later, almost as an afterthought, did Sparta allow itself to be drawn into the international political arena and, departing from its historical experience, emerge as a Mediterranean superpower.

SPARTA'S GOVERNMENT: MONARCHY, OLIGARCHY, DEMOCRACY—OR POLICE STATE?

The term "Sparta" needs some additional specificity since, as previously mentioned, the main settlement, rather than (as at Athens) consisting of a more or less continuous expanse of infrastructure enclosed by fortification walls, comprised five separate villages. Absence of a unifying enclosure would seem to go hand in hand with the survival intact of the villages (or, to cite the Spartans' own unique technical term, *obai*) long into postclassical and even Roman times. Four of the *obai*, Kynosoura, Limna, Mesoa, and Pitana, seem to represent the original disposition, while a fifth, Amyklai, situated a short distance to the south, was added later (but still early in the archaic period, ca. 750 B.C.E.). A sixth, Neopoleitai, "New Citizens," belongs to the age of revival in the postclassical times. The lack of fortification system was noted even in antiquity (Thucydides, for example, commented famously on the virtual dearth of infrastructure of any kind)[1] and can be understood only in terms of a total domination by the Spartans of any and all approaches by which the city might be assaulted militarily. But where society and politics are concerned, it is the persistence of the compound village structure in the apparent absence of a unified central town that demands our attention.

Did the Spartan citizens, for all their military cohesion and singleminded dedication to the almighty state, somehow conduct their public lives within spatially distinct ancestral communities? Probably not, or not entirely, because we know that the five *obai* were intersected by the three *phylai*, or "tribes," Dymanes, Hylleis, and Pamphyloi, the traditional divisions of the citizen body observed by Dorian Greeks everywhere they settled. At an early date, the Spartan poet Tyrtaeus writes of warriors, who are presumably Spartans, arrayed by Pamphyloi, Hylleis, and [Dymanes], armed with "hollow shields" and "brandishing man-killing spears in their hands." But, later, it is the *obai* that emerged as the primary military units and that probably served as the underlying framework for several fivefold boards of magistrates and commissioners. If these few surviving traces of public administration are true to the actual original state of affairs, we could find at Sparta the same basic transition from traditional personal associations (the *phylai*) to territorially based groupings (the *obai*) reflecting place of residence that was in evidence at Athens and indeed throughout Greece. But whatever their origins, these segmentations, *phylai* and *obai*, afforded the macro organization of the citizen state's people and territory that was the setting for Sparta's unique array of governmental institutions.

An organization of the citizen body had been in place from an early time, since both *phylai* and *obai* are mentioned in the foundation charter of the archaic and classical state. I refer to the so-called Great Rhetra, which is quoted, and ascribed to the legendary lawgiver Lycurgus, by Plutarch in his *Life* of the lawgiver. The reader should keep in mind that Plutarch's approximate date of composition (ca. 100 C.E.) postdates the approximate date of Lycurgus's legislative activity (ca. 600 B.C.E.) by as much as 700 years and is by any calculation centuries later than the final demise of the Lycurgan sociopolitical order. But Plutarch's text may be substantially genuine, as the apparent archaisms of its content and wording would seem to suggest:

Lycurgus got so enthusiastic about this form of government so as to obtain from Delphi an oracle that they call a *rhetra*. And this is the way it goes: "After constructing a shrine of Zeus Syllanios and of Athena Syllania, order the people into *phylai* and by *obai*, set up a *Gerousia* of thirty members including the *archegetai*, then from time to time convene an assembly between [the places] Babyka and Knakion, and there both introduce and rescind [legislative measures]. But to the People *[damos]* will be final authority and power." In these clauses, the part about dividing into *phylai* and *obai* has to do with distributing the population into segments, some of which he called *phylai*, others of which he called *obai*. The kings are called *archegetai*; and *apellazein* means "to assemble" because Lycurgus attached the source and authority of his polity to the Phythian god Apollo. The Babyka is now named Cheimarros, and the Knakion Oinos, but Aristotle says that Knakion is a river and Babyka a bridge.[2]

The text quoted (along with the parsing interpretation offered by Aristotle and, much later, Plutarch himself) concerns only what we would call the "constitutional" arrangements of the new polity (and Plutarch does in fact use the Greek word *politeia,* which has reference to the structure of the polis in all its dimensions). These arrangements are discussed in the immediately following paragraphs. The initially surprising thing is that, despite the limited scope of the Rhetra's few preserved clauses, it was believed in antiquity that Lycurgus's work had brought about an across-the-board reworking of Sparta's economy, society, and culture and that, in place of the inherited institutions shared by all other Greeks, a distinctive new regime had been installed that would set the Spartans apart throughout the remainder of Greek antiquity. The new regime went by the technical term *diagōgē,* or, as commonly translated, "Discipline." So thoroughgoing was the transformation that ancient Sparta stands out as one of human history's clearest proofs that, far from being enslaved by its inheritance from the past, a people sometimes *does* possess the capacity to radically transform even its most fundamental institutions. True, modern historians often prefer to think in terms of the working out of processes over lengthy periods of time rather than the revolutionary acts of a single statesman, but one way or another we know that the changes in question did in fact occur. So, with politics and society as our continuing focus, we will try to convey an impression of that transformation, beginning with politics (narrowly understood) itself.

At the top of the pyramid of institutional power stood the two kings, who possessed a double uniqueness. First, monarchy itself was an anomaly. Rule by a king (and queen) had been the prevailing political form of the Bronze Age (hence King Agamemnon and Queen Clytemnestra of Mycenae; King

Odysseus and Queen Penelope of Ithaca; and, at Sparta, King Menelaus and Queen Helen), but all indications are that monarchy had vanished with the collapse of the palace-state at the end of the Mycenaean period. At Sparta, however, monarchy did somehow survive (or was reinstituted). The second anomaly is that (in defiance of the literal meaning of *mon*archy), the Spartan kings were two in number, one being selected from each of two hereditary clans. True, despite the general regressive trend of Spartan arrangements, collegial kings did admittedly mark a kind of advance toward democracy. The one king might serve to check an otherwise unbridled authority of the other, and the rule that only one king might go on campaign while the other remained at home did afford administrative advantages in these times of slow and undependable travel and communications.

But the powers of the kings were checked not only by the presence of two kings but, more decisively, by the board of *ephors* ("overseers"). Numbering five at Sparta (ephors were found in other Dorian states, as well), members of the board served for one year only and were not eligible for a second tenure. All Spartans were qualified to stand for election, in contrast with the exclusive hereditary limitations imposed on the monarchy. But the ephors were opposed to the kings in a more important way, for every month they exchanged oaths with the kings. The kings swore to rule according to Sparta's laws, while the ephors swore to uphold the kings provided that they abided by their oath. Clearly, the ephors had the upper hand here, and their specific control over the kings extended to ordering their appearance before the board, adjudicating disputes between the two, and even initiating prosecution against them, while two ephors regularly accompanied a king on military campaigns. Summoning and presiding over the assembly, prosecuting lesser officials and conducting political trials, mobilizing Spartan troops, supervising the educational system (see later discussion), and negotiating with foreign governments—these were among the powers that without question made the ephors the actual chief executives of the Spartan state.

The rank-and-file Spartiatai exerted their citizen rights not only through standing for election to the ephorate and voting in these annual magisterial elections but, more directly, through their participation in the Spartan bicameral legislature. The upper house, the Gerousia, corresponded to the American Senate; indeed, *gerousia,* the body of *gerontes,* or "old men," means in Greek exactly what Senate, from *senis,* or "old man," means in Latin—the council of elders. According to Plutarch, the Gerousia comprised 30 Spartiatai, 28 plus the two kings, and members served for life. The Gerousia, by reason of the seniority of its members, enjoyed enormous prestige, but its powers were checked by the sovereign powers of the Apella, or Assembly, of Spartiate citizens. The interrelationship between the two bodies, the upper and lower houses, has struck scholars as reminiscent of the decree-making *probouleusis* of the Athenian Council of 500 and the Assembly (hence my term "bicameral"). It has even been suggested that it was precisely the Spartans who invented this legislative system—a suggestion that, if nothing else, is consistent with the very early date of Lycurgus's Rhetra, by which it was presumably brought into existence. But, however that may be, there can be no doubt that ultimate authority rested with the Spartiatai. They were the owners of the original 9,000 allotments of Sparta's agricultural lands. They and they alone served as the heavy-armed infantry to whom all other military personnel were subordinate. They and they alone were eligible for the ephorate and elected each year's new board. And they, sitting as the Apella, had reserved for themselves the right to modify or check what look to us like "bills" coming out of the Gerousia.

Monarchy? Yes, two kings, not one, but it's still rule by king(s). Oligarchy? Yes, the Spartiatai constituted only a very small fraction of the populations inhabiting Spartan territory—small even in comparison with the citizen elite at Athens—and in later antiquity that small number was allowed to dwindle almost to the point of extinction before the authorities finally were driven to recruit new citizens. Democracy? Yes, if "democracy" can legitimately be used to denote the Athenians' classical government, then certainly the term may also be applied to Sparta's regime of Homoioi, or "Equals." However limited the franchise may have been, the Spartiatai enjoyed nominally equal property rights, all could stand for the highest elective office (the ephorate) and vote, all enjoyed equal status in the almighty prestige-bestowing military organization, and so on.

The conclusion can only be that Sparta's government represented a combination of forms of polity as we moderns understand them. But was Sparta also, as many believe, also a police state? A possibility that, if true, would trump the academic question of just how the Spartan government is to be characterized and labeled? For the chilling answer to this question, we need only translate a memorable passage from Plutarch's *Life:*

The institution called the *krupteia* [or secret service] ... was something like the following: From time to time the magistrates sent into the countryside those most reputed for cleverness of the young warriors, equipped with daggers and minimal supplies but nothing else. By day, they scattered into hard to detect places, where they hid themselves and kept quiet. But at night they came down onto the roads and slit the throat of every helot that they captured. Frequently, too, they would go on patrol through the fields and dispatch the sturdiest and strongest of the helots at work there. Similarly, Thucydides, too, in his history of the Peloponnesian War,[3] recounts that the helots who had been singled out for bravery by the Spartiatai had wreaths placed upon their heads in recognition of their emancipation and made the rounds of the temples of the gods. But a little while afterwards all disappeared, more than 2,000 in number, in such a way that no one was able to say, either then or afterwards, in what manner they had perished. And Aristotle specifically says also that the ephors, upon their entry into office, formally declared war upon the helots, in order that there be no impiety in slaying them.[4]

True, only enslaved helots, not free perioeci or wayward Spartiates, figure as the victims of the *krupteia*. But the legitimated waging of warfare, and without provocation or even pretext, by the citizen authorities against the bulk of the state's population is certainly inconsistent with any present-day notions of civilized governance. Formally speaking, the terms "monarchy" (rule by one), "oligarchy" (rule by few), and "democracy" (rule by the *dēmos,* or "people") have reference in an ancient context only to the distribution of power (*archē* or *kratos*) among the *free* citizens of a state. But, on any less strictly technical understanding of a polity—including other ancient Greek states, such as Athens, where the unjustified slaying of a chattel slave was a serious crime—Sparta under the Lycurgan "Discipline" was arguably what we would call a "police state."

SPARTA'S ECONOMY, SOCIAL ORGANIZATION, AND EDUCATIONAL SYSTEM

As we've just seen, the engine that drove the Spartan military machine— the machine that enabled Sparta eventually to supplant Athens as Greece's reigning superpower—was domestic in origin. The state-slave helots and the nominally "free" but subject perioeci had to be kept pacified and working productively in support of the Spartiate citizen-class. To achieve this on-going goal, the entire structure of the polity would be redesigned in defiance of prevailing and elsewhere generally recognized Greek principles. The "way of life" of all other Greeks had to be jettisoned in favor of another that throughout antiquity would remain uniquely Spartan. So, using Plutarch's *Life of Lycurgus* once again as our guide, let's try to get an idea of what this new social order looked like in general outline. And then, with that outline as background, we can narrow our focus to the life of the individual Spartiate man and woman.

At the time of Lycurgus's activity as understood by Plutarch (and his sources), Sparta suffered under the effects of a grossly unequal distribution of the state's wealth. This was the "rich versus poor" situation that was to be typical of the historical Greek city-state. Since agricultural land, not cash or stocks, constituted in antiquity the fundamental form of wealth on which all other forms of wealth were dependent, it is not surprising that it was with land that Lycurgus began his work:

The second of Lycurgus's constitutional arrangements, and the most innovative, is the re-division of the land. For the inequality was terrifying, the many propertyless and helpless people were weighing hard on the city, and the preponderance of the wealth had become concentrated in the hands of a few. So, in order to drive out excess, envy, misconduct, indulgence, and the still greater and more ancient sicknesses of a polity, wealth and poverty, he persuaded them to put all the land in a pool and to re-divide it afresh, and to live together on an equal basis and with equal lands for their livelihoods.... Matching deed with word, Lycurgus distributed the land of Laconia to the *perioeci* in 30,000 lots while that assigned to Sparta town came to 9,000 lots—for this was the number of the lots of the Spartiatai. The lot of each was sufficient to yield [each year] 70 bushels of barley for a man and 12 for a woman [i.e., his wife], with a corresponding quantity of wet goods [i.e., wine and oil].[5]

Next, he undertook to divide up the movable property, in order to make inequality go away and level the playing field.... First, he invalidated all gold and silver coin and ordered that people use iron only. Then, he gave so little a value to so great a weight and bulk of iron that a sum of ten *minae* required a big storeroom in a house and a pair of oxen to haul it. With the approval of this measure, many kinds of injustice went away from Lacedaemon.[6]

With the abolition of money and of its potential use as a medium of exchange for goods and services, what was the nature of Sparta's economy? A polity that was to attain so high a pitch of development must have had an economy of some kind, after all. Mention has been made of the agricultural and domestic labor of the helots and how their productivity set free the Spartiatai for their military service as soldiers and as mothers and wives of soldiers. But precisely how was the wealth created by the helots conveyed to the Spartiates, in the absence of a medium of exchange such as the coins in use in other Greek city-states? The answer is, through the medium of the *syssitia,* or common dining halls. Instituted by Lycurgus (I will quote the key passage from Plutarch shortly), the *syssitia* were the linchpin of the Spartan economy, since each soldier's mandatory contribution of produce (in function amounting to a payment of dues) was literally the fruits of the helots' agricultural labor. No money was needed.

Because the citizen's purpose in life was to contribute to the war machine, it would not be misleading to think of these "common dining halls" as military barracks. From the description, with its implied chronology, of the male career illustrated by Plutarch in the following section, it is clear that Spartans lived more or less continuously with other males in these facilities from childhood (after they were taken from their birth parents) until marriage and, even after marriage, through their twenties. Obviously, such same-sex living arrangements must play a role in any appreciation of the patterns of personal behavior that, as we'll see in a moment, departed so radically from generally accepted ancient Greek norms.

At Athens, the years from the teens through, say, age 30 were the time that a youth received whatever education he was to acquire, depending on his personal circumstances, such as urban or rural residence, financial resources, availability of time, and so forth. And what about Sparta?

Lycurgus didn't put his laws in writing, for this [prohibition] is one of the so-called *rhetras.* For he thought that if the most authoritative and important elements contributing to the prosperity and excellence of the city were implanted in the habits and practices of its citizens, these elements would remain undisturbed and secure and would produce in the resulting mind-set a stronger bond than the necessity that education *[paideusis]* imparts to the young.

A Spartan's education, then, was to be severely limited. The boys were taught a concise and to-the-point form of speech, in their own (and our own!) times to be characterized as "laconic." Spartan poetry, so splendid in the pre-Lycurgan era, came to be largely restricted to didactic and uplifting songs in praise of men who had died in battle—or correspondingly censorious of the cowardly.[7]

SPARTA'S MEN: THE MAKING (AND UNMAKING)
OF A SPARTAN POLITICIAN

The father was not empowered to raise the newborn, but he took and carried it to a certain place called the Lounge, in which the elders of the tribesmen sat and examined the infant. If it was well put-together and robust, they invited the father to rear it, assigning to it one of the 9,000 allotments. But if it was ill-born and ill-shaped, they sent it to the so-called Dumps, a pit-like place on the slopes of Mt. Taygetus, on the theory that it was of no use to itself or to the state that a being not well born suited from the start for health and strength continue to live.[8]

For which reason, the women used to bathe the newborns not with water but with wine, thereby making a sort of test of their constitution. For it is said that epileptics and the sickly are convulsed and lose their minds by un-watered wine, while the healthy specimens are rather steeled by it and strengthened in the frame.[9]

But Lycurgus did not place children of the Spartiatai with mere purchased or hired pedagogues, nor was it permitted for each man to raise his son just any way he wished. But personally appropriating them all as soon as they reached seven years of age, Lycurgus grouped them into herds and, by subjecting them to the same culture and upbringing, he accustomed them to play and work together.[10]

Now these matters [relating to women] were incentives to marriage. I have in mind the processions of virgins and their disrobings and competitions within the sight of young men,...Nor was this all, for Lycurgus attached a kind of disfranchisement to unmarried men. They were debarred from viewing at the Naked Games. And in wintertime the authorities ordered them to process naked around the market square and as they processed they sang a kind of song composed against them—that they were suffering justly because they were in disobedience of the laws.[11]

And now that the boys had reached such an age, lovers from among the younger elite men started to keep company with them. And the older gentlemen, too, showed them attention, frequenting the gymnasia more often than before, standing by while the boys were battling and goofing off—not pointlessly but with the thought in their minds that in some way or another they were their fathers and trainers and guardians. Thereby, no opportunity of time or place was lost to advise and correct the boy who was going astray.

And there was more. From among the upper-class gentlemen was appointed a *paidonomos,* or child-guide. And the boys themselves, organized in troops, were marshaled under the most responsible and warlike of the so-called *eirenes.* They used to call *eirenes* those who were in their second year beyond the boys. And *melleirenes,* or Wannabe *Eirens,* was what they called the oldest of the boys. Now, this *eiren,* at twenty years of age, commands his underlings in the mock-battles, and in the dining hall uses them as servers at his meals. And he commands the robust ones to fetch the firewood, and the smaller fry the greens for cooking. And the boys get what they fetch by stealing, some by marching straight into the gardens, but others by finding their way with all stealth and caution into the dining halls of the men. And when a boy is caught, he receives many lashes with a whip since he is regarded as careless and unskilled at stealing. They steal whatever they can of their food, learning to set deftly upon any who are sleeping or not keeping careful watch. But, again, the punishment for getting caught is lashes and hunger. For the meal rations for them are paltry, in order that they, by taking it upon themselves to ward off starvation, be forced to be daring and resort to trickery.[12]

And the boys go about their stealing so conscientiously that one of them, it is told, having stolen the whelp of a fox and concealing it in his cloak, allowed himself to be mangled in the stomach by the beast's claws and teeth, persevering to the point of death in order to escape detection. Nor does this fail to win credence from the example of present-day ephebes, many of whom we have observed on the altar of Artemis Orthia meeting death under the lash.[13]

With the thought in mind of attacking extravagance still more and in order to take away the lust for wealth, Lycurgus introduced his third and finest constitutional arrangement—the institution of the common dining halls or *syssitia*. Thereby, they would gather to eat with each other from a menu of common, previously determined dishes and garnishes, and not dine at home while reclining in the dark on expensive couches and tables, at the hands of waiters and cooks being fattened like ravenous animals, and ruining their bodies along with their characters...They met in groups of fifteen (or a little more or fewer), and each one of the messmates contributed every month a bushel of ground barley, eight short gallons of wine, five pounds of cheese, two and a half pounds of figs, and, in addition, a quite small amount of cash for condiments.[14]

After finishing his meal, the *eiren* while reclining would order one of the boys to sing a song. But to another he would put a question requiring a carefully considered reply. For example, "Who is the best among the men?" or "What are we to make of this man's conduct?" As a result, they became accustomed right from the start to form good judgments and to get involved with the citizens. For when asked who was a good citizen or who was not distinguished, if a boy was at a loss for an answer, they took this as a sign of a spirit that was slothful and without ambition for excellence. And it was necessary that the reply both have supporting evidence and an expression condensed to a brief and concise statement. But the boy answering poorly was punished by taking a bite on the thumb from the *eiren*. Often, also, it was in the presence of the elders and the magistrates that the *eiren* punished the boys, thereby demonstrating whether the punishment was reasonable and necessary. And while administering punishment, the *eiren* was not restrained. But after the boys had left he would render account if he had exacted a harsher penalty than was needed or, at the other extreme, in an easy-going and relaxed manner.

The lovers shared in the distinction of the boys for good or for ill. And it is said that once when a boy in the pitch of battle let out an unbecoming cry, his lover was fined by the magistrates. So approved was this love between man and boy among the Spartans that even the unmarried girls similarly loved the fine and noble women. But there was no rivalry in love. Rather, those men enamored of the same boys made this an impulse for friendship with one another and continued to strive in common to make the boy beloved by them as good a person as possible.[15] And at that time [during war], relaxing the harshness of the Discipline for the young men, they did not prevent them from primping by attention to their hair and decoration of arms and clothing—delighting to see them, like show horses, prance and neigh in a contest. Accordingly, growing their hair out immediately after leaving the age of ephebes, and especially in times of danger, they took care that it look shiny and well-parted. The practice recalled some saying or other of Lycurgus's about a person's hair, that it makes the handsome still more attractive but the ugly still more terrible. And, furthermore, they followed a softer routine of exercises while on campaign, and [the authorities] imposed on the young men a regimen that was not so condensed or monitored. As a result, for the Spartans alone of human societies a war meant a respite from the preparation for war.[16]

SPARTA'S WOMEN: HOUSEHOLD, PROPERTY, AND INFLUENCE

With the Spartan women, too, departures from the cultural norms observed at Athens and throughout ancient Greek city-states are no less in evidence. Take, for example, their education:

But even to the women Lycurgus showed the greatest attention. He made the girls exercise their bodies in running, wrestling, throwing the discus, and hurling the javelin, in order that the fruits of their wombs might have vigorous roots in vigorous bodies and arrive at a healthier maturity—and that they themselves might . . . labor successfully and easily with the pangs of child-birth. He liberated them from softness and delicacy and all femininity by accustoming the girls no less than the boys to wear only a tunic in processions, and at certain festivals to dance and sing when the young men were present as spectators.[17]

None of this would strike a twenty-first-century American as unusual, but it would be difficult to find parallels in ancient Greece, least of all at Athens. Plutarch, writing hundreds of years after the final demise of the Lycurgan Discipline, interprets the training of females as a eugenic practice designed to produce fitter mothers and fitter offspring—the males, the next generation of Spartiate warriors; the females, the next generation of mothers of Spartiate warriors.

To a noticeable extent, the Spartan deviation from general Greek practice is simply a matter of degree. Take, again as an example, the persistent tradition that Spartiate wives and mothers vigorously incited their husbands and sons to valorous conduct on the field of battle. No one would deny the same to the womenfolk of other ancient Greek cities, but in Sparta's case the extremes to which the tendency was taken elevate the theme to a conspicuous—even dominating—role in the formation of the Spartan culture and mindset. First, mothers and their sons:

Damatria, having heard that her own son had been cowardly and unworthy of her, killed him upon his arrival. The following is the epigram on her: "The transgressor of laws, Damatrios, his mother killed—a Lacedaemonian by a Lacedaemonian."[18]

Another Laconian woman, having heard that her son had fallen in battle formation, said: "Let the cowards be mourned; but I, you, child, bury without a tear—you are both mine and Lacedaemon's."[19]

One woman, perceiving her son approaching, asked, "How's our Sparta doing" And when he said, "All have perished," she picked up a roof-tile, threw it at him and killed him, saying, "And so they sent you to us to be the bearer of bad tidings?"[20]

One woman, having sent off her five sons to war, took her place at the edge of town fretfully awaiting the outcome of the battle. And when someone arrived, she inquired, and he reported that all her children had perished. She said, "But that's not what I asked, you pitiful nobody, but how's our Sparta doing?" And when he said, "Sparta is victorious," she said, "Well then, gladly do I accept the death of my children."[21]

Another Laconian woman, presenting to her son his shield with exhortations, said, "Child, either this or upon this!"[22]

Another Laconian woman, presenting his shield to her son as he went off to war, said, "This shield your father always preserved for you. Do you, therefore, either keep preserving it or not be preserved yourself."[23]

Additional examples could be added, but the pattern is already clear enough. Spartan mothers bore and raised sons for warfare—and not for the sake of the sons' glory or for their own, the mothers', but for the greater good of the Spartan state.

Interestingly, no mention in these (or other) contexts is made of daughters, perhaps because their role in the Spartan polity, to function as the next generation of soldier-bearing mothers, was so clearly and emphatically articulated elsewhere and could be taken for granted.

But what is more than a little odd is that nothing is said of husbands or fathers in these stories. Where are they, the holders of the 9,000 allotments, the citizens, the backbone of the hoplite phalanx, the fathers of these war-dead sons? Since men of this age would have long ago left the all-male barracks, we can not think of a literal permanent absence from the family household. But other passages from Plutarch's "Sayings of Spartan Women" are relevant to the internal dynamics of that household. I have in mind the four "sayings" with which the collection comes to a close. All four concern Spartan women, taken captive by the enemy, who were being sold as slaves. Pivotal for our discussion is number 28:

Another, taken captive, and asked a similar question [i.e., what she knew how to do], said, "To manage a household well."

The Greek world for "household," *oikos,* might have reference to the usual run of domestic routines, but on a broader view of its nature and management the saying could easily be taken to embrace the household in all its dimensions—raising the children, maintaining the Spartan value system, and, as repeatedly affirmed in our anecdotes, rallying the household's human resources in the interests of the state. So consider, in this light, the remaining three "sayings":

A Laconian woman, when being sold and when asked what she knew how to do, said, "To be faithful."[24]

One woman, asked by someone if she would be good if he bought her, said, "Yes, and if you do *not* buy me."[25]

Another woman who was being sold, when the herald asked what she knew how to do, said, "To be a free woman." And when the purchaser tried to impose on her things not befitting a free woman, she said, "You'll be sorry for your ill will towards so valuable a possession," and did away with herself.[26]

Faithfulness, good conduct, the freeborn person's abhorrence of servility— these mandated qualities suggest that the Spartan wife and mother's "management" of the household embraced not only the propagation of children but, beyond reproduction, the articulation of the fundamentals of the distinctive Spartan ideology, as well. Women in any culture, however subjugated, are never entirely without influence, but here scholars are correct to think in terms of a more direct and incisive control. The Spartan mother inculcated her sons with the state's militaristic code of male honor and sent them off to war; if they failed to return, she accepted their deaths not as a personal loss but as a contribution to the greater welfare of the Spartan state.

And against such a wider cultural backdrop, it is also attractive to consider perhaps the most remarkable fact about the Spartan women preserved for us by a contemporary dependable witness. Aristotle states in his *Politics*[27] that in his own day (the late fourth century B.C.E.), women of the Spartiate class owned nearly 40 percent of the land of Lacedaemonia—apparently the result of male deaths (both fathers and sons) in warfare, leaving only females as heirs. The fact that, in comparison with Athens at least, females should actually own any land at all is remarkable enough. But the control of so large a fraction of the resource on which the economy and welfare of the Spartan state was entirely dependent points to an influence far beyond that of the "nagging wife" or the "power behind the throne."

Thus, Plutarch, even at his very far remove from the facts, may not have been far from the mark when he wrote:

For it is not true that, as Aristotle says, Lycurgus tried to bring the women under proper constraint, but rather he desisted because he could not overcome the great license and power which the women enjoyed on account of the many expeditions in which their menfolk were involved. During these expeditions, the men were indeed obliged to leave their wives in sole control at home, and for this reason paid them greater deference than was their due, and gave them the title of Mistress.[28]

"Politics and society," their intersection and interrelations, could not be more dramatically and graphically illustrated than in the case of Sparta. The study of "politics" cannot end at the examination of constitutions, elections, and factions, if only because, in the case of ancient Greece, adult citizen men alone were allowed to play the game. At Sparta, it was women who, literally and figuratively, made the men and made the men what they were. And they too, if Plutarch is right, not only directed and shaped the citizen households (itself a remarkable state of affairs) but also, empowered with unparalleled holdings in the state's most valuable resource, came to acquire as a consequence of sustained and repeated male absence an influence that extended far beyond the four walls of their private dwellings.

Acknowledgment of the unique position of women is actually, to make the final and perhaps most important point about this unusual Greek city-state, but a single illustration of Sparta's defiance—and successful, productive defiance at that—of its own past, of what we customarily call "tradition." Were it not for Sparta's eccentric example, an ancient historian might be tempted to see the ancient Greek city-state as simply a logical and predictable outgrowth of all that had gone before. Yes, to be sure, minor variations are easily found among the more than 1,000 documented polities, but these are merely the superficial surface clutter that is inevitably produced by differences in local conditions. What counts, the argument might go, is that deeper current of shared inheritance common to all ancient Greek communities that, local conditions notwithstanding, imposed a recognizably Hellenic stamp on all the city-states of ancient Greece. But the fact is, Sparta's eccentric jettisoning of that shared inheritance is too conspicuous—and, as defined by the Sparta's own values and goals, too successful—to be ignored. And, inferentially, no community, Greek or non-Greek, ancient or modern, can be viewed by the historian as an inevitable outgrowth of the customs or practices of the past. And so, too, just as Sparta willfully and consciously abandoned its orthodox beginnings (as attested by the remains of archaic art, literature, and constitutional arrangements), we must acknowledge that more typical-seeming city-states, Athens among them, despite appearances, actually did *choose* the presents and futures that unfold before us in our ancient sources.

Four

Conflict, Trials, and Ostracism

Ancient Greek civilization recognized the *agôn,* or "contest," as a fundamental feature of human society. For the Greeks, a human being was not just a "political" animal (as Aristotle put it, with reference to the *polis,* or city-state) but a competitive one, as well. Most of us are familiar with individuals or groups that want to keep score, lay down a bet, or get into the Guinness Book of Records, no matter what the nature of the activity. Getting ahead of others, defeating one's rivals, and (always to be kept in mind when dealing with the ancient Greeks) gaining recognition for one's victories seem to be widespread and enduring goals of civilized living, ancient and modern alike. Specifically, at Athens we find traces of various board games, informal wrestling matches, and cock-fights for spectator (and bettor), to mention only a few examples from daily private life. Where Athenian public life is concerned, formally organized and fully legitimated contests come in all shapes and sizes. The athletic contests that were the centerpieces of the Panhellenic Games at Olympia (hence our Olympic Games), Delphi, Isthmia, and Nemea are perhaps already known to readers, but less well known is the similar festival called the Theseia, celebrated at Athens in honor of the founder-hero Theseus (see chapter 7). The dramatic productions at the several festivals of Dionysus (City Dionysia, Rural Dionysia, among others) were actually contests in tragedy, comedy, and lyric, with prizes and appropriate recognition for the victors. And, again at Athens, the cityscape (and occasionally a village square, as well) would reveal to the visitor a plethora of monuments and inscribed tablets announcing to all who cared to view them the essential details of a proud winner's victory over his defeated rivals in all manner of *agônes.*

Politics in a democratic setting, too, is intensely competitive and engages essentially the same factors as when two boys wrestle in a gymnasium, when armed cocks fight to the death in the ring, when a dozen four-horse chariots round a tight turning post at Olympia, or when Euripides takes on his older hallowed rival, Sophocles. Someone has to win, and someone has to lose. The problem is that Greeks did not take defeat easily. And it is at this point that the positive and productive dimensions of competition begin to shade imperceptibly into its negative, potentially damaging flip side—conflict. And it is conflict, and the various modes of its resolution devised by the Athenians, that is the subject of the present chapter.

HESIOD'S *WORKS AND DAYS:* THE LITERARY EXEMPLAR

So pervasive was the competitiveness of ancient Greek society that it could be illustrated from almost any substantial surviving written source, but there is one that stands near the beginning of the literary tradition that is deserving of special attention. I do not refer to the *Iliad*—the story of the Trojan War and the earliest surviving work of Greek literature—with its "wrath of Achilles" (wrath directed at the Greeks' commander at Troy, Agamemnon), on which the working out of the narrative turns. Rather, I have in mind another archaic poet and a near contemporary of Homer's, a man of land-locked Boeotia in Greece's heartland—Hesiod. Some of Hesiod's poetic writings, including two major intact poems, the *Theogony* ("On the Origin of the Gods") and the *Works and Days,* have come down to us. The latter is concerned with proper agricultural practice for the small farmer (with a shorter section on maritime practice) but is relevant here in respect to its narrative thread: a rivalry between the author and his brother Perses about the allegedly unfair division of the patrimonial estate. Hesiod represents himself as a small farmer, and it is likely that, since personal property of all kinds typically moved from one party to another not through gift or sale but through inheritance, such disputes were common—and, since so much was at stake in the case of a farm, particularly virulent. To mark symbolically the significance of this dispute, and of disputes in general, Hesiod places near the opening of his poem the mythical tale of the two Strifes. Interestingly for our subject, the contest is not between Strife and Harmony (for the latter, by implication, is not left open as a possibility) but between Bad Strife (which causes war and battle and is loved by no one) and Good Strife (which is much better for men, because it arouses even the lazy to work—so vital to the farmer's well-being).

So, conflict is so fundamental to human society that it operates both at the level of the individual dispute and in a higher-order meta-contest among competing modes of conflict. The onset or emergence of harmony cannot be imagined. What makes this eighth-century poem from Boeotia relevant to another place and time—Athens two or three centuries later—is the fact that, prior to and almost certainly following the composition of *Works and Days* by the literate Hesiod, the poem's traditional core of wisdom-lore circulated orally at all levels of Greek culture. That conflict was a natural, expected, and pervasive element of civilized society was a proposition known to—and accepted by—every Greek, including the Greek of classical Athens.

CONFLICT RESOLUTION IN CLASSICAL ATHENS

Early on, even in soon-to-be democratic Athens, conflict resolution might involve family feuds, blood vendettas, hereditary curses, and the like—all explicitly documented in the chronicles of Greece before the classical period. But the transition to more civilized modes of resolution was a long and gradual one, with some identifiable signposts along the way. For example, Draco near the end of the seventh century b.c.e. codified and published previously unwritten customary law; Solon, archon in 594, made important judicial innovations; and the tragedian Aeschylus produced in 458 a trilogy called *Oresteia* ("The Story of Orestes") that dramatized in a mythical setting the progression from blood-revenge to judicial procedures. So, by the mid-fifth century at the latest, the transition had been accomplished. But, even with written laws, a system of law courts, and cultural reinforcement, conflicts remained as numerous and virulent as before, perhaps even more so.

Private versus Public Disputes

Before a dispute reached the courts, procedures existed for what we call mediation or (a more formal procedure) arbitration. The procedures in question are roughly classified by modern historians as private and public. In the former, the injured party was a private individual person, and responsibility for bringing action against the alleged perpetrator rested with him alone. In the latter, the whole of Athenian society was believed to have suffered injury, in which case any citizen was qualified to initiate action on behalf of the entire state.

Resolution through Arbitration

Private Arbitration

If a person believed that he had been injured by another, he normally lodged an accusation in the presence of witnesses. In the event that the accused rejected the accuser's charges and demands, the case then proceeded to informal arbitration. The two parties had to agree on the selection of the arbitrator (who often turned out to be a family member or friend of one or the other) and on the ground rules that were to be followed. Athenian law, besides calling for such agreement, presumably dictated that the arbitrator take an oath to decide justly and that his judgment would be binding. For most Athenians, informal arbitration would end the matter, since to proceed further might involve knowledge of the law, expenditure of time and resources, and, should the opponent be better equipped for a legal struggle, significant risk. But working against private arbitration was the likelihood that the disputants would not be able to agree upon an arbitrator. If so, the next step was to move on to public arbitration.

Public Arbitration

Public arbitration at Athens originated in the system of deme-judges instituted by the tyrant Pisistratus in the sixth century b.c.e. The tyrant's idea was that the judges would travel from deme to deme (like the American circuit judges of times gone by), making a trip into town unnecessary for country people. In the mid-fifth century there were 30 judges, but by century's end the number had been increased to 40 and the positions were allocated to the 10 tribes, four from each. If private arbitration had failed (or had not been attempted), the accuser (hereafter "the plaintiff") would present his accusation to the four judges for the tribe to which the accused (hereafter "the defendant") belonged. If the money involved in the dispute was not more than 10 drachmas, the judgment of the four judges was final and binding. If the sum was more than 10 drachmas, the law called for the case to be turned over to the arbitrators.

The public (or, as I shall call them in order to prevent confusion with public disputes, magisterial) arbitrators were all the citizens who had reached their sixtieth year (i.e., were 59 years old), the year that marked the termination of their military responsibilities. Apparently, they served during the civil year of their fifty-ninth birthday. From the chance survival of an inscription listing all the arbitrators for 325/4 B.C.E., we know that one year's class totaled 103 Athenians—indicating a rather substantial cohort of "retired" citizens. In keeping with the general high regard in which the accumulated experience and wisdom of the aged were held, these old-timers now had a chance to put that experience and wisdom to good use in the public interest.

The arbitration was conducted in a public place where (as with court proceedings) anyone who wished could watch and listen. The two parties presented all the evidence they had collected, and on its basis the arbitrator reached his decision—receiving for his efforts a fee of one drachma from the plaintiff. Unlike in a private arbitration (in which the two disputants had agreed upon an arbitrator beforehand), the municipal arbitrator's decision was subject to appeal—to the people's courts. Strictly speaking, appeal was made initially to the four tribe judges to whom the plaintiff had originally presented his case. The evidence already assembled for the arbitration was placed into two jars, one for the plaintiff, one for the defendant, and put under seal until the day of the trial.

Procedures for the settlement of private disputes helped to ease some of the burden on the court system. Classical Athens was an exceedingly litigious society, with up to a dozen judicial venues operating simultaneously throughout the civil year with its approximately 200 court days. To bring aggrieved parties to reconciliation prior to reaching the point of a trial was certainly in the public interest.

THE COURTS IN CLASSICAL ATHENS

In a very real sense, the system of courts (called in Greek *dikasteria* or "places of judgment") represented the ultimate institutional embodiment of the will of the People of Athens. Among the most important acts of the lawgiver Solon at the beginning of the sixth century B.C.E. was a provision for appeal against the judgments of magistrates to a court called the Heliaia. To be able to appeal a magistrate's act implies that that magistrate's authority was not final, and if, as seems likely, the Heliaia was actually the Assembly sitting in a judicial capacity, the implication is that the actual final authority rested with the People. By the classical period, appeal or "reference" (the Greek word is *ephesis*) was provided for in multiple circumstances, the court of appeal in the final instance being the People or some representative fraction thereof. But once the People had ruled, no further appeal was possible— and no clearer indication of the People's sovereignty could be found.

The Pool of 6,000 Jurors

"Some representative fraction thereof" is a somewhat wordy way of expressing the principle that, as we saw with the Assembly in chapter 2 and will see again with ostracism at the end of the present chapter, a sufficiently large segment of the total citizen-body could speak for the whole. A term familiar to many of us is *quorum* (the Latin for "of whom" in the plural number), by which is meant the minimum number of qualified persons who must be present in order to do business—that is to say, to reach decisions binding on the entire association, club, committee, or whatever. Under the classical democracy, the quorum for the Assembly was 6,000, which seems to have remained fixed despite fluctuations in the population (due, say, to military losses) but which in any case was probably never more than about 30 percent of the citizens (the percentage late in the fourth century B.C.E., when the citizen population is recorded to have been 21,000). To look ahead, 6,000 was also the quorum for the just-mentioned Assembly-like quasi-judicial procedure called ostracism. Where, in the present case, the courts are concerned, 6,000 is the number given by Aristotle for the size of the pool of dicasts (the jurors of the *dikasteria*) when he was writing in the later 300s B.C.E. It is an obvious inference that the same thinking underlies this 6,000 and that for the Assembly and ostracism: the pool of jurors was empowered to speak for all the citizens of Athens. But the thinking was more theory than practice, since, as we shall now see, any given jury impaneled for a particular legal proceeding was itself only a small fraction of the pool. Even a small fraction, however, might be representative if that number (200, or 300, or 500) had been selected at random. Was this the case?

Each year the Athenians chose by lot the 6,000 citizens for jury duty. The qualifications were, besides Athenian citizenship, minimum age of 30 and absence of any disqualifying legal encumbrance. Importantly, those citizens from whom the 6,000 were selected were volunteers. The point is important because it bears decisively upon the social and political complexion of the eventual pool and, consequently, upon that of any of the numerous juries actually impaneled from the pool. Because we have no data regarding the actual composition of any group of jurors (as we do for some of the more important boards of magistrates or even the Council of 500 in some instances), we have to fall back on general probabilities, but these probabilities are unmistakable in their implications.

To the surprise of only few, it all comes down to money, specifically the recorded amounts of compensation to jurors during the classical period. All government service under the democracy was compensated, but in the case of the courts the payment for a single day's work was relatively low: At first only two obols, then later (in apparent keeping with long-term gradual inflation) three, where the amount remained stalled for the remaining life of the system. Given one drachma, or six obols, as the minimum income per day required to meet the operating expenses of a typically small household, it is obvious that we are dealing here with supplementary income only—not to mention the fact that one might not be selected to the pool of 6,000 in the first place or, if selected, come forward on any particular day and be lucky enough to be impaneled. A juror was paid only if he sat on a jury, and the maximum number of actual court days has been estimated at about 200 per year. So, under these circumstances, who would volunteer for selection to the pool?

Obviously, not the gainfully employed adult male citizen heads of households. The few rich, if interested, might make themselves available, but if they did they would have to swallow their pride and accept the principle of one-man-one-vote. That leaves the poor, and the inactive poor at that, especially the older and "retired." And, when in literature, for example in the comedy *Wasps,* by Aristophanes, we do get a glimpse into the realities of an Athenian court, this is what we find—the old and poor. Probably most were members of extended households, such as the "retired" former patriarch who had stepped down to make way for an adult son and his family but who continued to reside on the property. For a contemporary parallel, such "retirement" is a frequent practice among the Amish in the author's own state of Pennsylvania; on the distaff side, also comparable are the many traditionally low-paying jobs originally intended to provide American wives and mothers with a small supplementary household income.

But our concern here is the implications any such imbalance in composition had for the outcome of trials before juries dominated, say, by urban-dwelling poor and old men. Those who have followed recent trials involving celebrities (athletes, musicians, media personalities, politicians, and so on) are already very familiar with the various aspects of jury selection—the social composition of the community from which the jurors are to be drawn, the actual selection process, the peremptory challenge, change of venue, and so on. We accept the notion, in other words, that people's judgments are significantly influenced by their personal profiles—age, gender, race, level of education, place of residence, and all the rest. So, with these experiences of our own as background, what are we to make of the classical Athenian judicial system in this regard?

Impaneling of the Juries

From the pool, jurors were impaneled to hear and decide particular cases. The numbers were in the low hundreds, sometimes with an additional one (e.g., 201, 301) to preclude a tie (which otherwise would have brought acquittal for the defendant). Hundreds? American juries typically number just 12. Why so large a number? The answer is suggested by the bewilderingly complex procedures reported by Aristotle's *Constitution of the Athenians* for the selection of the panels.[1] Why so complex? And why (as, sometimes, with our own system) did the impaneling not occur until the very day of the trial, and with the trial (unlike our own practice in many cases) scheduled to conclude on the same day that it had begun? Four private cases were expected to be completed within a single day. The answer to all these questions is the same: to prevent jury tampering by interested parties. Few Athenians, even the richest, could afford to bribe a jury numbering in the hundreds. And if impaneled jurors, physically insulated from contact by outsiders, proceeded immediately to their appointed venue, there would be little if any opportunity for bribery or other form of tampering in any event. And, as a final precaution, once a juror's identity on a certain panel became known (as it inevitably would) to all present in the courtroom, he was afforded some protection by the use of secret votes—and afterwards he could remain silent or lie if he had to! Iron-clad precautions against tampering, to say the very least!

Admittedly, different kinds of cases were assigned to different magistrates. Among these assignments were, for example, inheritance, family matters, and certain religious festivals to the archon; homicide and religious disputes to the archon basileus; all disputes concerning metics to the polemarch; and so on. These and the other magistrates were assigned to any of upward of a dozen different venues in and around the Agora. Charges of various kinds were heard on only certain days. So, to this small extent, there was an element of predictability in the system. But it is unlikely that a litigant, armed with these minimal bits of information, could make any headway in influencing the true obstruction to the accomplishment of any unethical designs—the large and randomly selected jury of his fellow Athenian citizens.

The Preliminary Hearing

The initial charge by the plaintiff was made to the appropriate magistrate, at which time that magistrate fixed a day for a preliminary hearing *(anakrisis)*. Both parties were present at this hearing, where they were examined by the magistrate and could also interrogate each others. At its conclusion, a day for the trial was set.

THE TRIAL

Evidence

Mention was made earlier of the evidence brought to the preliminary hearing, placed before the magisterial arbitrator, and put under seal to await its dispatch to the scene of the eventual trial. What do we know of this evidence?

Laws and Decrees

Litigants were responsible for identifying and obtaining texts of relevant laws, decrees, and other public documents. This probably meant a visit to the archives to peruse papyrus originals (now of course all perished in Greece's un-Egypt-like climate), rather than seeking out and reading the stone copies on public display (and in many cases preserved and still legible to this day!). The transcripts, once the trial had commenced, were read out by a clerk. Falsification was punishable by law.

Contracts, Wills, and Other Private Documents

Such evidence was admissible and is sometimes cited in our surviving forensic speeches, but, because forgeries could easily go undetected, private documentation normally had to be supported by witnesses.

Witnesses

In the absence of the means (such as formal signatures) designed to authenticate written texts, not to mention sound and video recordings, the sworn testimony of witnesses took on greater meaning in antiquity than it has in the modern world. A person whose testimony was sought by a litigant was obliged by law to appear at the trial and to testify. Witnesses might declare that a particular person had been named by his father at a certain time and place (thereby testifying to age, legitimacy, and citizenship); that certain parties had been engaged to be married (with similar possible ramifications); that a will naming certain properties and certain heirs had in fact been composed; and so on. Only firsthand knowledge was admissible, although hearsay reports regarding a deceased person were accepted. Originally witnesses appeared in person at the trial, gave their testimony under oath, and were subject to cross-examination, but later on a written deposition was taken in advance and read out in court, with the witness present in order to vouch for its authenticity. Women and children are never known to have been witnesses, despite the firsthand knowledge they must have had in many of the types of suits to come before the juries. Most peculiar to us is that if the testimony of a slave was sought, it could be obtained only under torture.

Courtroom Procedure

With the jurors assigned and in place, the charge against the defendant was read out by a clerk, and the defendant stated his response. The plaintiff made an exposition of the charges, followed by the defendant's speech of corresponding length. There followed two shorter speeches, in the same order, plaintiff then defendant, with the defendant being given the last word. In public cases, such as the trial of Socrates, each litigant was restricted to a single major speech. Time was kept by a ceramic clock, a jar with a spout near the bottom from which water would be evacuated at a known rate. Each litigant had to speak in person, but either might delegate time to one or more co-speakers *(synēgoroi)*. Silent parties, such as women or children, might be introduced in order to elicit the sympathies of the jurors—a tactic that Socrates in his *Apology* says that he will not resort to.

Officiating were, in addition to the presiding magistrate, one juror selected by lot to work the water clock, four to conduct the voting, and five to distribute the payments to the jurors at the conclusion of the trial.

Either speaker might (as does defendant Socrates) pose a question to his opponent, and the opponent was required by law to reply, but the opponent could not interrupt the speaker while his speech was in progress.

Most remarkable perhaps to us are the elements that were *not* present. There was no officiating person in the courtroom corresponding to a judge to provide legal information and instruction, only a magistrate and other functionaries exercising an essentially policing function. There were no lawyers or other legal professionals, paid or otherwise, representing either side of the litigation. Nor, behind the scenes, were there legal scholars corresponding to the *iuris consulti* (or *periti*) at Rome who prior to the trial advised any of the principals in proceedings. Copies of laws or decrees could be presented, but their interpretation was left, again, not to legal experts but to the litigants themselves and ultimately to the jurors. And, usually on the same day that the trial had begun, the outcome rested solely with these jurors, whose only qualifications were citizenship and minimum age and who, as we saw, had not been subject to any of the screenings that modern systems deem necessary or desirable.

It is these facts more than any other aspect of the system that somewhat diminish its purely legal character and gives it a decidedly political color. "Political" trials may, and certainly did, occur (and ancient Rome provides more than a few celebrated instances), but the general absence of a legal authority in the Athenian judicial system had the effect of reducing a trial to competition between amateurs for the votes of a large amateur jury. An Athenian trial was not unlike an Athenian election, with litigant "candidates" running for "election" by acquittal or conviction.

Litigants' Speeches: Composition and Delivery

Note has been made of the general absence of legal experts at all phases of an Athenian trial. This situation would seem to work against the defendant, but there was one welcome resource allowed to him by law: to hire a ghost writer (called *logographos* in Greek) to compose a speech in advance for his client's presentation. There is no reason to suspect that any of these speechwriters were particularly adept in legal matters, and the literary distinction achieved by some, such as Lysias and Demosthenes, suggests that what they offered was primarily rhetorical skills. A big question, however, remains unanswered to this day: Exactly what use did the client make of his professionally crafted text? Did he read out the speech from a text resembling the texts that have come down to us? Or did he recite it word for word from memory? Or, what is most likely given an obvious need for sincerity and spontaneity in the courtroom setting, did he internalize the material and attempt to re-express it in his own words? We shall probably never know the answer.

At all events, more than 100 such speeches have survived, in most cases probably because of the Big Names attached to them, such as the just-mentioned Lysias and Demosthenes, two of the canon of the Ten Attic Orators. Writings by famous authors were always in demand, both in schools and by a larger reading public. Some changes have occurred, such as the deletion of depositions or legal texts in which ancient readers presumably were thought to have little interest. Another limitation is that, with one lone exception, we have only the one side of the case, predictably the side supported by a speech of the famous writer, so it is very difficult to establish the facts of the case or to guess at the outcome of the trial. Even so, this large corpus of forensic oratory at once provides us with much information on the operation of the Athenian legal system, a treasure house of content about those areas of ancient life subject to litigation in a judicial proceeding, and some of the most distinguished examples of Attic Greek prose that have come down to us!

Votes and Verdicts

With the conclusion of the speeches, and after the voicing of any allegations of false testimony by witnesses for either side, came the vote for conviction or acquittal. By use of an ingenious system of balloting, the jurors filed by two urns, casting voting discs for plaintiff or defendant in such a way that the secrecy of one's vote was virtually guaranteed. Of the two urns, the bronze one contained the valid votes (hollow for the plaintiff, solid for the defendant), the wooden one the remaining invalid votes. Upon the completion of the count, the herald announced the result, majority ruling, a tie acquitting the defendant.

Next, in the event of conviction, the two sides proposed alternative penalties, between which the jurors alone were to decide. The jurors did not have the option of proposing a third option, and there seem to have been no prescriptions regarding the fitness of a particular penalty to a particular crime. Socrates' response at this stage, as we'll see in a moment, shows that the convicted defendant could suggest any penalty that occurred to him, however facetious or likely to result in the jury's deciding in favor of the plaintiff's alternative.

What motivated a juror to vote one way or another? Jurors had sworn to cast their votes justly, but how would anyone ever know what additional motivation might have been at work? Available evidence suggests four principal categories of motivation: (1) ideological (oligarchic or democratic, for example); (2) political (with narrower reference to past or upcoming elections); (3) patronal (as when local big men, such as Cimon in the village of

Lakiadai, would have been able to control their clients' actions); and (4) purely personal. When, in a moment, we turn to the trial of Socrates, the reader will have an opportunity weigh these and any additional factors bearing on the eventual outcome of that notorious judicial episode.

Penalties

Penalties in the event of conviction varied widely in type and severity but were not attached to any particular offense. The particular penalty meted out to a particular defendant, as we have just seen, came down to the proposals put forward by the two litigants and which of the two the jurors happened to have selected. Again, this represents a marked difference from the practice of modern legal systems.

Attested penalties included death (by being thrown alive into a pit, by being fastened to a board in a fashion resembling crucifixion, or by being forced to drink hemlock); exile from Athens; loss of civic rights (in the case of citizens); imprisonment; confiscation or destruction of personal property; and various financial assessments.

More needs to be said about the last item, financial assessments. In the absence of a public prosecutor (such as a district attorney), the law allowed any interested citizen to bring suit against another party on behalf of the state. Such practice was encouraged by providing a financial reward to the prosecutor if he should be fortunate enough to win the case. Inevitably, any such system would give rise to abuse, and in the fifth century unprincipled opportunists called "sycophants" were bringing frivolous suits against innocent individuals in the hope of collecting the reward. To discourage such practice, a law was introduced penalizing any prosecutor who failed to obtain at least one-fifth of the votes in the trial.

SOCRATES ON TRIAL: A LITERARY ACCOUNT OF AN ATHENIAN TRIAL IN 399 B.C.E.

Thus far, we have been discussing factual realities, and it is tempting to continue in this mode by drawing upon the preserved texts of the Ten Attic Orators in an effort to illustrate the actual operation of the Athenian judicial system. But an alternative plan presents itself irresistibly in the person of the philosopher Socrates who, as an historical fact, was brought to trial on multiple charges in the year 399 B.C.E. The several points of doubt expressed earlier regarding the use made of speeches composed by hired *logographoi* fortunately have little or no relevance here, since the "speech" of Socrates that has reached us is one of the so-called *Dialogues* of Plato called the *Apologia*, "Apology." This (to us) possibly misleading title (from Greek *apologeisthai*, to speak in one's defense) refers to the accused's speech (actually, speeches) before the court. Plato, we know from a passage late in the text itself, was present at the trial (as a spectator, not a juror), so, unless this is some sort of literary conceit, he was in a position to get the facts right. But it is also clear that the *Apology* is an after-the-fact remembrance by an eyewitness to an event of the past, perhaps the distant past, and thus differs fundamentally from the scripts composed beforehand by the *logographoi*. Besides, as will be almost painfully clear to anyone who reads the *Apology* with attention to its tone as well as its specific content, the philosopher's presentation, heavily laden with sarcasm and even disrespect for the jurors and the judicial system, borders on the self-defeating. It is therefore most unlikely to have been the production of a professional speechwriter working for pay and with the ultimate objective of securing acquittal for his client.

For the sake of correlating our analysis with the foregoing account of judicial procedure, we will proceed by topic: the pool of jurors; jurors, accusers, and accusations; courtroom, jurors, and audience; votes, verdicts, and (looking ahead to the companion early dialogues that take the story from the close of the trial to Socrates' incarceration and execution) punishment.

Jurors, Accusers, and Accusations

"Your honor, my client cannot receive a fair trial in this city." Public relations campaigns designed to influence in advance of a possible trial the attitudes of persons from whom a panel of jurors might eventually be selected. Dismissal of jurors. And on and on and on. Such is the stuff enveloping the preliminary stages of the American celebrity trials that have captured the attention of millions in the country and even around the world in recent decades. To a reader coming to the *Apology* with even a fleeting familiarity with these media events, it will immediately be clear that "contamination of the jury pool" was precisely the obstruction confronted at the outset by the accused, Socrates, but with the difference that there existed no procedural remedies for its correction prior to the beginning of the trial. Socrates is acutely aware of the problem, so much so that he adopts the gambit of dividing his accusers into two classes: first (and it is with these that we are concerned here), the "accusers" from long ago who, unhappy with the philosopher's conduct in public discussions and under the influence of defaming portrayals such as that in Aristophanes' *Clouds,* now harbor negative opinions about him, and, second, the three actual accusers (Meletus, Anytus, and Lycon) to whose allegations Socrates is now responding in the present trial. Striking a startlingly contemporary note, Socrates realizes that within the time allotted to him he must address his "first accusers" before proceeding to the formal charges now before the court. Socrates doesn't know who these accusers are, he cannot recognize or name them, he cannot pick them out among the 500 jurors he now faces, but it is a statistical certainty (although Socrates himself doesn't put it this way) that they are among the Athenians on whose votes his fate depends.

Socrates doesn't need to spell out the position in detail, since of course the jurors themselves know whether they are the persons concerned or not and in any event Plato's ancient Athenian readers could be assumed to have the necessary background information. The comic misrepresentation of the philosopher as a dishonest sophist in Aristophanes' *Clouds* would have been witnessed by thousands of Athenians back in 423 B.C.E. (our own version of the play, dating to the years 418–416, was never produced). True, that was 24 years previously, but we need to remember, as emphasized earlier, that jurors tended to be older, retired Athenians and that a person 60 years old in 399 would have been 36 in 423—plenty old enough to have received a lasting impression from the vividly conceived and produced drama: Socrates flying high above the stage in a suspended basket, pale wimpish disciples, the Thinkery burning to the ground at the play's climax. In a culture promoting the development of memory (after all, oral habits and culture were still very much with the classical Athenians), and in the absence of the superfluity of competing media to which the modern world is accustomed, recollection of so vivid a portrayal could easily have survived to influence people's thinking a quarter century later.

No less serious was the matter of the confrontational debates in the public square, the Agora. According to the *Apology*'s own account, a friend of Socrates', Chaerophon, had journeyed to the oracle at Delphi and asked the god Apollo if any person was wiser than Socrates. The reply: No one is wiser than Socrates. To the jurors Socrates explains that he interpreted this response as a command to test the proposition by examining people with a reputation for wisdom, with the result that, after taking on in succession politicians, poets, and artisans, he had found that none actually possessed the wisdom they claimed to possess. Now, Socrates realized that he himself possessed no knowledge worthy of the name, either, but, as he points out to the jurors, at least he, unlike his defeated elenctic adversaries, knew that he knew nothing—and that it was precisely in this respect, he concluded, that he, Socrates, might be the wisest of all people. The problem, however, he sees, is not with the probably relatively few actual debating victims but with the far more numerous onlookers—and it is in numbers that the impact on the jury of 500 had to be measured. And what had these onlookers witnessed? The public humiliation of prominent Athenian politicians, poets, and artisans. In a shame culture such as this one, such humiliation is perhaps the deepest of wounds, and onlookers as well as the actual victims are not likely to look with favor upon its perpetrator.

The imagined charges of Socrates' "first accusers" had been that he had criminally inquired into things below the earth and in the heavens, that he had made the weaker argument superior to the stronger, and that he had taught others to do the same—all recognizably traits of the itinerant teachers of rhetoric called the sophists and hung on Socrates at least in part under the influence of Aristophanes' *Clouds*. The actual, in-court charges were that he had corrupted the young men of Athens and that he failed to recognize the divinities of the state of Athens. Being a sophist was not, of course, a crime (for they, after all, had won the allegiance of the wealthy, who paid dearly for the instruction of their sons), but the allegation that Socrates had inflicted injury upon the next generation of citizens and that he had withheld belief (if only implicitly by neglect) in the gods of the state—now these were serious matters, whatever the actual legal niceties might have been.

Socrates was a war veteran, for he himself mentions his hoplite service at the battles of Amphipolis (422) and Delium (423). Years later, following the naval debacle at Arginusae, he had risked reprisal by standing up in defense of illegally accused generals when the democratic mob called for a trial en masse of guilty and innocent alike. Furthermore, Socrates, now at age 70, was speaking to a group of jurors fundamentally similar to himself—male, citizen, older, and probably urban. Prospects for a favorable reception might (to us) seem excellent, even allowing for unwelcome memories of past events, if only a persuasive—and conciliatory—speech could be presented. But Socrates represents himself as implacably opposed to a "sophistic" approach, to any reworking of the facts designed to place himself in a more favorable light—standard operating procedure among the trial lawyers for the defense of our own experience. Nor does he fail to point out that, as a result of his philosophical activity, he has been reduced to poverty, has neglected his household responsibilities, and generally has absented himself from the public life of the polis. Needless to say, this is not the way to win over a large cross-section of one's citizen peers, who presumably (like ancient Greeks generally) thought it a sacred obligation to pass on the ancestral property undiminished to the next generation, who by legal statute and universally accepted moral notions made the household the true basis of the commonwealth's culture and indeed its survival, and who, unlike many moderns, certainly did not regard the isolated intellectual as a praiseworthy "lifestyle choice." Did Socrates, therefore, believing that he did not under any circumstances have the votes he needed, resolve to declare his true colors—only to realize, too late, that a more conciliatory approach might have yielded a different result?

Courtroom, Jurors, and Audience

As noted in our discussion of procedure, magistrates (but not, again, as in our own experience, a judge or other judicial official) presided over the several courts, but even so it is clear from the *Apology* that they did not, or could not, maintain the level of decorum we are accustomed to. Socrates must repeatedly request the jurors not to interrupt or make a disturbance. No mention is made of a bailiff or marshal who might have been under the direction of the presiding magistrate. What we do learn of is the instruction to jurors not to communicate with each other. Since the maintenance of silence seems not to have been of high priority, here the purpose might have been to prevent attempts at bribery or other undue influence during the course of the trial itself.

Besides the magistrate or magistrates, litigants, and the jurors, the courtroom was also occupied by "auditors." In Socrates' trial, these included at least two personal friends, Plato and Crito, but there may have been others, on the prosecution's side as well, plus any unaffiliated spectators and curiosity seekers. Socrates' debates, it will be remembered, had always drawn a crowd of onlookers in the Agora, and it is likely that a similar confrontation in a public courtroom will have packed the house. Modern celebrity trials may have audiences both on the scene and, thanks to our media, beyond the courtroom, across the nation or even worldwide. And, in both ancient Greek and modern settings, the underlying principle is the same: In a democracy, the public has a basic right to witness the democracy's own acts.

Differing from modern practice (at least modern American practice), however, is the procedural provision that allowed the defendant (in this case, Socrates), while holding the floor, to cross-examine his accuser. Moreover, the law required the accuser to respond. The accuser had presumably been put under oath to respond truthfully, but Plato's text reveals nothing to this effect, and Socrates' questioning of Anytus is confined to one or two small points. Remember, too, that in this public trial, procedure did not allow for a second, shorter speech by accuser or defendant in which to rebut his adversary's claims.

Votes, Verdicts, and Punishment

Not surprisingly, it is arguable that the eventual verdicts of guilty and, in the penalty phase, of death by execution were brought on by Socrates himself, even if not with his full consciousness of doing so. At the conclusion of Socrates' speech, the vote was taken, and a majority of 280 ruled for conviction, while 220 voted for acquittal. The initial clue is Socrates' statement following the announcement of the vote that, had only 30 votes gone the other way, he would have been acquitted. The expression of surprise can only, in retrospect, color our understanding of his words to the jurors up to this point—words marked above all by condescension, sarcasm, and general contempt not only for his three accusers but for the judicial system itself, as well. And among these 500 jurors were, again, as a virtual statistical certainty and as Socrates himself strongly suspected, some of the "first accusers" from many years gone by. And what Socrates had given them was, on his accounting, essentially a replay of those earlier elenctic encounters in the Agora. If onlookers back then had been unhappy with what they saw and heard (as Socrates concedes in his discussion of the "first" accusers), those same Athenians, as jurors now, are unlikely to have been any less unhappy.

The penalty phase of the trial marks a continuation, and intensification, of Socrates' sarcastic, and certainly self-defeating, attitude toward his accusers and indeed the entire process. Going first, the accusers ask for the death penalty. Severe, yes, but by asking for the maximum penalty Anytus and his colleagues may have been doing the philosopher a favor by allowing him room for a lesser, but still substantial, penalty. Socrates himself contemplates exile as a possibility (and this option might well have satisfied even a hostile jury), but, at his age, he seems to be saying, giving up nearly everything but mere life itself was too great a penalty to pay. Sarcastically, he suggests as an alternative to the prosecution's proposal free meals for life in the town hall (actually a high honor reserved for Athenians who were victorious in the Olympian and Pythian Games). But he eventually relents by proposing a small fine, the money to be put up by his friends in the courtroom audience. With that, the second vote is taken, and Socrates' next stop is the state prison and a vial of hemlock.

OSTRACISM

Thus far we have studied conflicts and their resolution, in their constitutional and legal dimensions, from private and municipal arbitration through the various stages of a trial in the democratic courts. Now we turn to another constitutional and legal institution, which, like arbitration and the courts, dealt with conflicts—conflicts that, however, are difficult to detect and characterize. Furthermore, to mark another, more fundamental, difference with the judiciary, even though the operation of this institution resembled a trial in certain of its elements and even though its outcome could and frequently did resemble a criminal penalty, no crime had been alleged or proved, and it is debatable whether or not or in what sense that outcome really was a penalty. The institution I am referring to is ostracism.

"Ostracism" is an English word that many of us already know. In everyday use and in standard dictionaries, to ostracize means to exclude from a group or society, usually with connotations of disapproval. My dictionary lists among synonyms blackball (and blacklist), boycott, shun, snub, give the cold shoulder, and so on. All these are identifiably outgrowths of the ancient Greek (but specifically Athenian) *ostrakismos.* In its ancient Athenian legal setting, this term denotes the formal banishment of an Athenian citizen from Athens for a period of 10 years, but without the loss of property or other civil rights and with the opportunity to return to the city at the end of the decade in full standing. At no point had any criminal behavior, or allegation of such, played any formal explicit role in the imposition of the banishment. So understood, ostracism must always be carefully distinguished from the criminal penalty of exile (as obtained, for example, in the case of the historian Thucydides). Exile could be imposed only by a democratic jury in a formal criminal trial. Ostracism had only a short life at Athens, corresponding more or less to the fifth century B.C.E. (the exact beginning date is disputed), and on any accounting was a most peculiar institution. How did it work? Who were its victims? And what was its purpose or purposes?

Ostrakismos derives from *ostrakon,* Greek for a fragment of pottery (shard and potsherd are somewhat archaic synonyms). Ceramic pottery was the universal durable hard material of the domestic household, and every dwelling must have contained many ceramics of various size, shape, and function, intact or otherwise. When ceramic clay is fired in a kiln, it becomes virtually indestructible. Consequently, given an even modest incidence of breakage, shards must have littered all occupied areas of the town, while most other materials, such as leather or papyrus (the "paper" of ancient Greece), would, when discarded, have rotted away into oblivion. The universal availability of shards (or an intact ceramic that could be deliberately broken) would have made *ostraka* the ideal objects for the ballots in the quasi-Assembly of citizens that came as a result to be called *ostrakismos*.

According to Aristotle's *Constitution of the Athenians,* each year in the sixth civil month the Assembly voted whether or not to hold an ostracism. If the vote was affirmative, the procedure was conducted in the eighth civil month in the Agora under the direction of the archons and the Council of 500. Participation, as for a meeting of the Assembly itself, was purely voluntary and was of course limited to citizens. Participants were herded through 10 corrals (corresponding to the 10 tribes) that led them by the ballot urns. By this point, each participant had with him one *ostrakon* on which he had scratched, or had had scratched for him by someone else, the name of one Athenian citizen that he wished to be "ostracized." Once all participants had cast their *ostraka,* the 10 urns were emptied and the ballots were counted. On the most reasonable interpretation of the conflicting sources, a minimum of 6,000 ballots had to have been cast (corresponding to the known quorum of the Assembly, hence my use of the term "quasi-Assembly"), and, if the minimum had in fact been reached, the one citizen with the plurality of "votes"—and only he—would be ostracized that year. By "plurality" I mean the largest number, not a majority, which, given the large number of names attested by surviving *ostraka,* is unlikely to have been obtained by even the most unpopular of Athenians. The citizen had to leave Attica within 10 days and remain beyond the city's territorial limits for 10 years without possibility of return even for short visits (so far as we are informed).

As noted, the circumstances of the procedure's introduction are clouded in mystery. According to Aristotle, the law on ostracism was the work of the democracy's founder, Clisthenes, in 508/7, but it would not be for another 20 years, in 487, that the first ostracism (that is, the accomplishment of a citizen's banishment) occurred. Why so long a period before the first successful use of so novel an innovation? Perhaps Clisthenes saw in ostracism primarily its deterrent value (much like powerful modern weaponry that is never used over long stretches of time) and its intended purpose *was* being fulfilled during those two decades. Perhaps the very large quorum of 6,000 was never achieved because citizens believed that banishment of an innocent man for 10 years was not a good idea, however politically expedient. Perhaps, prefiguring a problem encountered in later classical times, the reason was simply what we would call "voter" apathy. We really don't know. But what we do know are the names and years of banishment for some of those citizens successfully ostracized in and after 487:

487	Hipparchus, son of Charmus (relative of tyrant Pisistratus and sons)
486	Megacles, of the Alcmeonid clan
485	Callias, son of Cratius, also of the Alcmeonids

484	Xanthippus (returned under amnesty in 480)
482	Aristides (returned under amnesty in 480)
about 470	Themistocles
461	Cimon
443	Thucydides, son of Milesias (not the same man as the historian)
417 (or 416? 415?)	Hyperbolus (the last citizen to be ostracized)

This list reads like a "who's who" of fifth-century Athenian politics. Even allowing for the strong possibility of unrecorded ostracisms of politically insignificant figures, it is remarkable that so many dominant leaders should have fallen victim. It is further remarkable, and perhaps more significant for our understanding of the procedure, that all points on the ideological spectrum are represented, from a tyrant's family (Hipparchus), to a renegade aristocrat (Megacles, Callias), to a traditional conservative aristocrat (Cimon, Thucydides), to a radical populist (Themistocles). This information bears importantly (but not decisively) on the third and final question posed earlier regarding the purposes of ostracism. It is inescapable that among them was the removal of one prominent politician in any year that the quorum was obtained. So understood, ostracism looks even less like a criminal trial and even more like (as some scholars have put it) a negative general election, with the difference that "victory" in the "election" that was ostracism meant virtual suspension of the so-called winner's public life for a full decade by means of his physical removal from the scene of political life, namely Athens itself. Conflict, or its prospect, must have been at the heart of so drastic and, from our perspective, so unfair a procedure. Conflict had been the legacy of the sixth century, starting with potentially revolutionary state of affairs addressed by Solon, continuing through the regional rivalries that issued in the final triumph of Pisistratus and a half century of tyranny, and culminating in the in-fighting and foreign interventions that led to the foundation of the democracy. Perhaps the Athenians thought the unjust treatment of a maximum of one citizen per year was a small price to pay for an increased possibility of political stability for all of Athens.

So far we have pictured ostracism merely in terms of large numbers of citizens in the Agora filing through gates by tribe and depositing their individual single *ostrakon*. But everything we know about Athenian politics argues for some kind of organized activity behind these thousands of individual choices, and, sure enough, evidence pointing clearly in that direction is forthcoming from one of the most remarkable archaeological finds from ancient Athens: a deposit of 191 *ostraka* found in a well on the northern slope of the Acropolis. All but one of the 191 bear the same name, Themistocles, and study of the lettering by experts showed that all were inscribed by as few as a dozen or so different hands, that is, different people. The imagination runs wild. That something mischievous, if not illegal, was in store is evident from the fact that the *ostraka* were never actually cast as ballots but rather tossed into the well before they could be used. And why was this one name inscribed in advance? As an innocent convenience to citizens who had already decided to "vote" against Themistocles? Or was a conspiracy afoot involving bribery ("here's one all ready to go, and a drachma for your trouble!"). Or, even more sinisterly, was an anti-Themistocles group passing the ready-mades off to nonliterates who were told that the name inscribed was that of someone other than Themistocles? Obviously, the procedure was subject to abuse and was almost certainly about to be abused in some way on this occasion.

The lone individual acting on a purely personal impulse is the subject of a famous anecdote recorded by Plutarch. Aristides (ostracized in 482) was approached by a nonliterate countryman who, failing to recognize the man, requested that he inscribe upon his *ostrakon* the name Aristides. When asked by the popular general why he wanted to ostracize Aristides, the countryman responded that he was tired of hearing him called "the Just." Whereupon, the anecdote concludes, Aristides took the shard and inscribed it as requested.

Conflict and its resolution were not limited to the fortunes of powerful political figures. Were less eminent Athenians in some way touched by the procedure of ostracism—as they clearly were meant to be and in fact were by the operation of the judicial system? An answer is suggested again by the record of the *ostraka* themselves, which now number more than 10,000. These, once cast by citizens, were discarded in the Agora and in Potters' Quarter, to be found by archaeologists. Among the scores of names attested are many, in contrast with a Cimon or Themistocles, who are utterly unknown to us, and in the large majority of cases only one or two *ostraka* per unknown person have been found. What is the explanation? Previously unrecorded major politicians? Hardly, given the relatively dense and detailed surviving sources for fifth-century Athenian public life. More likely, these ballots were inscribed and cast as expressions of a citizen's purely personal feelings—to get back at a rival in love, to punish a borrower who had failed to pay a debt, to get even with someone who had snubbed an invitation to a wedding feast. Perhaps we should think here of a milder version of the so-called curse tablets—sheets of lead punched with dire maledictions, pierced with nails, and tossed into a well—better to reach the nether regions of Hades and Persephone! So with ostracism, too, we can yet again discern the personal underpinnings of an ostensibly "public" political institution.

Five

The World of Men

THE ATHENIAN MALE FROM CRADLE TO GRAVE

With the completion of our discussion of conflict in public life, we have addressed two of the main categories of "politics" at Athens as traditionally defined and understood: constitutions and elections (chapter 2) and courts and ostracism (chapter 4). It was principally through the workings of these institutions that individuals and groups competed for a share of *ta politika*— "the affairs of the polis"—and from that competition emerged as winners or losers. Now is the time to widen our discussion and to consider political activity in the context of the society in which it operated and thereby, I hope, fulfill the promise of the book's title. Already in chapter 3, we looked at Sparta from just this vantage point, examining that city's political forms as expressions of the bizarre Lycurgan "Discipline" and the unique social order that that regime brought into existence. Fundamental to the Lycourgan Spartan society was, we saw, the utterly contrasting life careers of men and women of the citizen class. So, let us look at Athenian society in the same way, beginning with the life course of citizen men, and then map onto that framework the political activities of those same men.

A basic principle about Athenian citizen society that must be understood from the outset is that the line between the public and the private spheres was drawn in a very different place than in our own experience. Much of what we in the modern world regard as an individual's own personal affairs and no one else's business was, if not actually controlled, at least subject to governmental—that is, public—interference in classical Athens. American law, for example, does not limit the choice of women a man may marry by declaring that only children born to wives of a certain category will be eligible for citizenship—thereby indirectly penalizing marriage to any woman in a different category. American law does not confine fundamental rights—such as the right to inherit—to those of legitimate birth and thus to male offspring of the marriage just described. Ancient Athenian law, however, did both.

At the heart of Athens' governmental intervention in what we would regard as a citizen's private life was the definition of legitimacy, a distinction largely disregarded in the modern world. A child is said to be legitimate when it is born to lawfully wedded parents—in the case of classical Athens (in the language of the law on citizenship), to "duly betrothed" Athenian parents. Betrothal (an archaic synonym for engagement) was an agreement between the father (or other male guardian) on the bride's side and, on the male side, if not the groom himself, his father or other older male relative. Representation by a guardian was required on the female side not only because women had virtually no legal standing in such a matter but more particularly because if this was a girl's first marriage, she was only 14 years old or so, while the man was typically twice her age at his first marriage. At some later time, following a banquet at the bride's parents' home, the two set up housekeeping at some new location (but very possibly in the groom's parents' home) and, in keeping with an unquestioned cultural imperative, turned to the serious business of producing a typically small family—usually no more than two children.

Female and male children, given the operation of the societal ideals that are the subject of this and the following chapter, would look forward to very different futures. But at least for the first few days of life, the two genders seem to have been treated alike. Within a week of birth, in a ceremony called Amphidromia, "running around," the newborn was carried around the interior central hearth, probably to mark its formal acceptance into the physical house. A few days later, in the Tenth Day ritual, the putative father cradled the infant in his arms and gave it a name, thereby formally and publicly acknowledging paternity. Paternity is always problematic but was particularly so in the absence of blood or DNA tests and at a time when the citizen population at least was ethnically homogeneous—and everyone looked pretty much the same.

With the completion of these two ritual affirmations of acceptance and legitimacy, a female could look forward to eligibility for marriage (that is, since she was a legitimate Athenian, she would not, if married to an Athenian man, compromise the legitimacy of any children) and continuing inclusion within the closed circle of the citizen elite. For the woman, marriage, even at the tender age of 14, amounted to the principal (indeed, the only) remaining rite of passage and marked, to put the point in developmental terms, the transition from girlhood to womanhood, from child to producer of children, from the guardianship of her father to the guardianship of her husband. Nonetheless, to revert to the fundamental distinction with which this chapter began, the Athenian female's progress from girl to woman and wife and mother did not mean a transition from the private to the public sphere. Public life at Athens was the exclusive province of citizen men. But to characterize a woman's existence as fundamentally "private," that is, domestic, is not to disparage it. When my readers reach the following chapter, "The World of Women," they can decide for themselves from their own perspectives which gender, males or females, enjoyed the more enviable existence in classical Athens.

Where males were concerned, however, the recorded rites of passage *did* mark the progressive stages of entry into the public sphere. Briefly, these were, following the Tenth Day naming ceremony, admission to the brotherhood; admission to the clan; admission to the village association; and completion of a two-year stint of military training and guard duty. With the ceremonial presentation before the Assembly of a shield and sword at about age 20, the young Athenian now formally entered the citizen body as a fully legitimated citizen. The legitimacy claimed by his father had withstood multiple scrutinies by brotherhood, clan, and village; his age, likewise, had been established beyond any reasonable doubt; his preparedness for military service, the duty of all able-bodied citizen males, was a matter of record. And, of course, the achievement of citizenship also meant that the young Athenian had reached the age of political activity in the classical democracy. But to delve more deeply into the nitty-gritty of his public life, we need to take into account important distinctions regarding place of residence, degree of wealth, and occupation.

ATHENS AND ATTICA

To this point, our discussion of Athens has been confined to the town, the relatively small and compact settlement at the foot of the Acropolis enclosed within the so-called Themistoclean fortifications. After the mid-fifth century, the town's enceinte was connected by a system of "Long Walls" to the two ports, the older one at Phaleron and its replacement at Peiraieus, the latter enclosed by its own circuit fortification. So, when we speak of urban Athens, we're referring primarily to the settlement within these walls—the town and the port at Peiraeus. But the city-state of Athens' territory—called Attica—extended far beyond its fortification system. Extramural or (the term I'll use from this point on) rural Attica covered about 1,000 square miles (equivalent to about 80 percent of the state of Rhode Island). And, if we count only citizens, about 95 percent of Athenians were officially affiliated with a rural deme, as, for example, in the case of "Pericles, son of Xanthippus, of the deme Cholargus." Obviously, no aspect of ancient Athens can be adequately understood unless rural Attica is also taken into account. What, then, do we know about politics in rural Attica?

The usual, and easy, answer would be that, since all of Athenian territory and all Athenian citizens were governed by the same system of laws, and since the legislature (the Council of 500 and the Assembly) and courts and magistrates were recruited from, and governed, all of Athens (not just its urban settlements), politics out in the countryside was fundamentally no different from politics in town and Peiraeus. All Athenians, including rural Athenians, were eligible to attend meetings of the Assembly. All Athenians, including rural Athenians, could volunteer for jury duty, be allotted to the pool, and become eligible for allotment to a courtroom panel. All Athenians, including rural Athenians, were eligible for allotment to a magisterial board or for election to a military or financial board, subject only to rules regarding minimum age and nonrepetition in most instances. But the clearest such case, the one that would seem to clinch the argument that rural politics and urban politics were one and the same, is the Council of 500. Did its members not represent the villages according to a system of quotas based on population? Did not the tiny farming communities at Oinoe and Tricorynthus and a hundred others select and send to town each year a fixed number of their own fellow villagers—and replace them each succeeding year with a fresh delegation, thereby ensuring an "urban experience" for all? Did not the Council, if we go by the quotas, as it seems we must, consist overwhelmingly of farmers and other countryfolk? And, if all this true, weren't rural Athenians, at least in terms of their political lives, no different from their urban counterparts?

The view taken here is that, in contrast with prevailing opinion, the answer to all these questions is No. Rural politics at Athens was in fact fundamentally different from the politics in town and at Piraeus. But to see how this could be true, despite so many appearances to the contrary, we must first make a couple of negative technical observations. The first of these concerns a male citizen's village affiliation. That affiliation was signaled, as we saw in chapter 2, by the *dēmotikon* (or "demotic"), an adjective appended to every citizen's name, such as "Marathonian" or "Rhamnousian." Not only rural Greeks but every Athenian had a demotic, since the town too was segmented into four "villages" and Piraeus constituted its own big "village." And it was with reference to the demotic that representation on the Council of 500 (to take the crucial case) was determined. So, in any given year, the 10 councilors from Marathon were Athenian men who had the demotic *Marathonios*. But the actual real-world situation was probably not so simple. Any citizen's demotic did not necessarily reflect his actual place of residence at the time. Rather, all the demotics went back to Day One of the democracy in 508/7 B.C.E. (or soon thereafter), when Clisthenes is assumed to have declared that every Athenian was to have a village affiliation based on the place of his primary residence at that time. The problem is that Clisthenes made the demotic both (1) portable and (2) hereditary. If an Athenian relocated from the village of his Clisthenic demotic to another village, the demotic went with him and remained unchanged. If that same Athenian had a son, the son inherited the demotic of his father—and so on down the generations, irrespective of any descendant's actual place of domicile. And we know that such relocations occurred, and in disproportionate numbers they were relocations not from rural village to rural village or from town to rural village but from rural village to town. So, late in the fourth century, when Aristotle was writing the *Constitution of the Athenians,* it could well have been the case that a large number of the Athenians with rural demotics sitting on the Council of 500 were actually residents of the town or Peiraeus—and that their families had been so for generations.

The second negative observation concerns the absence of any trace of village or even regional representation throughout the remainder of the democratic government—Assembly, courts, and boards of magistrates. Indeed, in those cases where a source preserves, say, the names of the members of a board of 10 with their demotics, it is clear that no mode of representation was in effect, that the 10 were selected without respect to village affiliation. And so, as with the Council, these Athenian men serving in this or that governmental capacity could have been from anywhere in Attica, and, if we were guessing, we would guess that they were in disproportionate numbers residents of the town. After all, it was in the town, in and around the Agora, that the democracy's entire physical infrastructure was located. Absolutely nothing stands in the way of our concluding that Athens' democratic government was dominated by the urban citizen residents.

The Demes of Attica

Well, then what was the nature of political life in rural Attica outside the walls? To answer that question, we must first have a working understanding of the countryside in its demographic and societal dimensions. The key organizational unit was the "village," to which I have repeatedly referred already, but now it is time to start calling the village by its ancient Greek constitutional name, *dēmos,* or, in its anglicized form, "deme" (in order to prevent confusion with another use of the same word, *Dēmos,* to designate the People or citizen body). Presumably created out of preexisting villages or other settlements by Clisthenes when the *dēmokratia* was established, in 508/7 B.C.E., the demes numbered by a reliable count 139 in the classical period, and the system underwent very little noticeable change through the end of antiquity. As mentioned previously, only five of the demes were situated within the fortifications (four in around the central Acropolis-Agora town and a fifth at Peiraeus), with the 134 others distributed more or less evenly over the vast expanse of extramural Attica. Very little is known about the demes. Perhaps a hundred or so are merely names to us, and in many cases (but not all) an approximate location has been deduced from various clues. The better-known demes include those few that were the sites of large Athenian sanctuaries utilized by all Athens (such as Eleusis, Rhamnous, and Sounion), as well as the 40 to 45 or so from which inscriptions on stone recording the official acts of a deme association have been recovered. That, furthermore, we can say that we know something about the system as a whole (including a definitive number for the units, 139, just given) is owing to the preservation of many documents, again inscribed on stone stelae, pertaining to the composition of the Council of 500. The Council's 500 seats were apportioned to the 139 demes on the basis of numbers of citizens bearing a given deme's demotic (again, as we saw, not necessarily corresponding to the actual place of residence), and from the inscriptions can be reconstructed virtually the full list of demes and quotas. At a higher level of organization, the demes had been grouped by Clisthenes in regional entities called Thirds (and three Thirds, according to a complex plan, made up one of the 10 *phylai,* or tribes), and this macro-organization too seems to be reproduced in the documents of the Council (thereby, incidentally, providing valuable clues regarding the location of the many demes for which there are no visible physical traces on the ground).

When this detailed information about the number of demes, the size of individual demes measured in terms of citizen members, and the location (even if only approximate) of the demes is put on a map of Attica, we can begin to learn something about the nature of rural political life. The first point of importance to be noted concerns distance from the urban center, where, as I continue to emphasize, the seat of the democratic government was physically situated. All significant participation in the democracy of Athens transpired in town (or at Piraeus) or at least began and ended there. The only exceptions were the few procedures administered on location by the deme's chief executive officer, the demarch, in his concurrent capacity as representative of the central government in Athens. But if a citizen wished to attend a meeting of the Assembly, sit on a jury panel, serve on a magisterial board, or run for elective office, he had to get to town—and in many instances be prepared to stay there for a while, even for an entire civil year if he was to exercise magisterial responsibilities.

Now, just how feasible, in the case of the ordinary rural Athenian, was such a major disruption of one's domestic or working life going to be? Some of the more remote demes lay as much as 15 or 20 miles from town, and in some cases terrain would have imposed additional difficulties. Travel for most citizens would presumably be by foot. Farmers might conceivably ride on a slow-moving mule or ox-drawn wagon, but only the prosperous few would have had a horse at their disposal. At the town end, even a half-day's service in the Assembly or on a jury panel would probably have necessitated a layover for the night, thereby entailing additional expense for room, board, and stabling. In the case of jury service, the civic-minded citizen might go all the way to the Agora, only *not* to be selected by lot for a panel. And what of the protracted in-town duties implied by such magisterial titles as Town Stewards *(astunomoi)* or Road Crew *(hodopoioi)* or Wall Builders *(toichopoioi)*? Might a farmer, and head of a household at that, absent himself from home for the long stretches of time implicit in many types of government service? Even allowing for wife and grown sons (daughters would have married and joined their husbands' new households by the time they became useful laborers), hired hands, and slaves, an adult citizen male was on any accounting a sizable fraction of a farm's workforce—not to mention the necessity of his presence at home for any number of reasons.

Key to understanding the situation is the negative observation that, in contrast to the contemporary American way of looking at citizenship, ancient Athenians did not cultivate an ideal of participation in government or of exercising one's civic rights. With the sole exceptions of military service and payment of the occasional extraordinary tax, any citizen's involvement in democratic institutions or processes was entirely voluntary. True, the rate of participation by our standards seems relatively high, but we have to remember that all such participation was compensated and that, once allowance is made for citizens with rural demotics resident in the town, the urban citizen population by itself was probably sufficient to keep the legislature, courts, and magisterial boards in continuous operation.

Patronage in the Rural Demes

Not the urban phenomenon of politics based on the democracy but a quite different kind of politics was going on in the rural demes. From our ancient sources we have only one unambiguous example, but it is an excellent one: the fourth-century historian Theopompus's story about the prominent mid-fifth-century politician Cimon. The son of the wealthy aristocrat Miltiades, Cimon was affiliated with the tiny extraurban deme of Lakiadai. Here is what Theopompus says:

> Cimon the Athenian posted no guard over the crop in his fields and gardens, in order that those who wished of the citizens might enter and gather fruit and take whatever they wanted of what was in the plots. And then he made his house common to all. And he always provided an inexpensive dinner for many people, and the poor of the Athenians used to enter and dine. He attended to those who each day asked something of him, and they say he always led around with him two or three youths with small change on them and ordered them to give it away whenever someone approached him with a request. And they say he would make contributions for burials. And he also did the following many times: Whenever he saw any of the citizens poorly clothed, he would order one of the youths accompanying him to change clothes with the man. From all this, he enjoyed a high reputation and was first among the citizens.[1]

Two other versions survive from antiquity, which need be quoted only to the extent that they bear upon Cimon's activity in his rural deme itself. First, Aristotle in his *Constitution of the Athenians* makes not "the Athenians" (as in Theopompus) but the Lakiadai demesmen the recipients of Cimon's largess:

> For Cimon, since he owned property worthy of a tyrant, first performed the common liturgies in splendid fashion, and then sustained many of his demespeople. For any of the Lakiadai who so wished could approach him each and every day and receive what was necessary for a comfortable livelihood; and, as well, all his fields were unfenced, in order that anyone who wished might enjoy the produce.[2]

Next, Plutarch, working centuries later from already existing secondary sources (such as Theopompus and Aristotle), adds a few other relevant details and some interpretation in his account:

> And already being wealthy, Cimon spent the booty from his campaigns...on the citizens. He removed the fences from his fields, in order that it be possible for strangers and those in need of the citizens to take from the crops without fear. And every day he put on dinner in his home, frugal to be sure but adequate for many, to which who wished of the poor might come and have a maintenance without trouble, now at leisure for public affairs alone. But Aristotle says that it was not for all Athenians but for his demespeople the Lakiadai that he prepared the dinner for anyone who wished.

And well dressed young cronies attended him, each of whom, if any of the older town residents in shabby clothes chanced upon Cimon, would exchange cloaks with him. This practice left an impression of majesty. And these same young men, carrying a great quantity of coin, approaching the more dignified of the poor in the Agora, would quietly slip small change into their hands...(10.1–3). But proclaiming his house a public town hall for the citizens, and in the country providing for strangers to take and enjoy the first fruits of the ripe crops and all the fine things the seasons bring, after a fashion he brought back to life the fabled communism of the time of Cronus.[3]

The idea emerging most clearly from Plutarch's version is the model of town-career-with-country-base. That Cimon, speaker in the Assembly, elected general, and conservative leader, was a town politician there can be no doubt. But no less unambiguous in all three versions is his dominant position, rooted in personal wealth and farmlands, among his home demesmen. And that dominance was expressed above all in the dependence of his fellow villagers upon Cimon for food, clothing, and cash. However, and crucially for our understanding of the situation, the payback was not in kind (e.g., food) but in prestige ("high reputation," "first among citizens," in Theopompus's version). Asymmetrical reciprocity of this kind, arising out of economic (and the resulting social) inequalities, we might call patronage, and a modern investigator of a living culture of this type might call Cimon a Big Man.

As plausible as all this may appear to my readers, a professional historian of ancient Greece might be unhappy with an interpretation based, as is this one, entirely on noncontemporary literary sources. Theopompus, who appears to have been the primary source excerpted by both Aristotle and Plutarch, was not an Athenian (he was born on the island of Chios), and he wrote a full century later than Cimon's activity. Certainly, it would be preferable to have some contemporary documentation from Athens. Well, I would say to my critic, it's arguable that we do have such documentation. It comes to us in the form of numerous decrees from the rural demes bestowing honors upon persons who had benefited the village and its residents in some significant way. In more than a few cases, the benefactor is said to have performed his meritorious services in connection with lands, crops, the harvest, farmers, and the like—that is, in connection with just the sorts of things of concern to a rural and especially agrarian population. Most scholars have read these decrees as though they were decrees of the democratic legislature in Athens town, where the benefactors are war heroes, heads of foreign states, and, indeed, entire foreign states themselves. But it is attractive to view the rural honorary texts as thinly disguised forms of patronage: Local Big Man provides the means to bring in the crops; local villagers, his dependents, meet in the deme's assembly to reciprocate by bestowing honors upon him and inscribing their decree on a beautiful monument in the village square for all to see. Honors in exchange for food would be entirely suitable asymmetrical transaction in a patronal environment.

"Patronal," used in the preceding sentence, is from Latin *patronus,* "patron." At Rome, patrons were (what I am calling here) the Big Men, and clients were their economic and especially social dependents. Greeks and Romans were very different peoples, but beneath the surface the two environments had many elements in common—natural resources, climate, technology, neighbors, idea systems, and so on. Patronage, rooted in inequality, was surely the fundamental social institution of ancient Rome. We should not expect Athens, just a few hundred miles to the east and on only a slightly earlier schedule, to be all that different. Inequality, despite all the noise made by the *dēmokratia*, certainly continued to exist on a large scale. Recorded acreages of Attic farms, for example, reveal a variation of four or five to one, easily adequate to produce and maintain significant class stratification. My guess is that Athens was not in fact all that different. Outside the walls of Athens, in the world of men, politics meant essentially the interactions between what their Roman neighbors might have called "patrons" and "clients."

A traditional agrarian community dominated by a Big Man and ruled by custom seems to be at odds with the clearly visible remains of the arrangements of the democratic village. From contemporary inscriptions from the village sites, references in Athenian literature, and the occasional significant physical remains, we can piece together what looks like a central village hub duplicating in miniature the state's own town hub in and around the Agora. Hence, the typical characterization of the deme is that of *polis* in microcosm—a model that formally asserts, moreover, the diffusion of democratic ideology from the town to the countryside. This model concedes (correctly, I think) that the citizen residents of remote Attic demes did not in all probability avail themselves of opportunities in the distant town. But it also adds, less correctly, that these same citizens, in response to their isolation, brought about the development of their village into a quasi "little Athens."

This characterization is, however, an illusion—plausible, beguiling, yet nonetheless an illusion. Yes, the infrastructure, organizational arrangements, constitutional bodies and processes, and so on existed, but the uses to which they seem to have been put were quite at odds with their modern urban counterparts in town. The person honored by decree in Athens was a politician, a general, or a head of state. But the person honored in the village could just as easily have been the owner of the largest acreage on the best land who had opened his silos to his fellow small-holder villagers after a drought. The Assembly in town was dominated by a random rootless mass of landless urbanites ready to cast their votes according to political slogan, ideology, or whim of the moment. But, in the village assembly, a vote by the demesmen may have been dictated in advance by obligation or loyalty to the local Big Man. The Agora in town was the literal embodiment of the values and thinking of a large and dependent urban populace. But the village's agora was mostly for show, probably imposed from Athens through the medium of its agent the demarch—and consequently misleading with respect to the fundamentally different culture and social-political organization of a rural farming or pastoral community.

To get a more vivid impression of the cleft that separated the political life of the village from that of the town, we may turn to contemporary Athenian literature. As in our own times, the clash of cultures when country and town came into contact was a favorite theme of writers of more than one literary genre. Let us take, as a particularly apt and explicit example, the essay on *Agroikia*, or "Rusticity," by the late-classical writer Theophrastus. Theophrastus was not a native Athenian (he had been born in Eresos, on the island of Lesbos), but he lived in Athens and achieved fame as the successor to Aristotle as the head of the philosophical school in the Lyceum. Among his surviving writings is a collection of 30 or more brief sketches of personality types called the *Characters*. The one on "rusticity" goes like this:

Rusticity would seem to be an unbecoming ignorance, and the rustic the kind of man who takes a purge before he goes to the Assembly, who declares that thyme smells every bit as sweet as perfume, who wears shoes too large for his feet, and who talks at the top of his voice. He distrusts his friends and kinsfolk, but confides matters of great importance to his slaves, and tells everything that went on in the Assembly to the hired laborers who work on his farm. He will sit down with his cloak above his knee, so that his private parts are showing. Most things this man sees in the street do not strike him at all, but whenever he sees an ox or an ass or a billy goat, he stops to inspect it. He is skilled at eating while in the very act of taking food from the larder, and he mixes his wine too strong. On the sly he makes a pass at the slave girl who bakes the bread, then helps her grind the day's flour for the whole household, himself included. He feeds the draft animals while he is eating his breakfast. When someone knocks, he actually opens the door himself. When he puts on a feast, he calls the dog, takes him by the snout, and says: "This guy guards my house and farm." When he receives a coin, he bites it and, saying that it is lead, demands that it be exchanged for another. And if he has lent out his plough, or a basket, or a sickle, or a sack, he will remember it as he lies awake at night and get up and go out to look for it. On his way to town, he will ask anyone he meets the price of hides or herring, and whether it's a new moon festival day. If the answer is Yes, he announces that he'll get a haircut and buy some herrings at Archias's shop on the way to the barber's. He is also inclined to singing in the baths, and loves to drive hobnails into the soles of his shoes.[4]

Town-meets-country is a well-established theme in Greek literature, almost approaching the genre scene with its stock, stereotyped characters and routine topics. Theophrastus's sketch gives us a broad sweep across the entire spectrum of private and public life, in each instance the country practice on the one end of that spectrum standing alone in implied contrast with its town opposite number on the other. The perspective is by reasonable inference urban. An urban author (namely a scholar in the Lyceum) writing for an urban literate readership (since, so far as we know, only townspeople had access to education) does not need to point out how an urbanite behaves in these settings. Rather, it is precisely the urban experience and the urbane sensibility that are assumed as givens and that are the ultimate sources of amusement. By urban standards, the rustic and everything he does is to the townsman or townswoman intrinsically laughable.

Where politics are concerned, Theophrastus's rustic does not know how to keep his cloak pulled down when sitting at Assembly and, afterwards, back

home, rambles on to most inappropriate (and probably) captive listeners—
the hired hands on the farm! Apparently, farmer-at-Assembly was stock topic,
for we have another example in an even earlier contemporary source, the
comedy *Acharnians,* by Aristophanes, produced in the year 423 B.C.E. The
principal character, Dicaeopolis ("Just Polis"), who hails from a country
deme, opens the drama with a soliloquy from his seat in the assembly place
on Pnyx hill:

O Polis! Polis! I am always the first of all to come to the Assembly and take my seat.
And then, when I am all by myself, I moan, I yawn, I stretch, I break wind, I daydream,
I doodle, I pluck myself, I do some figuring—all while looking off towards the country,
lusting for peace, hating the town, but longing for my deme, which has not to this day
spoken the words "buy charcoal," "buy vinegar," "buy olive oil" nor even knew the
word "buy," but on its own produced everything with no grating Buy Guy in sight!
And so now I have simply come prepared to shout, to break in, to abuse the speakers, if anyone touches on any topic but peace.[5]

Apparently Dicaeopolis's behaviors are all too reminiscent of life in the
village. But can we learn anything by inference about the village's specifically political life? The village's deme association did, we know, have an assembly, called in Greek the *agora;* again, many decrees passed by its members
have survived for us to read. But if Dicaeopolis's and Theophrastus's rustics
are representative, the village's assembly must have differed markedly in
tone and ambience from its counterpart in town. No mention, to be sure,
is made in the decrees of a village Big Man, so his presence (and influence)
remain an inference from the content of the honorary decrees discussed
earlier. But, if I am right, he was often the honoree on whom, as "patron,"
the assembled villagers, as "clients," bestowed honors in exchange for material benefactions in a typical asymmetrical patronage relationship based on
reciprocity.

THE TOWN

My title "The World of Men" reflects the reality that only males of the citizen class enjoyed access to constitution, government, politics, and to public
life generally—whether in village or in town. Our two portraits of the countryman visiting the democratic Assembly provide a neat transition to the
town itself and its distinctive political forms and practices.

Chapter 2, "Constitutions, Governments, and Politics," dealt with these
subjects in detail, and no rehearsal of those discussions is required here. What
is needed is a more personal appreciation (and appreciation from the Athenian male's own perspective) of the institutions, rules, and numbers set out in
that earlier chapter. And, beyond that appreciation, we are looking for an understanding of the more day-to-day and interpersonal connections between
Athenians—men and boys—that underlay, shaped, and fueled the more visible and "official" politics of the town.

Hetairia, Symposium, and Personal Relationships

As it happens, we know quite a bit about the politics of the town—especially concerning the aristocrats residing or based there. One manifestation of aristocratic political life at Athens stands out in particular, the *hetairia,* or "association" (the related personal noun *hetairos* means "companion"). The *hetairia* goes a long way back in Athenian political history. Late in the seventh century B.C.E., according to Herodotus,[6] a *hetairia* was formed around an aristocrat (and, significantly, an Olympic running champion) named Cylon. With the assistance of an army provided by his father-in-law, the tyrant of nearby Megara, Cylon attempted to overthrow the Athenian government. The attempt was not successful, but the fact remains that a nominally private social circle was at the heart of the conspiracy. Two centuries later, the government (now the classical democracy) *was* overthrown, an episode in which Thucydides[7] says conspiratorial societies were recruited for "the dissolution of the *Dēmos.*" Not so overtly political at the governmental level but nonetheless potentially subversive of the political order were the so-called hellfire clubs. Several are known, such as *Ithyphalloi* ("Erect Penises") and *Kakodaimonistai* ("Evil Spirit Worshippers"), and their members seem to have been young, aristocratic males. Notwithstanding the groups' ostensibly cultic or ritualistic orientation, these names suggest deeper antisocial or iconoclastic purposes. Such juvenile delinquent gangs might well have been the perpetrators of the urban street violence (in fact, the scene was the Agora) reported later in the fourth century B.C.E. by Demosthenes in his speech *Against Konon.*[8]

Why the aristocratic orientation and membership? According to the present writer's comprehensive thesis worked out in *The Associations of Classical Athens: The Response to Democracy,* the *hetairiai* were fueled by aristocratic reaction to the leveling egalitarian ideology of the democracy established by Clisthenes and reigning supreme throughout the classical fifth and fourth centuries B.C.E. They provided an apparatus for the organization and eventually the execution of strikes against a form of government that was the very antithesis of everything aristocrats stood for. Claims to privilege based on high birth, continuing influence in all matters private and public, and maintenance of a distinctive (and much emulated) lifestyle were the planks of their platform. When we discussed ostracism in chapter 4, mention was made of the discovery of a cache of *ostraka* all but one bearing the name of Themistocles and of the fact that, to judge from the writing, only a dozen or so individuals had been involved in the production of the entire lot of 191 inscribed shards. A group of this small size working cooperatively against a prominent democratic politician is an obvious strong candidate for a *hetairia.* But, at the same time, we should not succumb to a simplifying model of innocent-social-group-temporarily-diverted-to-political-ends. An ideology, the ideology of reaction against democratic egalitarianism, was probably at the heart of the *hetairia* from the beginning. And, while visible outbreaks of violence seem indeed to have been rare, even such extreme measures were probably in fundamental agreement with the goals of these associations.

Symposium

Related in some uncertain manner to the *hetaira* was the *symposium*, or drinking party (the Greek word means literally "drinking together"). Mirroring the composition of the *hetairiai* and hellfire clubs, the symposium was normally attended only by males—specifically, aristocratic males both young and old. Small and exclusive, as we'll now see, the symposium might be regarded as the *hetairia* in its social and pleasure-seeking aspect, but since we are dealing here with terminology no more formal or institutionalized than English "party" and "club," there is no need to press the evidence for an exact correspondence.

"Symposium" refers to only a single phase—albeit (for the participants) the most important phase—of a rather lengthy social gathering. A libation (the ceremonial dedication of a liquid) and prayer opened the party, followed by a meal (*deipnon*) and then the *symposion* proper. At the end came a closing libation and prayer and, last, the *kōmos*—a procession through the streets by the now drunken revelers. Prior to the exit of the *kōmos,* the setting of the party had been a private residence, specifically the *andrōn,* or men's room, the design and dimensions of which tell us much about the nature of the event. Square in floor plan but with a single doorway set off-center, the space was equipped with usually seven (two against each wall, one on the wall with the doorway) or more couches. The symposiasts reclined on the left elbow, two on each couch, in which position they ate from low tables set before them and were served by slave wine stewards. Entertainment might be provided by female musicians (who are entirely nude in some pictorial representations) or by professional lyric poets. The guests also played a game called *kottabos* ("wine-throw") in which the players, while still reclining on the left elbow, would fling the last drops of wine from their cups at various targets placed in the center of the couches.

Resemblances to certain contemporary social events in the modern world may spring to mind, but in the ancient Athenian case it is important to emphasize the ideological character of the proceedings. Needless to say, only a select few could ever hope to be invited to so intimate a gathering. The symposium immortalized by Plato in his *Dialogue* of that name, for example, included among its guests, in addition to Socrates, a leading politician-general, Alcibiades, and a leading tragic poet (perhaps, among contemporaries, second only to Euripides), Agathon. Things were done just so, in a set way, in a set order, as in the case of the preprogrammed orchestration of the wine service with the purpose of postponing full drunkenness until just the right (final) moment. As in Plato's symposium, discourse might be very elevated, and any performance of exquisite lyrics would appeal only to a cultivated musical and literary sensitivity—naked flute-girls and vomiting symposiasts notwithstanding. And why all this orchestration (as I have termed it)? Why not simply get drunk and proceed directly to sex with the flute girls? Well, exclusion, above all else, seems to have been determinedly at work. The symposium's larger setting was, after all, a democratic regime where social leveling continually threatened the aristocrat, and his traditional claims to social preeminence, with extinction. Ritual, elaborate proceedings, and high culture—what better way to keep the riff-raff out! But also important, and complementing the exclusivity, was the promotion of internal group solidarity, of interpersonal cohesion. Such a bonding manifested itself publicly in the symposium's final scene, when, in the *kōmos,* the drunken aristocrats took their until-this-point private social affair onto the streets of democratic Athens.

At this point, the symposium was transformed into a political phenomenon. To be sure, the *kōmos* might have ended in the muggings in the Agora recorded in the just-cited speech of Demosthenes, *Against Konon,* but it is also attractive to link the symposium with the overtly political activities of the *hetairiai.* Mention has already been made of the conspiratorial societies that Thucydides says were instrumental in the overthrow of the democracy late in the fifth century. Earlier, during the Peloponnesian War and on the eve of the departure of an Athenian naval expedition to Sicily in the year 415, unidentified parties jinxed the expedition by going around the streets at night mutilating statues of the god Hermes—an act of sacrilege that could only be interpreted as an ill omen. Soon, another sacrilege was rumored to have occurred on previous occasions: performances in private homes by private individuals of the mysteries (strictly, initiatory rites) of the goddesses Demeter and Persephone. Among the accused was one of three commanders of the expedition, the aristocratic politician Alcibiades (see chapter 7 for his political career). We think at once of the Themistocles *ostraka,* the hellfire clubs, the muggings in the Agora, the conspiratorial societies at century's end—all with their signs or hints of youthful, male, and especially aristocratic associations. While details remain hard to pin down, there can be little doubt that in the *hetairia*-symposium nexus is to be found a major wellspring of Athenian political life.

Athletics, Gymnasium, and Palaestra

At the beginning of the previous chapter, the subject of conflict was introduced with a general discussion of the *agōn,* or contest, so fundamental to the Greeks' combative approach to social relations. The inclination to compete manifested itself easily and naturally in athletics, but careful note must be made of the ways in which the Greeks' athletics differed from the modern world's. With few arguable exceptions, ancient Greek competition was between individuals, never teams—thereby contrasting sharply with the generally corporate organization of Greek societies. While measurements were taken and recorded where technologically possible (distances jumped, weights lifted, competitions won), the overriding goal was to win by defeating one's rivals. Furthermore, the ultimate object of winning was to achieve personal glory, to secure enduring fame, to enhance one's prestige among one's peers, and to ennoble one's family connections and descendants. Thus, the prizes at the Panhellenic Games were typically wreaths of olive (Olympia), laurel (Delphi), or celery or parsley (Isthmia and Nemea). Prizes could also have considerable intrinsic value, such as the bronze cauldron called a tripod or a fine painted amphora filled with costly olive oil, but it is not clear that the winner would convert such a prize into cash, any more than a modern athlete would normally sell or hawk an Olympic gold medal or a Super Bowl ring. Greek athletics were all about winning, defeating the competition, and, above all, achieving popularity.

Once popularity was achieved, athletics could, and did, play various roles in Greek political life. Athletic accomplishments might easily be translated into a victory in an election or other political endeavor. Examples from Athens are straightforward and unambiguous. As previously mentioned, late in the 600s B.C.E., an aristocratic Athenian named Cylon attempted to overthrow the government with the aid of the army of his father-in-law, the tyrant of Megara. Cylon's sole recorded claim to prominence at the time was a victory in the 220-yard dash in the Panhellenic Games at Olympia. Since foreign intervention could never have been popular at Athens (or elsewhere), we can surmise that Cylon saw the Olympian laurels as a key to his acceptance as Athens' new ruler. Two centuries later, Alcibiades (the same man soon to be implicated in the scandals perpetrated on the eve of the Sicilian Expedition) came before an assembly of Athenians and, in support of his political position, instanced his showing at the Olympic Games of 416 B.C.E.—seven entries in the four-horse chariot race, carrying off first, second, and fourth places! Throughout the fifth century, unnamed Athenian victors at Olympia and Delphi were rewarded with a daily free meal for life in the town hall. Since the hall also played host to prominent visitors from out of town, this was Athens' way of showing off its celebrity athletes. The underlying logic is explicitly laid bare by Alcibiades in the speech re-created by Thucydides. His victory had brought glory to Athens (as well as to himself), and it was only fitting that Athens reciprocate by supporting his policy proposals. Thus, we can find here the same asymmetrical exchange that we saw marked relations between Big Man and underlings, with the difference here that the Big Man is an Olympic champion! Athlete as Big Man, athlete as patron to an adoring citizen clientele!

At a less exalted, everyday level, sporting activity could be found among males of all classes. Particularly notable is the *gymnasium* (from Greek *gymnos,* "naked"), an approximate equivalent of the modern community center with its assortment of social and cultural as well as strictly athletic facilities and activities. Within the gymnasium, or standing alone, was the *palaestra,* or wrestling pit. Wrestling was pursued by males of all ages. Popular in part because of its extreme simplicity, wrestling required no formal facility, no equipment (especially when, as was apparently the case, the wrestlers were nude), no particular skills necessarily, but, above all, it was a simple form of toe-to-toe individual combat and thus good preparation for boys who would one day enter the arena of political (as well as military) combat. From Plato's *Dialogues,* which are occasionally set in a gymnasium or palaestra, we learn that the boys and men present often came from aristocratic, and therefore potentially political, families. Accordingly, it is quite probable that athletic competition did indeed set many an Athenian on the path to victory in the *agōnes* of the democracy.

ARMY, NAVY, CALVARY

Whatever political dimensions these athletic activities possessed, it remains an essential truth of ancient Greek civilization that their origins and continuing reason for existing were fundamentally military. Just consider, for example, the javelin throw, the running race in infantry armor, and the horse-drawn chariot race. It is appropriate, therefore, to conclude our discussion of the world of men in politics by turning to the quintessential male public role, at Athens and elsewhere in Greece—military service.

Military service, at least in classical Athens, was both a duty and a privilege of citizenship. Under normal circumstances, every citizen male would undergo late in his teens two years of mandatory training in the so-called Ephebic College (an ephebe was a youth of 18 years). After graduation, the young Athenian would remain eligible for call-up through his sixtieth year, that is through the year that he turned 59. Mobilizations occurred at irregular intervals depending upon the city's war footing at the moment. The campaigning season in any given year was basically the warm and relatively clement summer when seas were navigable and the earth dry enough to allow infantry and cavalry maneuvering. But a war might drag on for decades, as did the 27-year long conflict with the Peloponnesians (431–404 B.C.E.). Citizens in the service of Athens were responsible for supplying themselves with their equipment, while the per diem allowances mentioned in the sources were probably barely sufficient to cover daily expenditures. Clearly, since farm or shop would have to go without the labor of an able-bodied man, no citizen could expect to come out ahead by serving his city in the military.

Economic factors were at work in another, far more consequential, way, as well. Wealth, and the social distinctions tied to wealth, underlay the segmentation of the Athenian military into three main branches. Accordingly, each branch came to acquire a distinctive political or ideological orientation. So, let us take them up one by one with special attention to the "politics" of soldier, sailor, and cavalryman.

Army

At the heart of the land army was the hoplite, or heavy-armed, infantry. Hoplite armor comprised helmet, breastplate, shield, greaves (resembling the shin guards worn by young soccer players), sword, and spear. Thus equipped, hoplites were deployed in a long line called the phalanx. Crucially for our concerns, the effective operation of the phalanx depended upon the skill and strict discipline of the soldiers. Specifically, the need for cooperation and uniformity required the stifling of the individual impulse, and the habit of mind thus instilled took on a decidedly egalitarian complexion. At the same time, the requirement that each hoplite purchase his own expensive panoply of armor, which put hoplite service out of the reach of the poor, justifies our thinking of the very sizable infantry corps (up to a fourth or third of the citizen body at any given time) as a sort of "middle class." And how would such class membership translate into political attitudes? Many maintained their prosperity through farming and therefore tended to favor a traditional agrarian regime of lifestyle and values. Consequently, hoplites would tend to favor cordial relations with old-fashioned land-locked polities such as Sparta. And when, after the Persian Wars, Athens undertook a massive reorientation toward the sea—maritime empire, reliance on the navy, and overseas adventure—the conservative hoplite class stoutly resisted. Not naval victories but the great hoplite land battle against the Persians at Marathon was their rallying call and enduring icon.

Navy

It was during the Persian Wars of the early fifth century that Athens began its turn from land to sea. Under the leadership of the politician-general Themistocles, the proceeds from a lucky silver strike were put toward the construction of a fleet of 200 triremes—the fleet that defeated the Persians in the great sea battle off the island of Salamis. With the return of peace, Athens by stages converted the once voluntary anti-Persian alliance into a tribute-paying empire headquartered at Athens and controlled by the Athenian legislature. The consequences for the male military-age population were enormous. Each trireme required a crew of 170 or so rowers, not counting officers and on-board hoplite marines. Rowers consequently were drawn from the great mass of poorer citizens, usually (it is believed) landless urban residents of the town and harbors. But even their large numbers did not meet the demand, for we learn that resident aliens and even slaves served as rowers alongside Athenian citizens. As with all public service, navy duty was compensated by state treasury, and in the case of the many poor rowers even a small per diem might mean an appreciable improvement in quality of life. Since rowers were paid only when the fleet was in operation, they naturally favored naval war operations, the expansion of the maritime empire, and the collection of tribute (for public expenditure sometimes to their own personal benefit). This large clientele of citizen voters was courted by the radical democratic politicians such as Themistocles, Pericles, and Alcibiades (see chapter 7).

Cavalry

Tactically, a mounted contingent was a vital component of Athens' land force, but its provision and maintenance posed two formidable barriers: expense and training. Throughout antiquity, horses were a badge of wealth, often enormous wealth. The animals were costly to acquire and maintain and, compared to stock animals, orchards, or field crops, represented a much less economical use of farmland. Not only was it difficult enough to learn to ride under the best of conditions, but the absence of tack in the ancient world compounded that difficulty. No wonder that only a leisured few with animals at their personal disposal ever achieved the skills requisite for mounted military service. Thus, the corps of 1,200 Athenian riders we learn of at the outbreak of the Peloponnesian War would be found(had we more information about specific individuals) to be wealthy aristocrats with family traditions of horse ownership and breeding. Enjoying enduring prestige even under the egalitarian democracy, the riders were even more conservative than the hoplites, favoring as they did good relations with Sparta and a restrictive oligarchic constitution.

The impact of military service and of specific membership in this or that branch cannot be overstated. All voters—adult citizen males—were military personnel of some kind. After the decline of the archonship (in the train of the introduction of the lottery for selection of the annual boards), the only effective political leaders remaining were the *stratēgoi,* or "generals." ("Generals" must have quotation marks, because the *stratēgoi* included naval as well as land-based commanders.) No separation of military and civilian authorities, so familiar to us, was ever conceived of, much less implemented. Moreover, many important policy issues, such as war or peace, expansion or maintenance at status quo levels of the empire, and even much domestic spending, necessarily engaged a citizen's military status, experience, and sympathies. To say that Athenian politics can be understood only in the light of its military dimensions is a conclusion well justified under the circumstances that we have here briefly sketched. In "the world of men," it would never have occurred to an Athenian citizen of the classical period to separate his virtually lifelong military training, obligations, and activity from his political participation in the democracy.

Six

The World of Women

When we turn to women, we must continue to keep in mind some of the definitions and qualifications underlying our study of politics and society. The term "politics," again, has wider reference to the affairs of the polis or city-state. While including the familiar politics of campaigns and elections, ancient Greek *ta politika* actually embraced the whole of public life—and, in the process, captured as well some of what we call "society." So, although there is no disputing (as we saw in the preceding chapter on the world of men) that only adult males of citizen descent were eligible to acquire and exercise the rights of citizenship, narrowly defined, it is a fact that women of the citizen class did enjoy some of the privileges reserved for "Athenians." It is the goal of the present chapter to explore in its various dimensions the female participation in *ta politika* of classical Athens.

METHODOLOGICAL PRELIMINARIES

Any attempt to characterize the place of women with regard to politics and society must take into account the findings and insights achieved by the academic study of women in classical antiquity during the preceding half-century. The women's movement, feminism, and, in academia, women's and gender studies have vaulted the subject of women, previously hardly recognized at all, to the level of major topic of investigation. That it had not been such previously is perhaps understandable in view of the fact that the evidential record is dominated by male authors writing about the affairs of males for a largely male audience—and that turns out to mean, above all, the men's world of politics (in the narrow sense). As a result, while the public lives of males are lavished with attention in the ancient sources, only very rarely do females rise to the level of subjects in their own right. A few (non-Athenian) lyric poets (such as Sappho), the occasional funerary epigram over a woman's grave, and the fictional roles played by females in works of literature are representative of the meager sources on women produced in antiquity. So, while it is undeniably true that women (as well as children, slaves, nonmainstream subcultures, and so on) historically have been largely neglected by classical scholars, it is also undeniably true that the lives of women of ancient Greece for the most part went unrecorded, that the subject is a difficult one to study—and that for these and other reasons interpretation is hotly contested.

Contestation in the present case comes down, as it often does, to underlying—and usually unexpressed—assumptions. Before proceeding further, let's take a minute to briefly identify a few of these, with an indication of the positions buttressing our own analysis.

1. Contrary to the design of many a book and article on ancient Greek women, females cannot be studied without studying their male counterparts simultaneously. True, ancient Athenian women suffered in comparison with women today, but it is equally true that ancient Athenian men suffered as well, albeit in different ways.

2. Ancient can be compared only with ancient, modern with modern, but not ancient with modern. To be sure, we're all free intellectually to make any comparisons we wish, and the principle bolstering the study of the past is that such study has some value for the present. But where the genders are at issue, and a past regime of genders is being brought into expressed or implicit comparison with present regimes, there is admittedly a strong temptation to juxtapose ancient women (usually unfavorably) with modern women or even with modern men. Since the contexts in the two cases are utterly different, it is questionable that anything of value could possibly flow from such an exercise.

3. Difference does not imply, or even suggest, superiority or inferiority. Ancient writers and their texts routinely mark variations between male and female, not infrequently to encourage gender-appropriate behavior. Thus, cowardly male soldiers are conventionally likened to women. And the mythical female Amazons, who, rejecting marriage and domesticity, adopted the male role of armed soldier, were defeated in short order by an army of Athenian men. But no ancient authority declares that a male husband soldier is ipso facto superior to a female wife and mother or that a female housekeeper is inferior to a male agricultural laborer. The ancient concern is with the maintenance of the gender roles, and it is deviation from one's (as they saw it) divinely ordained gender script that tends to be chastened.

4. Not all ancient voices can carry equal authority. Some seem to speak for the status quo and to faithfully reflect prevailing norms, while others are disgruntled and cantankerous rugged individualists who speak only for themselves. To the latter category belongs the embittered farmer-poet Hesiod, whose telling of the Pandora myth (Pandora was the first human woman and, in the poet's rendition, a curse to men) and slighting comments on the real women of his own day are unmistakably misogynistic. But it is difficult to square Hesiod's "hatred of women" (the literal meaning of misogyny) with the attitudes generally detectable elsewhere in the ancient record. If anything, male-poet-who-hates-women might be merely a literary persona, a mask worn by Hesiod (and later by Semonides and the Roman poet satirist Juvenal) akin to our own "battle of the sexes" banter. But it is not at clear that such literary productions are reflective of more deeply embedded cultural estimations and value.

5. Modern analogues to ancient Greek categories may not really be appropriate. Where politics is concerned, we saw in the preceding chapter that a large majority

of male citizens at Athens were practically disfranchised by the seating capacity of the assembly place (specifically, 6,000 places for a citizen population of 30,000 or so) and that rural Athenians, by reason of their physical remove from the seat of government in town, were unlikely to have participated in democratic processes of any kind on a regular basis. So, were Athenian citizen males, considered as a collectivity, really so privileged after all? *The* major public role of women, namely reproduction—to marry, to head a household, to bear and raise the next generation of citizens and mothers of citizens—was a much praised, even hallowed, contribution to the commonwealth. So, were Athenian citizen-class females, considered as a collectivity, really so downtrodden after all? An absolutely necessary preliminary to any appreciation of ancient Greece for our own benefit is first to establish how these matters were understood in terms of the conditions of that remote place and time.

MARRIAGE, CHILDREN, CITIZENSHIP, AND LEGITIMACY

From birth until marriage, the rites of passage of the citizen class female were identical with those of the males: Amphidromia (acceptance into the household), Tenth Day ceremony (naming and acknowledgment of paternity by father), and upbringing at home by parents, wet nurses or nannies, and, sometimes, female slaves.

First marriage occurred ideally at age 14 or so, according to the unanimous testimony of Greek writers. Marriage at so young an age would not be legal in many modern societies, but the practice is comprehensible in its ancient context. Since legitimacy of birth was highly valued, female virginity naturally enjoyed a comparable valuation, since a virgin could not possibly be pregnant by another male at marriage. But if menarche (first menstruation) occurred appreciably later than in modern advanced societies, it is likely that ability to conceive was not a factor determining age at marriage. Betrothal (the Greek word corresponds to our "handshake") was an agreement to a marriage arrived at by males (with the bride being represented by her father, an uncle, or another close relative) and was soon confirmed publicly by a feast at the bride's parents' residence and a parade to the new abode of the couple. Marriage marked the primary rite of passage for females: from girlhood to adulthood; from her parents' home to a new home (that might well be her husband's parents' home); from the guardianship of her father to the guardianship of her husband. To put the matter in legal terms, an Athenian woman remained dependent upon a male, whether father or husband, throughout her life, and this dependence echoed across the full spectrum of her existence, private and public. But it does not follow that that woman's life was devoid of political significance.

Marriage for Athenians—both male and female—was something different from marriage in modern Western societies. Readers of this book might think of matrimony as an essentially personal and preponderantly private undertaking, an expression of attraction, affection, love, and commitment. For ancient Greeks, however, these largely emotional considerations seem to have taken a back seat to more practical concerns. Through a marriage, an alliance of sorts was created between two households that might well prove useful on some future occasion. Parents of the bride, though under obligation to provide a dowry, would be relieved of the burden of supporting a daughter who in ancient Greek culture could never be a wage-earner. Meanwhile, the groom's family would be gaining a substitute for any daughter it had lost to marriage, particularly if the new daughter-in-law was to reside with her husband in his parents' home. For the new husband, marriage normally meant promotion from adult but socially immature single to head of his own household, even if he and his wife were compelled by economic necessity to share space with his aging parents.

But our concern here is with politics, and for political purposes the feature of marriage that counted was that only a "duly betrothed" Athenian man and Athenian woman could produce children who upon reaching adulthood could lay legitimate claim to being Athenian. In the case of sons, only the "legitimate" child could become a citizen and, perhaps even more important, inherit his father's property. For daughters, only the "legitimate" female child could ever enter into a marriage that, in the succeeding generation, could produce the next round of "Athenians." Marriages could, and presumably did, occur between parties one or both of which were not "Athenian," but such unions were penalized and stigmatized, since any children were statutorily barred from full political in-group membership.

Thus, Athenian women, no less than citizen males, possessed the capacity to bestow "insider" status upon their children in the context of marriage to an Athenian husband. No foreign woman, no female slave, not even the daughter born out of wedlock to Athenian parents possessed such capacity, so the distinction is a meaningful one. But a stiff price had to be paid in exchange for the privilege of bestowing legitimacy. A child was "lawfully" begotten only if its father was the mother's lawful husband. Since no attempt (or, at least, no successful attempt) seems to have been made to prevent male extramarital sexual activity, the full burden of monogamy fell upon the wife. Married men enjoyed extramarital sexual relationships with lovers (male as well as female), prostitutes, and slaves, thus foisting upon married women alone the role of gatekeepers to the privileged circle of the citizen body.

PUBLIC ROLES OF ATHENIAN WOMEN

The importance of Athenian women's domestic roles is undeniable, but we should be wary of falling into the trap of supposing that women's lives were confined to the private sphere while men, often absent from the home, held sway in the public sphere. For one thing, it is clear, as noted previously, that the line between private and public was drawn rather differently than in modern societies. Nowhere is this basic truth more clearly illustrated than in religion, where the female presence is continually before us in the records of classical Athens. Since religion, contrary to our own modern experience, resides almost entirely on the public side of the private-versus-public divide, and since ancient religion possessed unmistakably political aspects, women's religious roles clearly must play a part in the present book and chapter.

First, what do we mean by religion in an ancient Greek setting? We don't mean a system of beliefs about a higher power or powers set out in scriptural writings and expressed in the workings of highly organized churches, synagogues, and mosques. Ancient religion was not primarily concerned with belief, since belief in the existence and interventions of gods and goddesses seems to have gone largely unchallenged, notwithstanding the all too visible manifestations of skepticism on the part of an educated elite in our surviving sources. Nor was what we call "faith" needed to maintain such belief as it is in today's world in the face of modern science and our ever widening knowledge of human societies and their cultures and histories. Rather, ancient religion focused on the performance of ritual acts in the setting of individual cults of a multitude of divine beings whose assistance or cooperation could by such acts be secured in the service of human society. And by "human society" I refer not merely to the doings and fortunes of a worshiper's private domestic household (although, of course, the interests of the household do play a prominent role) but also, and just as important, to the larger, public world of the state in virtually all of its undertakings. For ancient Greeks, religion was an indissoluble part of public life, and, again, the key significance of female participation in it is front and center throughout the records of classical Athens.

Public female presence in religion, to begin, is detectable even in the fragmentary survivals of the village demes—the more than 100 rural farming communities sprinkled over the vast expanse of extramural Attica.

Particularly noticeable are the priestesses of female or female-oriented divinities in at least 10 villages: Acharnai, Aixone, Cholargeis, Eleusis, Erchia, Halai Aixonides, Melite, Lower or Upper Paiania, Peiraieus, and Phrearrhioi. Although the vast majority of the demes have no left no written traces of their internal arrangements, it is clear that the presence of a priestess of a village cult was widespread, perhaps universal. Documents from Cholargos and Erchia identify the priestesses as "officers," so there can be no doubt about the importance of their roles in the local organization. Divinities mentioned include Alkmene, Artemis, Athena Hippia, Demeter Chloe, Demeter and Persephone, Hebe, Hera, the Heroines, and Semele. Two male divinities occur, too, but they are not without significance for females: Dionsysus, whose worship, as readers of Euripides' *Bacchae* know well, was favored by women, and Plouton, an apparent surrogate for Mother Earth, the mother of all female divinities.

Festivals, too, might have a predominantly or even exclusively female orientation. Examples are Theogamia, Skira, and the Thesmophoria, the last-mentioned being recorded in no fewer than six, perhaps seven, demes. The so-called Rural Dionysia is a special case, since it, unlike most of the others, was celebrated across Attica, possibly at the instigation or even under the direction of the state government in town. Female presence in the person of the hero-protagonist's daughter is memorably indicated for one rural deme in a scene from Aristophanes' *Acharnians*. Another Aristophanic comedy, *Women at the Thesmophoria,* is of course set in the festival just mentioned, but the location of that setting is probably the town, as we'll see when we come to Aristophanes' "women" plays in the following section.

And why these striking exceptions to the general absence of women in what we would regard as Athenian "public" life? Multiple causes are at work. Girls and women play prominent roles in popular myths, which, if not the "scriptures" of Greek religion, at least put into circulation vivid and memorable narratives of many of the divinities in question. From the rosters in the preceding paragraphs, Artemis, Athena, Demeter and Persephone, Hera, and Semele, plus Dionysus, are among the "stars" of classical mythology. Female divinities, too, were centered on female concerns, above all reproduction in all its aspects, extending from conception and childbirth to marriage and domestic values generally. And let us not forget, since domestic values are in play, that the god's or goddess's temple was something like the residence of a human family. A temple was the home of the divinity; the cult statue represented a likeness of that divinity that had to be anointed (i.e., bathed), sacrificed to (i.e., fed), and draped with ritual textiles (i.e., clothed)—so, naturally, these sacred duties devolved upon the female human performers of these roles in the human household.

Was formal recognition made of the public importance of these demeswomen, or of demeswomen generally? Sepulchral inscriptions might be thought a promising candidate. But since females were not citizens (although a term in Greek *politis* meaning something like "citizeness" enjoyed occasional use), when a girl or woman is named on her gravestone, she does not have a demotic of her own but uses only her father's or husband's. At the local community level, a very rare word, *dēmotis,* corresponding in form to *politis,* should mean "demeswoman" and, if so, might meaningfully serve to distinguish the womenfolk of the villagers (that is, mothers, wives, and unmarried daughters of the Athenian citizen class) from other females resident in the deme. Accordingly, the more common and seemingly informal phrase "women of the demesmen" encountered in our sources might actually be technical and reflect the special public status enjoyed by these mothers, wives, and daughters in cultic and perhaps other village affairs.

And what of women of the citizen class at the state level? Recognition of women's roles in an isolated rural environment is one thing, such recognition in the high stakes world of the Big City quite another. Perhaps surprisingly, in intramural Athens throughout all periods of antiquity, the female presence in the town-centered cults of the state was as significant as it was visible—and significant in crucially political ways.

Take, as a particularly illuminating example, the priestess of Athena Polias. Her cult-title here—in contrast to Athena *Parthenos,* the Virgin Athena, whose Parthenon was the principal temple on the Acropolis—has reference to an older temple on the *polis* (properly, the Greek word for the citadel), the so-called Old Athena Temple. In accordance with the almost invariable practice of matching divinity and priestly officer by gender, this priesthood was held by a female. And also, as with many cultic offices, this priesthood was hereditary, in this case in the aristocratic clan called the Eteoboutadai. Admittedly, Athens was no less a man's world where the city's cults were concerned, and religion generally was subject to direction and funding by an all-male central democratic government. But even strictly ceremonial and symbolic roles count for a lot. As candidates for the priestess's political importance, consider two famous episodes from the chronicles of Herodotus on the Persian Wars.

As we learned in chapter 2, Clisthenes, on the eve of his creation of the democracy in 508/7 B.C.E., had successfully curried the favor of the poorer citizens but remained opposed by his conservative aristocratic rival, Isagoras. To strengthen his cause, Isagoras appealed to the Spartan Cleomenes, who proceeded to send an order to Athens calling for the expulsion of the Alcmeonidae—among whom was Clisthenes himself—on the grounds that the clan was still tainted by blood-guilt from their role in the failed coup d'état by Cylon a century earlier. Clisthenes left the city, but Cleomenes with his Lacedaemonian force entered Athens anyway and attempted to dismantle the Council and transfer its powers to 300 partisans of Isagoras. When the Council demurred, Cleomenes with Isagoras and his followers seized the Acropolis:

For when Cleomenes had ascended the Acropolis and was about to seize it, he was on his way into the crypt of the goddess in order to address her when the Priestess, before he could pass through the doors, stood from her throne and said: "Lacedaemonian stranger, go back and do not enter the shrine. It is not lawful for Dorians to enter here." And he said, "Woman, I am not a Dorian, but an Achaean." And so he, giving no heed to the admonition, made his attempt and at that point, again, he and the Lacedaemonians were expelled from the Acropolis.[1]

For the second episode we leap forward to the Persian Wars when, in 480 B.C.E., King Xerxes with his vast army was poised to invade Attica. Meanwhile, the Peloponnesians remained at home, fortifying the Isthmus in preparation for defense of their own territory. The allied fleet was now recalled from Artemisium to a position in the straits between the Attic coast and the island of Salamis:

While the rest of the others occupied Salamis, the Athenians returned to their own territory. Upon their arrival, they made a proclamation that the Athenians, as each was able, were to save their children and household members. Most of them were dispatched to Troezen, but some to Aegina and some to Salamis. They hastened to make the evacuation, partly because they wished to serve the oracle, but especially because of the following reason. The Athenians say that a great snake used to live in the temple as a guard of the Acropolis. This is what they say, and they continue to place monthly offerings for it, in the belief that the snake exists. The monthly offerings are honey-cakes. Now in the past the honey-cake was always consumed, but on this occasion it went untouched. The temple Priestess told them of this, and the Athenians even more readily departed from the town in the belief that the goddess herself had abandoned the Acropolis.[2]

Both times the priestess's role could fairly be called pivotal in that on her utterance depended the outcome of an epochal military-political episode in Athenian (and, in the second instance, Greek) history. The role was also intermediary in that she served to transmit the will of the gods to her human fellow Greeks. For a more explicit illustration of the mechanism we need only look to "the oracle" mentioned in Herodotus's Salamis narrative. The reference is to Apollo's oracle at Delphi, the site of the god's great panhellenic sanctuary in central Greece. Physically housed in a crypt at the rear of the god's temple, the oracle was staffed by both female and male temple personnel. (The Greek word for crypt is *adyton,* "the place that may not be entered," the same word used by Herodotus to refer to Athena's temple at Athens.) As with the two examples from Herodotus, the intermediary was a woman, in this case Apollo's priestess, the Pythia (so called from Pytho, the ancient name for the sanctuary site at Delphi). Even though male priests seem to have administered the sanctuary, at the heart of the oracle's operation was this old woman who, in a state of divine possession called alternately *ekstasis* or *enthousiasmos* ("ecstasy" and "enthusiasm" being complementary aspects of the same condition), mouthed the words that Greeks believed to be the response of Apollo. The oracle enjoyed immense popularity and prestige throughout Greece. Its authority was revered by all, from humble petitioners asking about a marriage or purchase of farmland to mighty states seeking advice on matters of war or peace. The oracle's 1,000-year run made it far and away the most enduring of all ancient Greek religious institutions.

By why a woman, especially in this man's world? Besides the underlying reasons for female presence in Greek religion already aired, it seems that the Greeks supposed that women enjoyed a sort of privileged pipeline to the divine. For more recent parallels, we might think of fortune-tellers, palm readers, telephone call-in consultants—all, in this writer's personal observation, female. The underlying psychology is identical with that in evidence in other ancient manifestations of the divine possession of females. Striking examples are Dionysus's "mad" followers the Maenads, their "madness" signifying the same divine possession experienced by the Pythian priestess. Relevant, too, are such gender-specific notions as female *hysteria* (anciently attributed, incredible as it may seem, to a displaced uterus). Women enjoyed, it was believed, a special access to the gods and so could, as priestess, oracular voice, or fortune-teller, more readily convey their will or their foreknowledge of the outcome of events to their fellow humans.

ARISTOPHANES: *LYSISTRATA, THESMOPHORIAZOUSAI, EKKLESIAZOUSAI*

To a reader coming to our subject with a preconceived notion of women in ancient Greece as an oppressed class of home-bound domestic servants devoted to the promotion of men's interests, the foregoing discussion may come as something of a pleasant surprise. But the fact remains that, at Athens at least, citizenship, strictly defined, remained the exclusive domain of adult Athenian males of legitimate descent. However, the relative eman-cipation of Athenian women (in comparison with foreign women, female slaves, and undoubtedly many non-Athenian Greek women of all categories) might open up expectations that things could conceivably be other than they were, even the formal logical possibility that women could be citizens. A woman with an Athenian in-group identity who could bestow citizen status upon her legitimate sons, who played visible public roles in the state's cultic establishment—that woman might well be a candidate for participation in government, if only in the active imagination of a comic poet.

There was in fact such a poet, the Athenian citizen Aristophanes, whose surviving intact comedies (11 in number) range in date between 425 and 388 B.C.E. Aristophanes was the foremost representative of the Old Comedy (to be followed later by the Middle and the New). The genre's distinctive characteristic is topicality. Old Comedy productions were topical in that they dealt with the affairs and events of the day, they responded to matters of con-temporary concern, and they often put on the stage literal or thinly disguised representations of real, living people. By contrast, Middle Comedy (includ-ing the last surviving play of Aristophanes) and New Comedy were to steer clear of the pitfalls of contemporary reference and seek the safer ground of a "comedy of manners" resembling our own television sitcoms. The topical-ity of Old Comedy recognized few limitations. Anything goes, seems to have been Aristophanes' guiding philosophy. Nothing was off limits, and, predict-ably, given the prevailing climate of conflict and disagreement—political, cultural, and ideological—that marked late-fifth-century wartime Athens in particular, it was not long before our poet found himself in deep trouble with persons more powerful than himself and indeed with a wider Athenian public. *Babylonians,* produced in 426, provoked a legal prosecution by one its targets, the politician Cleon (see chapter 8). *Clouds,* produced in 423, un-fairly ridiculed Socrates to the extent that the philosopher alluded to the play's harmful effects on his reputation when on trial for his life a quarter-century later, in 399. It is no wonder that the genre's run was a short one and that topical productions of this kind before mass audiences were not to be seen again in Greek (or Roman) antiquity.

Nonetheless, within Old Comedy's brief span of about a century, its many known poets managed to air many controversial issues. Among these was the matter of citizen women—their place in society, their aspirations, their frustrations. Three of the intact plays of Aristophanes, *Lysistrata* (411 B.C.E.), *Women at the Thesmophoria* (also 411), and *Women in Assembly* (392 or 391), are among the most explicit and sustained examinations of contemporary women's concerns that have reached us from classical antiquity. But before we attempt to assess their content and meaning for politics and society, we must first note a few important relevant facts about the setting and organiza-tion of these comedic productions:

1. All Attic comedies (as with tragedies and satyr plays) were staged initially at one of the public state festivals of Dionysus in Athens town before potentially very large audiences.

2. Audiences certainly included noncitizens (such as metics and slaves), but it has been disputed whether women were present. However, the fact is that indications of the presence of women are abundant (for one thing, since women played prominent roles in religion generally, it is difficult to imagine why they would have been excluded from festivals of Dionysus), and so the burden of proof is upon those who believe that women were *not* present.

3. Poets were competing for prizes; hence, the immediate objective was to please a panel of judges. Even so, we learn much about audience reaction and (again in Socrates' case) the enduring memories generated by these one-shot productions. Only later, it is assumed, were texts available for consumption as reading material by a literate public.

4. All actors in Attic drama (tragedy as well as comedy) were males. Masks, padding, and female dress seem to have succeeded in creating the illusion of genuine women, since no poet is ever found exploiting the obvious comic potential of a male masquerading as a female. But everyone present, including any women in the audience, knew full well that all concerned—poets, actors, chorus, and judges—were males. Therefore, the question arises whether these "women" plays are really about women, their lives, concerns, and aspirations, or are rather men's representations of women's lives, concerns, and aspirations. Scholars have proposed strikingly different positions on this, the central issue for the present chapter. My readers will have to come their own conclusions.

Lysistrata (411 B.C.E.)

By the year of Aristophanes' production of *Lysistrata,* the Peloponnesian War with Sparta had worn on for two full decades, with no immediate end in sight (and in fact the Spartan victory was not to come until 404). In an effort to bring about a peace, an Athenian woman, significantly named Lysistrata, "Demobilizer," organizes a Panhellenic conspiracy of the wives of combatants on both sides. Lysistrata's "Happy Idea"—around which the play's plot, as typically in Old Comedy, is organized—is this: The wives will cease to perform their domestic duties until their soldier husbands agree to put down their arms and return home. The plot is sometimes characterized as a "sex strike," and indeed much of the humor centers on the effects on the men of their wives' refusal to cooperate sexually with their desperate husbands and eventually on the women's own unmet conjugal needs. But much is also made of babies that need their mothers' attentions. And the play's men do not avail themselves of the alternative sexual outlets (prostitutes, slaves, other men, for example) that we know were available to real Athenian men and that actually receive dramatic mention in Aristophanes' text. Were sex, and sex alone, the focus of the women's conspiracy and of the men's response, the plot would not unfold as it does. Rather, in keeping with the orientation of Greek society, the centrality and transcendent importance of the household is the real issue here. No typical Athenian citizen could plausibly be represented as subject to manipulation *solely* by his wife's withholding of sexual favors. Nor could even a comedy succeed on so silly a premise that international affairs are governable by bedroom sex, so Aristophanes has a more serious second conspiracy running concurrently with the "sex strike" as subplot. The older Athenian women will occupy the Acropolis, where the state treasury is located, and thereby cut off the funds needed to prosecute the war. Main plot and subplot converge when, with the successful occupation of the Acropolis, the older women are joined there by the younger striking wives.

Graphic portrayal of a seizure of the Acropolis, even by old women, must have awakened memories of distant and not-so-distant history before any audience, particular a wartime audience. Late in the seventh century, Cylon had stormed the citadel in his abortive attempt to overthrow the government. And King Xerxes, at the head of a Persian army, had sacked the old Polis within living memory, in 480 B.C.E. That Athenian women could now be cast in the role of traitor (Cylon) or conqueror (Xerxes) would, in some minds, have testified to the latent political potentialities of citizen females. But what of the ordinary housewives and mothers driving the Happy Idea that implementation of the 1960s slogan "make love not war" could indeed alter the course of human events? To answer this question, we must be careful to distinguish between the leader, Lysistrata, and her rank-and-file followers. Readers of chapter 2 will recall the signs of an ideological gulf separating leader and follower in the ancient Greek (and Roman) political world.

Lysistrata herself is no ordinary or typical woman. No reference is made to a husband or children, the cultural sine qua nons of ancient Athenian womanhood. But light is shed on her identity by her doubly significant name. As mentioned, a name meaning Demobilizer has special significance for the plot (notwithstanding the fact that real women are actually known to have been so named). The name Lysistrata, as scholars suggest, would also recall to the audience Lysimache, the priestess of Athena Polias at the time of the play's production. Furthermore, by an easy extrapolation from priestess to priestess's goddess, the protagonist resembles no one so much as Athena herself. Manless and childless, the armor-garbed female who had no mother did things no mortal Athenian woman is ever found doing: advising heroes, leading armies into battle, and serving as protectress of the city itself. Given such an association, Lysistrata's capacity to rise above the insistent domestic preoccupations, her strategic and tactical prowess, and, indeed, her panhellenic vision of a Greece at peace are rendered believable. By contrast, the rank-and-file (who, though given names, do not, in conformity with the convention of ancient comedy, correspond to any known living women) seem never to be able to think outside the box of their domestic routines.

Let's see if we can illustrate plot and characterization by a selection of contrasting speeches, first by Lysistrata herself:

Early on, under press of our usual restraint we endured <in silence> whatever you men were doing, because you wouldn't let us make a peep. But you weren't making us very happy. Nonetheless, we were keeping close tabs on you, and many was the time that we'd hear at home that you had decided poorly on some major matter. And then, suffering on the inside we'd ask with a laugh, "What was decided by you men in the Assembly today? About adding a rider on the stele on the peace treaty?" "What's that to you?" my husband would say. "Why don't you keep your mouth shut?" And I would shut up.[3]

[But later on] we would hear about an even worse decision of yours, and then we would ask, "Hubby, how can it be that you're handling this so foolishly?" And right away he'd give me a dirty look and tell me that if I didn't keep to my knitting he would draw a bead on my head: "War will remain the business of men!, period."[4]

[To the magistrate] "Correctly"?, how so, you idiot, if it wasn't permitted to us [women] to offer advice even when you were making bad decisions?[5]

Then, again to the magistrate, in a memorable tour de force of female domestic imagery:

If you had a brain in your head [to the Magistrate], you'd administer everything in the style of our wool-working.... First, just as with a fleece, wash out all the dung from the City, put it on a bed and beat out the Bad Guys, pluck out the thorns, and the ones who conspire and make snags for public offices... card them and snip off their heads! Then comb everyone into a Unity Basket of Goodwill—you know, the resident aliens, any foreigner friendly to you, anyone who owes to the treasury,... mix these people in too. And, by Zeus, the cities too, all the ones colonized from Athens, imagine these as flocks of fleece sitting separately here and there, bring them together and collect them into one big bobbin. And from this bobbin weave an overcoat for the People![6]

This last speech forecasts the essentially domestic and therefore (according to the cultural norms of ancient Athens) essentially feminine new order. Reversal, as often in comedy, is the dominant operative narrative path. But the working out of the play's Happy Idea is not really a reversal of roles. Yes, the women do prevail when their wills win out over the determined but self-destructive mishandling of the state's affairs by their menfolk. But, even so, for all of Lysistrata's Athena-like idiosyncrasy, they remain very conventional wives and mothers. Far from taking over the government and placing themselves in the positions of men (much less exchanging roles with the men), each returns to her home, with its domestic calm restored, once the immediate goals of the wives' plottings—an end to the war—have been achieved. So, if reversal there had been, it was only a temporary one and a reversal not of roles but of temperament. The simmering frustrations evidenced in the speeches of Lysistrata had broken out in a temporary display of independence and determined cooperative political action. And, in its face, the men, no less uncharacteristically, had caved in rather than forgo conjugal sex or change a diaper. So much fantasy and nothing more, but, nonetheless, as I have been suggesting, a credible acknowledgment of Athenian women's potential for genuine political action.

Women at the Thesmophoria (411 B.C.E.)

Later that same year, 411 B.C.E., Aristophanes produced the second of his three surviving "women" plays, *Thesmophoriazousai*, or "Women at the Thesmophoria." From our book's perspective, "*Thesmo*" marks a decided advance in the playwright's portrayal of Athenian women as political beings. The plot, again, is a simple one. In contrast with *Lysistrata*, the object of the women's attention is not a war but the Athenian tragic poet Euripides. The poet, they allege, has made women his targets by exposing in his plays their scandalous behavior—drunkenness, adultery, baby-switching, and the like. So, to get even, the women celebrating the festival of Demeter and Persephone (the "Thesmophoria" of the play's title) will hold an assembly in order to deliberate on the matter and punish Euripides for his misdeeds. Opposing efforts by the poet and his Inlaw, the latter of whom infiltrates the assembly in women's dress, end in Inlaw's exposure and capture and in a series of attempts by Euripides, also in women's costume, to rescue him. Finally, Euripides strikes a deal with the women ("let my kinsman go, and no more abuse of women in my plays")[7] and the Happy Idea becomes a Happy Ending as all make their way back home as the curtain falls.

In the *Lysistrata,* the cooperative efforts of the women are loose and informal. After all, the women come from all over Greece and so can hardly be portrayed as commandeering specifically Athenian political institutions. But the "women at the Thesmophoria" are exclusively Athenian, and, consequently, their assembly, procedures, and actions may resemble those of the all-male democratic legislature. Consider the following dialogue as an illustration:

Euripides [to Inlaw]:	Come on, get a move on, and make it quick! The signal for the assembly at the Thesmophorium, don't you see! As for me, I'll be on my way.
Inlaw [to an imaginary female maid]:	Over this way, Thratta. Hey, Thratta, take a look-see! The torches are burning. Check out the crowd on its way under the smoke!...Let's see, where can I find a good seat for hearing the speakers? You get out of here, Thratta. Slaves aren't permitted to listen to the speeches.[8]
Critylla [one of the assembled women]:	Offer prayers to the Olympian gods and to the Olympian goddesses, to the Pythian gods and the Pythian goddesses, to the Delian gods and the Delian goddesses, and to the other gods! If anyone plots evil in any way against the Demos of Women; or negotiates with Euripides and the Medes in any way against women; or aims either to become a tyrant or to help bring in a tyrant; or denounces a woman who has substituted another's child as her own; or is a mistress's go-between slave and has spilled the beans to the master;...invoke a curse that this person and his family along with him perish miserably. And pray that the gods grant to all you other women all that is good![9]
Mica [another of the assembled women]:	By the Two Goddesses, it is not out of any personal ambition, my fellow women, that I have risen to speak. No, it's because I have long unhappily endured watching you be dragged through the mud by Euripides, son of that green-groceress, and hearing all the bad things said about you. With what insult has this man not besmirched us? Where has he not denigrated us? Where, in a word, where there are spectators, tragic actors, and choruses, has he not called us his lover-keepers, man-chasers, wine-guzzlers,

> Benedict Arlenes, chatterboxes, total sickos, the curse of
> men's lives?...Accordingly I move that by hook or by crook
> we brew up some kind of destruction for this man, either
> poison or some other m.o.,...just as long as he gets oblit-
> erated! This then is the gist of my presentation. The details
> I will draft with the Secretary's assistance.[10]

The content is comic. The speakers, women and Inlaw alike, in alternately defending themselves or Euripides, succeed only in drawing even
more attention to the riotous goings-on of the women—hence the humor.
The framework is quasi-constitutional, an approximation of the assembly
of Athenian citizen males, though only an approximation, for the scene remains the all-women's festival of Demeter and Persephone. Roles have been
reversed in a way that they were not in *Lysistrata,* but Aristophanes has yet
to take the final step by representing his Athenian women as actually seizing
the real Assembly and thus, by reasonable extrapolation, the entire government and the state itself!

Women in Assembly (Late 390s B.C.E.)

That final step is taken two decades later, in the late 390s, long after
Athens' eventual capitulation to Sparta and loss of her maritime empire,
with the production of *Ekklesiazousai,* or "Women in Assembly." This time
around, it is not a war, as in *Lysistrata,* that motivates the women. Nor, as
in the *Thesmo,* is it the alleged misdeeds of a particular poet or other man.
Rather, the theme is not tied closely to any specific event or specific person
but is simply the general matter of mismanagement of the government by
men—represented as an ongoing and deeply embedded inherent structural
defect of public Athens. Accordingly, so serious a theme (almost too serious to possess comic potential!) begets a serious Happy Idea. The aggrieved
women will disguise themselves in their husbands' clothing, occupy the Assembly at dawn, and, before anyone can stop them, vote the men (and their
constitution) out and themselves (and their constitution) in! Nothing less
than an outright revolution will, and does, transpire.

And how is this grand scheme worked out on the stage? Under the leadership of Praxagora ("Public Activist"), private property will be abolished and a
welfare state of full entitlements substituted in its place. Family and household will be abolished in favor of communal "free love" and promiscuous
reproduction. And, with the elimination of all inequalities of wealth, social
pedigree, and physical attractiveness, the underlying conditions that made
men's government so misguided and ineffective will be removed. So somber
a script points to some of the differences between what the Greeks meant by
komoidia and what we mean by "comedy," and indeed utopian speculation
of this kind would later more famously take a far more serious turn in Plato's
Republic, among other writings of political theorists. To a reader already ex-
posed and attuned to *Lysistrata* and *Thesmophoriazousai,* the proceedings

reach the level of entertainment only when the new Female Order is put to practical real-world tests—and of course it fails predictably, and miserably. Take one of the two such scenes as an illustration, the one in which the new principle of sexual access is under scrutiny. A dashing young man, fresh from the (obligatory) communal feast, now attempts to visit his young girlfriend. Strictly against the rules! Before he can visit her, he must, according to the new constitution, serve the sexual needs of three old hags, each uglier than the one before. But Hag Two and Hag Three collide in pressing their claims in the absence of a procedure that will decide between them. The hapless hunk is dragged off the stage by the quarreling pair, and he never does make it to his girlfriend's. A classic reductio ad absurdum, and a very funny one under inspired direction by the poet.

So, what we seem to have in this play is a total reversal of roles. The men, who have remained at home when their wives departed at dawn wearing their clothes, must now don the women's clothing, do wifely domestic chores, and even (as would a citizen-class married woman) make excuses when venturing outside the house. But the superficial change of clothing does *not* betoken a change of orientation, values, or temperament, at least not on the women's side. The women remain fundamentally women and, as such, impose upon the state their characteristically wifely and maternal attitudes and routines. State as household, with its governors, women, feeding, clothing, and disciplining its members!

Neither Aristophanes nor any other ancient Greek writer or thinker, save alone Plato, chose to take further the notion of a political woman. A comic poet is of course limited by what is entertaining, if not always actually funny. *Women in Assembly* comes perilously close to not being funny at all, and some would say that the poet's next (and last) surviving play, *Wealth,* is far more social commentary than "comedy" as we understand it. But, funny or not funny, these playful romps of Aristophanes do clearly, when all is said and done, envision nominal females who are more like men than is allowed by cultural norms—and it is precisely on the score of gender that a potential for a political life in this society initially depends. The mythical paradigm is (again) provided by the armored, manless, and childless Athena, who, born from Zeus's head, has no visible mother! But *komoidia,* in order to be entertaining, must be rooted in reality, and, what is more, in the more familiar reality of the lives led by most people—such as the thousands seated in the Theater of Dionysus who constituted an Aristophanic play's one and only intended original audience. That the genuinely political woman could not exist except on the dramatic stage must be conceded, but the fact that the mere idea found an apparently welcoming mass audience is surely not without significance for our understanding of ancient Greek politics and society.

ASPASIA

If we are searching for a woman at Athens who played an authentic political role in historical reality, we must venture outside the closed circle of citizens. The one notable such woman is the infamous Aspasia, the mistress of the popular general and political leader Pericles. From the Ionian city of Miletus, Aspasia was not Athenian but rather an alien permanently residing in Athens. Probably largely because of her association with Pericles, she inevitably became a subject of malicious gossip. Ancient traditions report that she was a prostitute or even a madam of her own brothel—a predictable (and possibly baseless) slander likely to arise in the case of a foreign woman with a less than fully legitimate relationship with a controversial political figure. The Greek word for mistress is *pallakē,* a not necessarily pejorative term, but in an age when marriage provided the sole route to full legitimacy, such a woman could never achieve respectability, not even when on the arm of Athens' first citizen. Consider what Plutarch has to say about her in his *Life of Pericles:*

Some say that Aspasia was highly esteemed by Pericles because she was a wise and politically savvy woman. After all, Socrates sometimes visited her, bringing along his cronies. And Pericles' own friends brought their wives to listen to her despite the fact that she presided over an establishment neither orderly nor respectable inasmuch as she maintained young female "escorts." Aeschines says that Lysicles the sheep-dealer, of ignoble family and humble of nature, became the most important man of Athens by living with Aspasia after the death of Pericles. Yes, there is some truth in the *Menexenus* of Plato (even if the first part is written with tongue in cheek), when it states that this woman had the reputation of associating with Athenians as a teacher of rhetoric. Nevertheless, it appears as if Pericles' affection toward Aspasia was rather more erotic in nature than anything else. For his legal wife was a relative of his who had previously been wed to Hipponicus and had borne to him Callias "the Wealthy." While married to Pericles, she bore him sons Xanthippus and Paralus. Afterwards, when they found living together to be unsatisfactory, with her consent he married her off to another man, while he himself took Aspasia and cherished her exceedingly. It is said that he would embrace and kiss her warmly both when he left for the marketplace and when he returned each day.[11]

Where politics is concerned, there is no reason not to take seriously the claims made about her by Plutarch and others. She is reported, says Plutarch, to have given instruction in rhetoric. According to the *Menexenus* of Plato, just mentioned, Aspasia actually composed what was perhaps the most celebrated pieces of ancient Greek rhetoric, Pericles' own *Funeral Oration* delivered over the dead of the first year of the Peloponnesian War and re-created by Thucydides in the second book of his *History.* If that is true, then perhaps we can also credit the report that she caused Athens to go to war with Samos or, on Aristophanes' account, that she was a factor in the outbreak of the ultimately disastrous war with Sparta. Given Aspasia's high profile and impact on events, her role in rumor and propaganda might be assessed in the light of the better-known case of the Egyptian queen Cleopatra in the final chapters of ancient Rome's equally destructive Civil Wars. In the ancient world as today, it is always easy to demonize an opponent by launching attacks, truthful or otherwise, upon a woman or women associated with him. But, as with Cleopatra, we cannot be sure where probable fact ends and rumor-mongering begins.

As to Aspasia's influence in matters political, however, there is little in these traditions that is intrinsically incredible, since a foreigner would not have been subject to many of the cultural barriers that obstructed a citizen-class female's intellectual aspirations at Athens. Besides, a highly educated and intellectually challenging *hetaira* in a domain normally peopled only by men would make for a more plausible object of Pericles' attentions than a mere prostitute, however skilled in her craft. And there can be no doubt that the bond between general and mistress was a strong one. After the death of Pericles' wife, the two produced a son who bore his father's name—an unmistakable sign of the general's deep affection and unabashed public acceptance of Aspasia. That acceptance extended to the full legitimation of the younger Pericles, for he is reported to have attained an honor accessible only to citizens, election to the board of generals. Sadly, the son met an ignoble end by execution after the Athenian navy's disastrous defeat at Arginousae when all 10 commanders were condemned by an angry Demos. But the fact that the People should have allowed an "illegitimate" to reach the highest elective office (even if only to turn upon him later) may represent as much a favorable verdict upon Aspasia as an enduring veneration for the memory of their great general.

SPARTA

Spartan women, as we saw in chapter 3, bore little resemblance to their Athenian counterparts. True, they could not become citizens and, equally true, their roles remained fundamentally domestic. But, as we saw, Sparta's unique circumstances and distinctive social organization thrust the matrons of the Spartiate elite into a prominent—and politically influential—set of public roles.

Seven

Some Ancient Greek Politicians

Not surprisingly, the typical ancient Greek historical writer, like the typical Greek on the street, tended to write history not as the working out of impersonal forces but as the very personal achievements, deeds, or misdeeds, of Great Men (and the occasional Great Woman). The approach is embodied in public historical art and architecture, in the sometimes lengthy biographical excurses in historical narratives (even analytical deep thinkers such as Thucydides succumbing to the temptation), and, most conspicuously, in the enduring popularity of the genre of *biographia*—literally, "the writing of a life." The genre's most well known (and enduring) exponent was Plutarch, a Greek from Chaeroneia, in Boeotia, writing under the early Roman Empire (approximate dates ca. 50–120 C.E.). Plutarch had no personal knowledge of his classical Greek subjects from a half-millennium in his past (a span such as that which separates us from Elizabethan England), but he was a man of affairs, had some good secondary sources at his disposal, and composed his *Parallel Lives* with attention to historical accuracy. Accordingly, it is a reasonable plan to draw upon Plutarch's biographies of classical Athenian political figures as a way of illustrating ancient Greek politics and society in the "lives" of the careers of specific individual people. Most (but not all) of the biographies in this and the following chapter are based in whole or part on a Plutarchian *Life*.

Given the many (indeed, hundreds) of known political families at Athens alone, our roster of politicians must of course be highly selective. To mention but one important criterion of selection, I have viewed "politicians" as initially products of the governmental machinery, that is, appointment and especially election to higher office. As a result, readers will not find here, for example, such prominent public speakers on policy issues as Demosthenes and Aeschines, who played crucial ideological roles in shaping Athens' response to the rise of Macedon. But however counterintuitive such omissions might seem in the light of our modern (and therefore anachronistic) expectations, there is little risk of our distorting or skewing our appreciation of ancient Greek "politics" (and society). To an overwhelming extent, the principal actors in Greek (and Roman) public affairs, political, diplomatic, and military, were occupants of official governmental positions.

FOUNDING FATHERS

The notion of "founding father," so familiar to the English-language reader, is not entirely without basis in the ancient Athenian tradition. Greek culture, like its counterpart Roman culture across the Adriatic, was uncompromisingly patriarchal, and so any "founder" could only be male and was accordingly conceptualized as a kind of father (rather than a mother). "Founder" itself may be seen as a special case of the Greeks' obsession with etiology—with the origin, cause, or explanation of things—so prominent in myth, art, and historiography. And an etiology, unlike a modern scientific attempt to get at the origins, will invariably be expressed in terms of the specific choices and acts of a specific recognizable human being, a kind of "hero," if you will. Two specific manifestations, relevant here, are the "first finder" motif so prominent in Greek myth (Prometheus, who gave fire to humankind, is a well-known instance) and the *ktisis,* or "foundation legend," that stood at the beginning of many a city-state's proto-history. By contrast, and with the exception again of the uncharacteristically deep-thinking Thucydides, we find little interest in underlying causes, in generations-long processes, or in random accidents. How could you write a biography about a cause or process or accident? And if such an account could be produced, what sort of readership could such an account expect to find? Greek writers condensed, telescoped, and simplified, reducing the complex and lengthy realities we have come to expect from the modern discipline of history to a specific point of time and place, and then they anthropomorphized what is really an indistinct faceless process as a charismatic individual's heroic achievement.

Theseus

Theseus, the founder-king of the city of Athens and its ancestral "national" hero, illustrates clearly the ancient Greek take on the patriarchal "father" of the state. But just as Theseus was of course not a literal father (unless of a successor king), so is his story a pastiche of myth, appropriation from other, non-Athenian traditions, and outright fanciful invention, hardly literal "history" in any familiar sense of that term.

Once upon a time, goes the story told by Plutarch in his *Life of Theseus,* Aegeus, king of Athens, despaired of ever having children. But when he sought help from Apollo's oracle at Delphi, the king received a typically riddling directive. When he asked about having children, the god instructed him "not to loosen the wine-skin's shaft" until he had returned once again to Athens. Stopping at Troezen, in the Peloponnese, on his way home from Delphi, Aegeus mentioned the puzzling oracle to King Pittheus, who at once interpreted the words as a reference to sexual intercourse. Evidently desiring a grandchild by Athens' king, Pittheus arranged for his guest to sleep with his daughter, Aethra. Upon his departure, Aegeus, suspecting that Aethra was with child, placed a sword and a pair of sandals beneath a large rock with the following instructions: Should her child be a son, she should tell him, when he reached manhood, to lift the rock, remove the sword and sandals, and depart in search of his fortune. In the course of time, the son, Theseus, set out with sword and sandals from Troezen to Athens, taking the hazardous route along the shore of the Saronic Gulf. Several muggers and monsters were encountered and all dispatched by our young hero: Periphetes with his iron club, Sinis the "pine-bender," an enormous female pig, the foot-washer Sciron, a wrestler called Cercyon, and the murderous pervert Procrustes. These were the Six Labors of Theseus, patently modeled upon the Twelve Labors of Heracles—the most popular and admired of ancient Greek "national" heroes.

Arriving at Athens, Theseus, still unknown to himself and others as Aegeus's son, found his birth-father the king now married to the foreign witch Medea—who was now pregnant with Aegeus's child. But Medea, by use of her magical powers, recognizing the young visitor as her husband's son and, as legitimate heir to the throne, a rival to her own unborn child, attempted by various devices to do away with him. First, she sent him against a bull on the loose on the plain of Marathon, in the hope that he would be killed in the process. Failing in this, she then attempted to poison him at a banquet, but Aegeus caught sight of the guest's sword, recognized Theseus as his son, and dashed the goblet from his hand in the nick of time. Exit Medea back to Asia.

But Theseus's troubles had just begun. Athens remained enslaved to Minos, the king of Cnossus, on the island of Crete. Every year, the Athenians had to send to Cnossus as tribute seven virgin girls and seven virgin boys. The victims would be cast into the dark maze called the labyrinth, where they would be eaten alive by the Minotaur—a monstrous half-human, half-animal "bull [Greek *tauros*] of Minos." The young Theseus volunteered to be one of the seven boys and, upon arrival at Crete, fell in love with Minos's daughter, Ariadne. Betraying her father, Ariadne came to her lover's aid by supplying him with a sword and a ball of thread. Attaching the thread to the door and paying it out as the youths descended into the maze, Theseus slew the Minotaur with the sword, followed the thread back to the entrance, and thereby freed Athens from Cretan rule. Buoyed with his success, however, Theseus committed two errors of omission. On the return voyage to Athens, he abandoned Ariadne on the island of Naxos. Then, while sailing into port at Athens, he neglected to follow the plan and change his sail from black to white in order to signal success—at which his father, Aegeus, in his despair hurled himself from the Acropolis to his death. Even a hero isn't perfect, and in Greek myth the price that must be paid for the accomplishment of his quest is invariably an innocent victim—or, in Theseus's case, victims.

Savior of Athens, Theseus now succeeded to the throne and, unencumbered by the self-sacrificing girlfriend who had brought him success at Cnossus, was free to marry. To secure a wife, Theseus journeyed to the land of the Amazons, where he abducted their queen, Antiope. In response, the Amazons invaded Attica and encamped near the Acropolis, only to be roundly defeated by the Athenians under King Theseus's leadership. Repeating his earlier act of perfidy, Theseus abandoned Antiope as he had done Ariadne and married the Cretan princess Phaedra (she, ironically, like Medea, descended from the Sun god). Phaedra, in the course of events, fell in love with Theseus's son with Antiope, her own stepson, Hippolytus—a passion that eventually issued in Phaedra's suicide, Hippolytus's violent death by the wish of his own father, and the ruin of Theseus himself.

All this perhaps makes Theseus an unlikely candidate for "founding father" of Greece's first city, but the tradition was to become the vehicle for a host of innovations that shaped the construction of the historical classical city-state:

Theseus was credited with the synoecism of Attica—that is, with the consolidation of the countryside's myriad village communities into a single unified constitutional entity with the town of Athens at its center.

Theseus was credited with the institution of classical Athens's preeminent religious event, the Panathenaic festival, whereby that unification of Attica was ceremonially commemorated.

Theseus was credited with the foundation of the popular Assembly.

No less significant, dominant themes of the legend could serve as precedents, and as validations, of future political practices, more generally understood. The hero's successive alliances with foreign women—a Cretan, an Asian Amazon, another Cretan—are paradigmatic of the historical "dynastic" marriage, above all when such marriage forged a link with another state or people. Theseus's popularity was grounded in essentially military heroic achievement, whether Athens' liberation from foreign rule (Minos; the Six Labors) or its defeat of an invading army (Amazons) or even (in still another adventure, not retold here) an expedition to the Underworld. Complementing his foreign adventures was the founding father's own birth from a "foreign" (that is, non-Athenian) woman, the daughter of Troezen's king. And balancing these external linkages and accomplishments was our hero's spectacular record of progressive constitutional innovation, culminating in the patently anachronistic creation of the classical polity a thousand years before its time. True, it really didn't happen this way, but the storyteller's (or image-builder's) purpose is clear: to establish Athens' high antiquity in the hallowed Bronze Age, to thereby put the legitimacy of the city's institutional arrangements beyond the reach of contemporary partisan politics, and (again) to provide uncontested models or paradigms for the conduct of contemporary political leaders.

Solon

With Solon the Lawgiver we emerge from the mists of storytelling about the heroic Bronze Age and arrive at a historical Athenian that we can believe we really know. True, another lawgiver, Draco, who is credited with the first publication of previously unwritten customary law, had preceded Solon by a generation, but very little is known about him (in fact, he may not even have been human, since Greek *drakōn* means "snake"!). But Solon is securely anchored chronologically by the year of his archonship, 594 B.C.E., a date that we may take as marking the beginning of reliably documented Athenian political history. Solon's constitutional, legal, economic, and social innovations (which we discussed in chapter 2) represent a watershed in the development of the government of Athens, and some of his progressive measures lived on under the classical democracy centuries later. For all that, however, Solon did not actually *create* the democracy, as some Athenians liked to claim. Rather, as with Theseus, such false (or exaggerated) claims represent the retrojection—sometimes demonstrably ideologically motivated—of contemporary realities to an earlier age. The older an institution, a procedure, an idea, the better. The more hallowed, idealized, and sanctified by the passage of time (as was certainly the case with Solon), the better. In the fourth century B.C.E., even a real, historical personage from the beginning of the sixth remained (unlike America's own Founding Fathers) comfortably beyond the reach of destructive nitpicking criticism or iconoclastic debunking.

Well, what do we know of this Solon? Again, as with Theseus, we have a *Life* by Plutarch, and the opening sentences of that text are richly informative regarding the lawgiver's family background. According to most authorities, Plutarch writes, Solon's father was Execisides, "a man of moderate property and power among the citizens, but from a leading family, since he was by ancestry one of the Codridae." And his mother, according to one authority, was a cousin of the mother of Pisistratus, the future tyrant. Eventually, the two men became close friends—indeed, Plutarch retails the dubious report that Solon may actually have been passionately in love with the younger man.[1] At all events, to say that Solon was highly placed in aristocratic social circles would be an understatement. The question that naturally arises in a book about politics and society is whether, or in what ways if any, Solon's personal background was a factor in the design and purposes of his comprehensive and, as it turned out, enduring institutional and policy reforms.

In chapter 2, "Politics and the Constitution," we introduced Solon's new system of income classes and its use as a criterion for determining the level of a citizen's participation in government. From the richest to the poorest, Athenians were classed as "500 Bushel Men," "Knights," "Two Oxen Men," and "Thetes" (probably propertyless laborers). Viewed ideologically, there can be no question that the new system amounted to an assault upon the fundamental principle underlying aristocratic domination of public life— the rule of descent, whereby an Athenian's place in society was determined by his family background, particularly on the father's side. Now, after Solon, an enterprising cultivator of nontraditional cash crops or a somewhat disreputable trader or a petty moneychanger suddenly was eligible for election to the state's highest office, however lowly his origins might have been. Was this a revolutionary measure intended to bring the impoverished masses into control of affairs? Before jumping to any such conclusion, let's consider the details—and the devil that may lurk within them! For one thing, the aristocratic holders of traditional agrarian inherited wealth had not been disqualified; they remained eligible to run for the archonship (and board of generals)—and, to be sure, their names continue to recur among the office-holders attested in later times. For another, lower-income Athenians, possibly a majority even if only the Thetes could be counted, were by implication formally *dis*qualified from all but membership in the Assembly and eligibility to run for insignificant administrative boards under Solon's supposedly progressive new nontraditional system. To many scholars, it has appeared that the chief beneficiary here was a somewhat expanded class of rich Athenians, the old-guard aristocrats now supplemented by *arrivistes*—wannabe aristocrats—that is, an enlarged and reinvigorated aristocracy.

Solon's judicial reforms, discussed in chapter 4, "Conflict, Trials, and Ostracism," do indeed look like an attack upon upper-class privilege, but the effects (and so the intent?) were reformist and, again, regulatory. Solon had no wish to overthrow the ruling elite; rather, he appears to have strengthened it by curbing its excesses and restraining its reckless abuse of privilege—all, it is clear, to its own long-term benefit.

Solon's sumptuary legislation seems to point in the same direction. "Sumptuary" refers to consumption, especially extravagant consumption, and the legislation was concerned with its regulation. Sometimes the purpose of such legislation is purely moral or religious, but the case of the ancient Athenian Solon was not so straightforward. Initially perplexing is the fact that women seem to have been the prime target. Major aspects of a citizen female's life, private as well as public, became subject to various confining restrictions: food, drink, and feasts; walks outside the house; trousseaux (that is, the clothing and other personal effects a bride takes into her marriage); and attendance and demonstrations at funerals. Was Solon anti-woman, a male chauvinist who believed that women had acquired too much personal property, public visibility, and influence and had to be reined in? Or was his purpose moralizing after all, with women, as often in later history, designated to bear the full burden of upholding society's values (while, on the male side, Solon is recorded to have instituted public brothels staffed by slave prostitutes)? More likely, however, his targets were actually men, specifically the aristocratic menfolk (fathers, husbands, and so on) who had traditionally used women as symbols (or "trophies") of their wealth, high pedigrees, and social prominence. But, if so, it was only the style or visible public face of the aristocracy that was at issue, not its existence. Arguably, Solon, by attempting to remove some of the more formidable and inimitable class markers, was animated by the statesmanlike goal of easing the way of the Johnny-come-lately "500 Bushel Men" in particular into the newly expanded ruling elite,

With the economic reforms, too, expansion of an already-in-place sector, in this case the crafts or industrial workforce, is in question. Solon offered citizenship to any free Greeks who, accompanied by their families, would take up permanent residence in Attica in order to practice a trade. Paralleling his expansion of the aristocracy, Solon seems by his invitation to foreign "guest workers" to have been enlarging the middle-class workforce. To Solon is ascribed (possibly anachronistically) a reform of the Athenian system of weights, measures, and coinages. A Solonian law called upon the Council of the Areopagus to punish any Athenian man who, upon investigation, was found not to be earning a livelihood. Still another ordained that an Athenian could not in his old age claim support from his adult son if he had not previously taught that son a gainful trade. Again, regulation, this time on the male side, and, again, the underlying intent was probably a disinterested concern for the public good, rather than moralizing. And throughout, as with the case of women, aspects of what the modern reader might regard as a citizen's own business became subject to public intervention and control.

Clisthenes

Both Theseus and Solon were, in later classical times, popularly identified as the founders in some sense of the democratic Athens, but, to more discerning observers (and to us), that distinction properly belongs to Clisthenes. The reasons underlying the conflicting ascriptions are not simply historical error or misunderstanding but are rather rooted in contemporary ideological issues that cannot concern us here. It is supremely ironic, therefore, that no ancient historian, not even a later biographer like Plutarch, has left us a "Life" of this pivotal figure who had so much to do with the emergence of Athens' classical Golden Age. Except for a brief excursus in Herodotus and the usual, routinely recorded details pertaining to family background, Clisthenes is little more than a mere name, known only by inference from his attested constitutional innovations. But, for all their brevity, those biographical details do tell us what will become in this and the following chapter a familiar tale. Clisthenes was the son of the aristocratic Megacles of the Alcmeonid clan and of Agariste, daughter of Clisthenes of Sicyon. By the chance survival of a fragmentary inscription, we know that our Clisthenes was archon eponymous in 525/4 B.C.E., during the ascendancy of Hippias, son and successor of the tyrant Pisistratus. Years later, when the Alcmeonids, and Clisthenes with them, were forced into exile, the former archon induced the Delphic oracle to pressure Sparta to overthrow the tyranny in Athens. With the eventual fall of the Pisistratids, Clisthenes then had to compete with the conservative Isagoras for supremacy, but the latter's own appeal to Sparta to intervene resulted in Clisthenes' withdrawal from Athens for a second time. Then, and only then, did Clisthenes, as Herodotus famously put it, "take the People into his faction," force the departure of Isagoras, and, installed once again in Athens, carry in the year 508/7 B.C.E. the program of reforms that were to go by the name *dēmokratia*, "rule by the People."

Highborn aristocrat? Son of a foreign (as well as aristocratic) mother? Opportunist who cooperated with an oppressive regime and thereby attained the highest elective office? Ally of the city-state that would eventually emerge as Athens' chief political and military rival? Radical ideologue and "man of the People"? Yes, there are contradictions and inconsistencies here, but they conform to a pattern that will, as I said, recur—here in Athens, elsewhere in Greece, and, equally famously, at ancient Rome.

THE CONSERVATIVES

By definition, a "conservative" is a person inclined to conserve existing conditions—ideas, customs, institutions, and so on. Already a radical innovation, by mid-fifth century B.C.E. the democracy had undergone additional liberalization. If greater precision is desired, a landmark event conventionally cited in this connection is the dimly understood progressive legislation of the reformer Ephialtes in 462. From that time on, a traditionally minded Athenian politician was faced with multiple challenges to any such conservative inclination. Specific areas of change, especially institutional change, may be mentioned to illustrate the point.

Militarily, the adoption of hoplite armor and battle tactics by the Athenian infantry had, even as early as the Athenian victory over the Persians at Marathon in 490 B.C.E., forced a reevaluation of the importance of the ordinary citizen. Prior to the hoplite reform, the military had been dominated by a minority of aristocrats, specifically the more recent practitioners of the Homeric-style individual duel of champions, the commanders who owed their position to membership in prominent families, and the elite of mounted horsemen. But the adoption of the hoplite phalanx (or battle line) not only introduced a new panoply of armor (a heavy set of protective helmet, breast plate, and shin guards in addition to spear and sword) but also (and more important for the present discussion) brought with it new manpower requirements: a greatly enlarged front-line corps of soldiers subject to a distinctly egalitarian—and democratic—code of conduct. Thousands of identically armed infantrymen, arrayed in uniform parallel files, would now be required to suppress any individualist or elitist impulses in favor of the interests of the group. The values on which the success of hoplite warfare depended (and in the absence of which defeat was the inevitable outcome) were equality, cooperation, and sacrifice of one's personal welfare in the service of Athens. Commanders, furthermore, whatever had been the previous mode of their selection, were now, from the beginnings of the democracy, subject to election by vote of the People. Since virtually every able-bodied citizen male between the ages of 18 (or so) and 59 prosperous enough to outfit himself with the necessary armor was potentially a hoplite infantryman subject to immediate call-up, it is easy to imagine how the small and dwindling numbers of the old blue-blood families might feel themselves to be, and in fact were, losing their grip on the reins of political leadership.

While the hoplite triumph at Marathon in 490 had vaulted the corps of citizen land soldiers into lasting preeminence, a decade later, in 479, in response to the renewed and larger invasion headed by King Xerxes, the

Athenian navy's no less incisive triumph over the Persian fleet off the island of Salamis had secured the lasting political presence of the masses of rowers (as well as commanders and marines) of Athens' fleet. The navy's nominal strength stood at 200 triremes, and each trireme required a nominal 170 rowers. Urbanites, landless in all probability, and certainly less prosperous (since they presumably could not have afforded the hoplite armory necessary for membership in the infantry), these sailors, by virtue of their numbers and even more radical political ideology, posed an even greater threat to aristocratic claims to preeminence and leadership than the hoplites.

The democracy had, as we saw in chapter 2, emerged from a political crisis involving factional conflict and the intervention of a foreign army, namely Sparta's. The new government can be understood as an expression of the balance of powers in Athens at that time. And the great victories at Marathon and Salamis, which transpired shortly after the creation of that government, continued to underpin and validate the ideology of egalitarianism embodied in democracy. Thus, aristocrats would continue to be challenged not simply by the mass participation of citizens in the legislature, magistracy, and courts (and that was challenging enough!). Perhaps more daunting, it was also the enduring memories of the decisive military achievements of the People that continued to sustain the democracy and insulate it from aristocratic reaction.

The triumph of the popular sovereignty went far beyond mere domination of constitutional organs of government. Appropriation is perhaps the most suitable term for characterizing the incorporation of once private aristocratic custom and lifestyle into the fabric of public democratic institutions. For example, religious cults (sanctuary, priesthood, and calendar) once controlled by powerful clans to varying degrees became subject to regulation by the democracy. Victories in the Olympic or Pythian Games, once a pinnacle of aristocratic striving to be celebrated by an ode of Pindar, were essentially co-opted by the state in the form of public honors (such as the free dinners in the Prytaneion immortalized by a comment of Socrates' in Plato's *Apology*), by representations of the private individual's achievement as Athens' achievement, and by the establishment of the state's own Games in the image of the panhellenic prototypes. Public festivals invited the participation of members of leading families, such as the virgin female Basket Bearers in the annual Panathenaia. And the depiction of this particular festival on the frieze that encircled the outer walls of the inner chamber of the Parthenon is but one of several known such appropriations in highly visible pictorial or sculptural programs on public buildings. All carried great symbolic weight, and all carried the same underlying message: that any individual's achievement, those of aristocrats not excluded, potentially belonged to the People as a whole and might be publicly represented as such.

Miltiades and Cimon

Miltiades was born into the wealthy clan called Philaidai that was based in eastern Attica. Elected archon for the year 524/3, Miltiades was dispatched on a foreign mission to the Thracian Chersonesus by the tyrant Hippias. Hippias, again, had succeeded to leadership upon the death of his father Pisistratus in 527. While in Chersonesus, Miltiades married the daughter of the Thracian king, Olorus. Eventually driven from his new foreign homeland, Miltiades joined in the rebellion of the Greek Ionian cities against Persia, but when the rebellion failed he fled to Athens. After escaping prosecution for misconduct while abroad, he was elected one of the 10 generals for the year 490/89—the year that was to see the battle of Marathon. The fifth-century tradition represented by Herodotus makes him primarily responsible for the great Athenian-led victory. After Marathon, Miltiades commanded an Athenian naval force against the island of Paros, failed in the attempt, was put on trial at Athens, condemned, and fined, but he died of an infection before the fine could be paid.

The fine, it turned out, would eventually be paid by Cimon, Miltiades' son by his Thracian wife. Marriages and children continue to tell the tale of the son and his aristocratic family. Cimon's sister Elpinice married Callias, son of Hipponicus, from one of Athens' richest families. Notwithstanding the probably politically motivated allegation that he had an incestuous relationship with this sister, Cimon himself married the Alcmaeonid Isodice, while another marriage was to an unknown woman from Arcadia in Greece. From these unions issued the sons Lacedaemonius, Eleos or Oulios, and Thettalus (as well as additional sons of questionable historicity). These crudely significant made-up names memorialized the father's hereditary and/or political connections with Sparta and Thessaly.

In 479, Cimon was a member of an embassy to Sparta and in the following year assisted Aristides in forming the maritime alliance against Persia called the Delian League. Elected general numerous times, Cimon commanded League operations until late in the 460s. In 462, he prevailed upon the People to send him to Sparta to help the authorities there suppress a revolt of the helots, but the distrustful Spartans rejected Cimon (evidently on the suspicion that the Athenians would join forces with the helots) and sent him (and his army) back to Athens with his tail between his legs. This humiliating setback led to Cimon's ostracism the next year and played an indirect role in setting the stage for the liberal reform program of Ephialtes.

Despite Cimon's occasional cooperation with anti-Spartan and pro-Empire politicians, his career does in the main seem to have conformed to the pattern of high birth, foreign and Spartan sympathies, dynastic marriage, and generally the practice of traditional politics.

The Two Athenians Named Thucydides

Thucydides, son of Melesias, was an aristocrat born at the turn of the fifth century B.C.E. Upon the death of Cimon, with whom he was connected by marriage, Thucydides emerged as the principal opponent of the "liberal" politician-general Pericles. Plutarch in particular reports on Thucydides' opposition to the Periclean building program (which produced the Propylaea and the Parthenon, among other structures), quoting some inflammatory purple rhetorical flourishes about decking out Athens like a prostitute. Despite the organization of his supporters as a bloc within the Assembly, Thucydides suffered ostracism (in 443) at the hands of his enemies and, after his return to Athens at the end of his 10 years of banishment, was legally prosecuted in his old age.

The Athenian citizen who wrote *The Peloponnesian War* identifies himself as Thucydides, son of Olorus. Given the rarity of the non-Greek name Olorus, the historian must be related to the Thracian king Olorus, whose daughter Miltiades married; and, given the comparative rarity of the (Greek) name Thucydides, he is almost certainly related to the son of Melesias. The conjunction of these two coincidences should, in the absence of any contrary indications, identify the historian, too, as a traditional early-fifth-century aristocratic "conservative."

But there are contrary indications. True, Thucydides' *History* does for the most part live up to the modern estimation of its author as an "objective" historian, but sympathies, likes, and dislikes, are on occasion betrayed, despite his seeming best efforts. Among the more obvious of these is his sympathetic, even congratulatory, portrayal of Pericles, who, in the following section, I will group with the "liberals." But how can this be? A conservative sympathetic to a liberal? To understand the phenomenon, we must grasp the fundamental distinction between the ideological and cultural dimensions of ancient Greek politics. To take the cultural dimension first, it is undeniable that Pericles was a high-born aristocratic and that he maintained his aloof "Olympian" personal style to the end of his life—and that it was these "conservative" elements of family background, routines, and demeanor that seem to have particularly appealed to his fellow aristocrat (and undoubted acquaintance) Thucydides. Thus, we are brought back once again to the themes of this chapter and, indeed, of the entire book—the political roles played by the pursuit of prestige, personal contacts, and, especially, cultural style.

A cultural identity, conservative or otherwise, does not determine a person's ideology, certainly not for Thucydides, for in his case the cultural elements arguably outweighed the matters of political philosophy and program. To see that this is so, one need only compare the historian's treatment of Pericles with that of his successor, Cleon, also a general and public speaker. Both championed the growth of the Empire, both favored and energetically prosecuted the ruinous war against Sparta, both curried the favor of the poor and landless urban voters—and, negatively put, both of necessity broke with Athens' traditional agrarian past and its "conservative" ideology. But, as much as the historian adulated Pericles, he held in contempt his successor and fellow "liberal," Cleon. And why? Cleon, like his father, was blue collar, literally dirtying his hands in the disgusting business of leather-tanning; his personal deportment, clothing, and manners lacked the polish of the high born; and his speaking style was crude, even vulgar. No matter that the two men's political views were at the level of fundamentals hardly distinguishable.

Aristides

As a final example of a "conservative" Athenian politician, let me introduce Aristides. The subject of a Plutarchian *Life*, Aristides was linked by friendship to Clisthenes (founder of the democracy) and was probably a cousin of the richest man in Athens during his day, Callias son of Hipponicus. Since both were highborn aristocrats, family background alone is sufficient basis to include Aristides here among the "conservatives." On hand (but not necessarily a general) at the battle of Marathon in 490 and apparently elected archon in 489/8, he would also figure prominently during the second Persian invasion a decade later, deploying a hoplite force in the allied operations off the island of Salamis and being in command at the decisive Panhellenic victory on land at Plataea. Soon thereafter, Aristides teamed with Themistocles in bringing about the rapid refortification of Athens over the determined opposition of the Spartans who, with characteristic paranoia, suspected aggressive intentions directed toward themselves. Altogether, then, a war hero and, given his family wealth, a solid "conservative" if there ever was one.

But the actual situation is not so straightforward. Though probably closely related to the richest man in Athens, even in antiquity Aristides could be represented as poor. Between the two Persian invasions, Aristides was ostracized, which, given the nature of the ostracism procedure, can only indicate a very substantial body of hostile sentiment. Nor are his "conservative" credentials as clear-cut and unambiguous as might be suggested. To help rebuild Athens' walls is one thing, but immediately thereafter, in 478, the reliable Thucydides (as well as Plutarch) credit Aristides with assessing the tribute payments for the member states of the Delian League. Initially a voluntary alliance dedicated solely to the defense of the Greek states against the Persians, the League was eventually converted by Athens into an empire, by which point the new walls and the payment of "dues" for common defense had acquired an entirely new—and "liberal"—meaning. Aristides could, by the time of the outbreak of the Peloponnesian War, in 431, in retrospect be characterized as one of the architects of the distinctly unconservative maritime Athens that had turned its back on the city's traditional agrarian orientation and culture.

Further muddying the waters is the ancient disagreement, or confusion, regarding Aristides' character. According to ancient anecdote, Aristides was "The Just," and, as such, he could be opposed to the scheming deceiver Themistocles (discussed later, under "The Liberals"). But the fact is that Aristides, as mentioned, cooperated with Themistocles in the refortification of the town, a project that, if Thucydides' detailed account can be believed (and it can), was a consummate example of scheming and deception. Indeed, an ancient pun on Aristides' deme name Alopeke styled him "more fox [Greek *alōpēx*, "fox"] by nature than by deme." Chances are that Aristides was no more just than any other successful politician of the day and that the sobriquet "The Just" is the product of a typical ancient schematizing opposition to a trickster Themistocles. Plutarch's pairing and comparison of Greeks and Romans in his *Parallel Lives* is but one late example of a tendency that can be traced to the very wellsprings of ancient Greek historiography. And, beyond the wellsprings, isn't schematization of this kind part and parcel of all politics, not the least the politics of our own day? Demonizing one's opponent, building up one's own (or one's candidate's) image, selling that image to the electorate—it's all so familiar. Aristides as poor but just defender of traditional values could easily have been the centerpiece of a public relations campaign to reinvent the image of an actual moneyed aristocrat.

THE LIBERALS

The English term "liberal" is vague and highly charged, meaning one thing to one person or group, another to another person or group. Latin in origin, *liberalis* marks the freed person in contrast with the slave and, because a freedman or woman had once been a slave (or descended from slaves), the *liberalis* must be further distinguished from an *ingenuus* (or *ingenua*), a person born free. Among various English meanings, a particularly common sense of "liberal" preserves the notion of former servitude or at least a state of liberation from involuntary confinement. "One who is open-minded or not strict in the observance of orthodox, traditional, or established forms or ways" is how one dictionary puts it.[2] Adherence to "tradition," that is, may be understood as a form of (self-imposed and voluntary) servitude. So the quality that sets the following "liberals" apart from their "conservative" (that is, more traditional) opposing numbers is a willingness or tendency to break with the values or practices of the past in pursuit of their political objectives.

Themistocles

Themistocles is the first well-documented major political figure at Athens under the new democracy. Indeed, his impact was so great that he might well have been grouped, along with the democracy's architect, Clisthenes, as one of Athens' Founding Fathers. But, unlike Clisthenes, "politics" for Themistocles has reference not only narrowly to legislation and elections but, in the broader sense of *ta politika,* to military matters and, his most lasting contribution, to his decisive role in the reorientation of the city away from its agrarian past and toward a maritime engagement with Greece overseas.

For Themistocles, family background was rather obscure in terms of reputation. His father was Neocles, hardly among the most distinguished people at Athens, by deme a Phrearrhian, of the tribe Leontis. On his mother's side he was, so they say, of non-Athenian stock:

> Here I lie, Abrotonom, a woman of Thrace by descent, but I lay claim to have given birth to the Great One among the Greeks—Themistocles.

Working, as always, let us remember, from preexisting literary sources centuries after the event, the biographer cites a second authority to the effect that the mother was Carian and a third that the Carian city in question was Halicarnassus.³

Plutarch, for reasons that are unclear but perhaps to make a better story by contrasting humble origins with future greatness, seems to be overstating the case for obscurity. Granted, the father, Neocles, may have been unknown to him (and his sources), but at this early date (Themistocles' birthdate has been estimated at 524 B.C.E.) nothing follows from such "obscurity" regarding high or low birth. In fact, there are slight indications (that cannot be gone into here) that his father hailed from an aristocratic clan (namely the Lycomids). But it's the mother's side and the use of the derogatory "bastard" (Greek *nothos*, here translated as "non-Athenian") that reveal the amateur essayist's failure to understand the actual facts of the situation. The deduction of illegitimate status from the mother's foreign origins is based on the anachronistic retrojection to a much earlier time of Pericles' law on citizenship, according to which the mother as well as the father had to be Athenian in order for the child to be Athenian. To the contrary, rather than indicating low birth, a foreign mother, if the daughter of royalty, could be (and often was) the mark of an international arranged dynastic marriage.

Right off the bat, and at a young age, it seems that politics took hold of Themistocles and that an impulse for fame overpowered him entirely. As a result, from the beginning, in his striving to be preeminent, he recklessly incurred the enmities of those who were powerful—and already preeminent—in the city, especially Aristides son of Lysimachus, who was always going up against him. And yet it seems that his enmity with this man had an entirely childish origin. Both were lovers of the handsome Stesilaus (a native of the island of Ceos), as the philosopher Ariston has recorded; and it was a consequence of this that they continued to be rivals in public affairs. For all that, it was the dissimilarity of their lifestyles and characters that seems to have increased the disparity. Aristides was placid by nature and gentlemanly in bearing. His public activity aimed not at personal favor or reputation but rather was all about The Best—consistently, that is, with Security and Justice. Accordingly he was forced into opposition with Themistocles, who was always stirring up the People and bringing on grand initiatives—and was always obstructing the growth of his influence.

For Themistocles is said to have been so distracted concerning his reputation and, under the influence of a desire for glory, such a lover of great deeds, that though he was still a young man when the battle against the barbarians at Marathon occurred and the generalship of Miltiades was talked about everywhere, he was seen to be engrossed in his own thoughts a lot of the time, to lay awake at night, to refuse invitations to the usual drinking parties, and to say to those who in their amazement put questions to him concerning his change of lifestyle that "the battlefield trophy of Miltiades won't let me sleep!" Now while other people thought that the loss by the barbarians at Marathon was the end of the war, Themistocles took it to be only the beginning of greater contests, and for these he anointed himself on behalf of all Greece and put his city into training in anticipation of the future that was still far off.⁴

The cautious Aristides versus the visionary innovator Themistocles? Such is the stuff of public opinion, of much postclassical historiography and biography, and of the essentially moralizing writing (the *Lives* as well as the *Moralia*) of the Roman-era Greek scholar Plutarch. Just as we moderns, in thought and practice, polarize our political personalities into two opposing camps, liberals and conservatives, so did the ancient Greeks and their successors. And, in antiquity, as in today's world, the end result of polarization is more often than not an exaggerated, overdrawn schematization that does violence to the complexity and essential messiness of reality. But does this observation mean that Plutarch's moralizing portrayals of Themistocles (and of Aristides, as well) must be jettisoned? That the baby has to be thrown out with the bathwater? Certainly not. To address Plutarch's central point, we can be reasonably confident that it was indeed a desire for a high reputation (or "glory") that was the dominant value in Themistocles' attitudinal repertoire. Why? Because, as we learn from contemporary documentation (inscriptions as well as historians), *philotimia,* "love of honor," was indeed the value consistently cultivated, acknowledged, and rewarded in Athenian public life of the classical period. Even if we concede the doubtful exception of Aristides (and Plutarch's Christian environment may conceivably be at work here), the politicians of ancient Greece were less interested in disinterested altruistic benefactions to society than in enhancing their reputations in the eyes of their fellow Greeks—superiors, peers, and inferiors alike. Honor (Greek *timē,* hence *philotimia*) had remained, ever since the fictive Homeric "society" of the *Iliad* and *Odyssey,* the dominating, primary value of a man's (and a woman's) striving in family, social, and public life. Wealth counted, to be sure, and great achievements, too, but they always served a higher purpose, the amplification of the actor's personal honor, as inwardly experienced but also, and far more important, as publicly acknowledged by others.

And what were Themistocles' "great achievements"? Early on, as archon, Themistocles spearheaded the development of Piraeus as the city's principal harbor—a role it was to play throughout antiquity and down to the present day. During the decade following the battle of Marathon, when a rich vein of silver was discovered in southern Attica, against popular opposition (shortsighted demagogic politicians wished to distribute the windfall to the entire citizen body), Themistocles prevailed upon the People to construct new triremes, raising the fleet's strength to 200 ships. Only a few years later, the Persians invaded once again, and the new fleet was to prove, at the great sea battle off Salamis, in 479, the salvation not only of Athens but indeed of all of Greece. Themistocles himself, as general, was the architect of the successful allied strategy, brilliantly overcoming Spartan intransigence and cunningly outwitting his opposing Persian numbers with their vastly superior military armament. The next year, 478 B.C.E., saw the creation of the Delian League, a voluntary alliance of Greek cities dedicated to maintaining vigilance against yet another Persian invasion, but by midcentury the League had been converted into an aggressive, acquisitive Athenian Empire administered by the People and narrowly serving exclusively Athenian interests. The backbone of the imperial military force was the fleet so providentially constructed under Themistocles' direction.

Moreover, the new port at Piraeus was now linked to Athens town by the Long Walls constructed, again under Themistocles' direction, in the years following the final retreat of the Persian invaders. A half-century later, and long after Themistocles' departure from Athens, these fortifications played a key role in Athenian strategic calculations in the early stages of the Peloponnesian War against Sparta and its allies. Piraeus gave Athenian shipping access to overseas imports and safe haven for the fleet, while the Long Walls guaranteed contact with the town even when, as actually happened during the Peloponnesian War, a large invading force was occupying the countryside of Attica. Themistocles, it is no exaggeration to say, had laid the foundations for Athens' classical imperial greatness. But not to be forgotten is Plutarch's (and our) point, that driving the achievements of this Great Man was not a craving for wealth or power or even some political ideology (so familiar to us observers of the modern world) but the characteristically ancient Greek "love of honor."

Ephialtes

Few figures of importance in Athenian political history are more shadowy than Ephialtes, but, as his reforms seem to occupy a pivotal position in the development of the democracy, he plainly cannot be omitted. True to the pattern of many politicians in the Greco-Roman world, Ephialtes' fragmentary resumé contains military service of distinction, for we know that he commanded a naval force against Phaselis on the Asia Minor coast, a harbor town of commercial importance that was eventually to become a member of the Athenian Empire. Since conservatives, too, like Cimon, regularly engaged in overseas military expeditions (Cimon, as just noted, led a force against the island of Paros late in his career), it is not on this head that conservative and liberal politicians are to be distinguished. Politicians of any stripe played parts in Athens' imperialist ambitions—just as their ideological counterparts were to do later at Rome, in Italy.

The two, in fact, seem to have become the principal rival leaders at Athens at midcentury. Either during Cimon's absence at Sparta, in his abortive effort to relieve the revolt of the helots, or, upon his return, in the wake of his public humiliation and presumable loss of political face with the voting public, Ephialtes sponsored legislation depriving the Council of the Areopagus of some of its traditional powers. The year was 462/1 B.C.E. The powers in question were the monitoring of magistrates (namely the preliminary examination before entering office and the audit following departure from office) and the presiding over trials of impeachment of these same magistrates. These functions had allowed the old council to indirectly control the state's affairs, since the fundamental function of a magistrate was, after all, to implement the policies adopted by the legislature. While the Areopagus continued to retain the right to try cases of homicide, bodily wounding, and arson (plus some vestigial authority over religious matters), magisterial oversight now passed to the organs of the Clisthenic democratic government.

To the extent that the Areopagus had retained to this point any of its ancient authority, Ephialtes' reform was a serious blow to aristocratic privilege.

Its membership had always consisted of outgoing archons, aristocrats all, but (as already frequently mentioned), starting in 487/6, the archons had been selected by the lottery and, consequently, by 462/1, the year of Ephialtes' reform, the importance of the Areopagus may have declined appreciably. Nonetheless, ancient writers ascribe a leadership role to the old council even after the Persian War, so it remains a tenable view that Ephialtes was indeed a liberal reformer aiming to empower the young democracy at the expense of the aristocratic class. And what of Cimon? He was ostracized the following year. Ephialtes himself suffered not ostracism but assassination. Are these events connected? The pitifully few ancient sentences about this pivotal period that have come down to us make any reconstruction extremely hazardous, but rivalry between opposing conservative and liberal leaders of political factions must certainly be the most attractive scenario.

Pericles

With Pericles we finally encounter a political personality about whom we have a relative abundance of reliable information. Besides the (always welcome) late *Life* of Plutarch, a somewhat younger contemporary (and almost certainly an acquaintance), Thucydides the historian gives us much about the man down to his death in 429 B.C.E., a victim of the plague that struck Athens early in the Peloponnesian War. And by midcentury the democracy was inscribing on stone some of the very acts of government in which Pericles had played a part. From these (and other) sources emerges a personality that clearly exemplifies some of the themes—connections, perception, and style—that distinguish the ancient Greek politician.

Pericles, from a modern perspective, without question stands toward the liberal end of the ideological spectrum. He instituted payment for jury duty. He undertook a massive public building program on the Acropolis that, besides glorifying Athens, brought years of gainful employment to large numbers at public expense. He flouted the cardinal principal of the highborn by authoring a law that ordained that a person's mother as well as his or her father must be taken in to account when deciding who may or may not be an Athenian citizen. And, having thus empowered Athenian womanhood, he defied aristocratic convention still further by marrying a foreigner who (even if she was not the former brothel keeper that Pericles' enemies made her out to be) certainly remained beyond the pale of respectability. Such were the more memorable acts of Pericles' domestic policy. And foreign policy? Pericles vigorously promoted the formation, growth, and maintenance of the Athenian Empire and, with that Empire in place, emerged as the architect (and, until his death, the guiding spirit) of the city's eventually ruinous war with Sparta. A liberal, certainly, but an imperialist and hawkish one as well.

Pericles' family background was undeniably aristocratic, certainly on his mother's side. His mother, Agariste, was an Alcmeonid and the niece of the founder of the democracy, Clisthenes, and the granddaughter of another

Agariste, from Sicyon—that is, highborn and with a "foreign" connection. Xanthippus, Pericles' father, had been prominent in Athenian politics early in the fifth century, even suffering ostracism (a sure mark of political prominence). As for Pericles himself, although Thucydides gives little of a personal nature regarding his hero, we do learn of a rural estate, and his instruction in music and rhetoric is a clear indication of an upper-class upbringing. Plutarch, whose overriding interest was, after all, the personal moral qualities that made the subject of his *Life* the man that he was, gives us the following:

Pericles, while young, was exceedingly watchful of the People, since he was thought to be similar in appearance to the tyrant Pisistratus. And since it was also noted that his voice was sweet and his tongue facile and rapid in conversation, exceedingly old people [i.e., who remembered Pisistratus, who had died in 527] were struck by the resemblance. Since wealth and background of distinction were his, as well as friends of the greatest influence, and accordingly fearing that he would be ostracized, he had nothing to do with politics, although in the military he proved brave and capable. When Aristides died, and Themistocles was banished, and campaigns were keeping Cimon outside of Greece for the most part, under these circumstances Pericles began to devote himself to the People, choosing the cause of the many and the poor over the wealthy and the few—contrary to his own nature which was anything but populist. Fearing, however, that he would fall under suspicion of tyranny, and observing that Cimon was exceedingly aristocratic and especially endeared to the Beautiful People, he gave his support to the Many, thereby securing safety for himself and power against his adversary.

Right away, too, he applied a different pattern to his lifestyle. For he was now seen using one street alone in town on his way to Agora and Council House. Invitations to dinner and all other such frivolity and socializing he passed on, so that during that time of his political activity (which turned out to be long) he went to none of his friends' for dinner, except that when his cousin Euryptolemos married he stayed for the libations, then immediately got up and left.... And so Pericles, seeking to avoid familiarity and overexposure, made his approaches to the People at intervals, not speaking on every question nor coming before the public all the time. Rather, like the trireme Salamis (as Critolaus puts it), he presented himself only for big emergencies; and he managed everything else by delegating to his friends and other public speakers.[5]

These paragraphs of Plutarch's reveal much of Pericles' personality, but it is a personality that embodies some of the cultural realities that were basic to the ancient Greek politician's public (as well as personal) profile. We now discuss some of these realities.

Connections

Why did Pericles go to such extremes to avoid social gatherings? It was a fact known to all that he had been born into an aristocratic, politically experienced, and successful family—or, rather, two such families. Given the unquestioned acceptance of the rule of descent, Pericles was consequently heir to an extraordinarily far-reaching and politically useful web of connections. "Who you know," not "what you know," was the formula that could easily write his ticket for political success in elections as spokesman of the blue-blood elite. Accordingly, it is clear why Pericles was doing all that he could to avoid any such expectations, since the potential following that he wished to nurture consisted not of the aristocrats of his own class but of the landless urban poor of the general citizen body. Avoidance of something (in this case, inherited aristocratic connections) serves to prove that something's dominating presence. But, in Pericles' case, essentially what he was attempting to do was to exchange one set of connections for another by becoming patron to a mob clientele.

Perception

Pericles feared that in his fellow Athenians' eyes he physically resembled the hated tyrant of the sixth century, Pisistratus. Actually, the two men had little in common, but it was not the facts but the perception that counted. From the beginning, an overriding concern of Pericles' publicly observable political activity was to avoid any perception of resemblance to the pre-democratic tyrant.

Style

For all his attention to avoiding unwelcome associations and perceptions, Pericles, the Man of the People, did not attempt to mask the aloof and superior personal bearing that was the inheritance of his aristocratic upbringing. Far from it. That bearing was to be the key ingredient of his success as speaker and campaigner. What set Pericles apart from other political aristocrats was his successful effort to put that much admired celebrity profile to work in the interests of *hoi polloi*. "The Many" may have hated aristocrats, but they also, despite themselves, loved the aristocratic style. It was all right if Pericles maintained the outward appearance of the highborn noble—provided that, in doing so, he directed his efforts to the service of the People.

Alcibiades

No selection, however brief or selective, of ancient Greek politicians could fail to include Alcibiades, first because of the sheer impact of his career and, second, because he illustrates as well as anyone some of the themes running throughout the present book. Take, to begin, his family background and personal associations. Alcibiades' father, Cleinias, had outfitted a trireme at his own expense (thereby, as the holder of a liturgy, by definition qualifying as a member of the propertied class) and with the ship acquitted himself honorably in the sea battle against the invading Persians off Cape Artemisium. When Cleinias perished in military action at Coroneia, in Boeotia, the youngster was reared by his first cousins once removed, the sons of Xanthippus, one of whom was none other than Pericles. The relation with Pericles was through his mother, Deinomache, the daughter of Megacles of the aristocratic Alcmeonid clan. High birth, wealth, military heroism, the tutelage of Athens' premier political leader—a background more distinguished and conducive to future political eminence would be hard to imagine.

But Alcibiades was manifestly more than the sum of his inheritance and relations by birth and marriage. Intellectually gifted, he had abilities that brought him attention and preeminence among his peers in several areas of endeavor. Early on, he won his way into the circle of youthful male followers of the philosopher Socrates, eventually earning an invitation to the drinking party that was the real or fictional subject of Plato's *Symposium* ("drinking party" being the literal meaning of the Greek *symposion*). At the same time, it must be conceded, on Plato's and, later, Plutarch's evidence, that the old man's physical attraction to the beautiful boy as much as anything else marked him out as a favorite. The word "beautiful" is an imperfect representation of the sources' repeated comment upon Alcibiades' face, physique, and demeanor, with at least one such comment characterizing his looks as strikingly feminine. But, for all that, Alcibiades was no sissy who cultivated interests assigned to females in this regimented gender-role-bound macho regime. To the contrary. Among his recorded pursuits were horses and horse racing—the consummate mark of good breeding and aristocratic lifestyle—and one that he took to the highest level by entering multiple four-horse chariots in the Olympic Games. Such a pursuit is not, however, to be equated with an interest in sports common among younger males in our own culture, even if we are willing to grant that Alcibiades did in fact possess considerable athletic ability and motivation. Closer parallels would be the Kentucky Derby at Churchill Downs or the Gold Cup at Ascot Downs in England, where elite society—hardly limited to owners of competing horses, much less to horse lovers—annually turn out in all their finery for what are essentially high-class social and fashion events.

According to the values and ideals of ancient Athenians, Alcibiades had it all: high birth, inherited wealth (making physical wage-earning labor unnecessary), good looks, talent soon to be manifested in public speaking or philosophical exchange or musical performance, and success in pursuits appropriate to a male of his aristocratic class. Alcibiades was first and foremost a celebrity, and, were he alive today, his image, his lovers, his doings both personal and public would be a constant topic of supermarket tabloids, television talk shows, and fan-driven Internet sites. True, he was a politician (winning election, for example, to the post of general), and an ideology might be found buried within his political acts, but all this was merely a secondary manifestation of the personal magnetism and celebrity profile that characterized this Golden Boy of classical Athens.

Alcibiades' political and military achievements, infamous as well as famous, were recorded in antiquity beginning with his contemporary Thucydides and continuing through the surviving *Life* by Plutarch. The entire career belongs to the time of the Peloponnesian War, especially its later and final stages. At first, the young aristocrat was a promoter of diplomatic offensives, but his alliance with Peloponnesian Argos did not, as he had hoped, succeed in weakening Sparta. As the war wore on, the ambitious politician's blatantly imperialist vision (which he shared with his former guardian Pericles) led him to champion the disastrous expedition against Sicily. But, after the fleet, with Alcibiades as one of the three commanders, had reached its destination, he was recalled to Athens to stand trial on charges, in whole or part trumped up by his political enemies, of religious sacrilege. Rather than face a likely conviction, however, Alcibiades fled to Sparta, where, turning traitor, he put his insider's strategic knowledge to use in the service of the enemy. At length falling out of favor at Sparta, Alcibiades spent the next decade in exile in Persia, eventually returning to the Athenian side as a naval commander in the Hellespont. Forced to withdraw once again, first to Thrace, later, once again, to Persia, he fell victim at war's end in Phrygia to the intrigues of his oligarchic enemies in Greece.

No single word, phrase, or slogan can comprehend the sheer virtuosity, shifting allegiances, successes, and failures of the prodigy that was Alcibiades, but shining through it all was something resembling what we call personal ambition. Resembling, yes, but really not the same, for the Greeks drew the line rather differently between the personal and the nonpersonal, or rather did not draw it at all. Take, as an example, his speech delivered before the Athenians in support of the expedition to Sicily, as recreated by Thucydides:

I also believe that I deserve a command, because all the things that make me notorious are really an honor to my ancestors and to me, as well as an advantage to the state. For example, because of my magnificent performance at the Olympic Games, the other Greeks, who came expecting to find us exhausted by war, decided that our city was even greater than it is. That was because I entered seven chariots, more than any other private citizen ever, and won first, second, and fourth prizes—and I also comported myself in a style worthy of such victories. It's the way of the world to respect things like that. People think there is power behind performance. And again, when I distinguish myself here at Athens with a dramatic performance or some other such thing, it's only natural for my fellow citizens to envy me. But to foreigners they are a sign of strength. So this folly of mine isn't so useless after all, since at my own expense I benefit not only myself but the city.[6]

Flair, style, the winner's touch of a person who is good at everything he tries—in short, his celebrity is now about to be converted successfully into political influence. The word "charismatic" (from Greek *charisma*, "grace" or "charm"), if a single word be needed, perhaps best sums up Alcibiades. But politics based on personal qualities, or at least on those particular qualities emanating from aristocratic breeding and display, was on its way out. New paradigms for the political career at Athens were now being tested and approved, even at the very time that the ultimately traditionalist Alcibiades was at the height of his powers. So, let us now proceed to the next chapter and take a look at some of these new-style challengers from outside the old-guard aristocracy.

Eight

Some More Ancient Greek Politicians

CLEON AND THE "NEW RICH" ENTREPRENEURS

Pericles' death, in 429 B.C.E., marked a watershed in the history of politics at Athens. The general had dominated the operation of the democratic government as speaker and author of legislation, and his sudden unforeseen departure (he died in the plague that swept through the city early in the Peloponnesian War) created a vacuum of leadership. The eventual heir to Pericles' mantle was Cleon, who was to prove the most successful, and infamous, of the new breed of *dēmagagoi*—literally "leaders of the people" but disparaged by their enemies as "demagogues" (with all the negative connotations of the English word). What set these leaders apart from Pericles was, first, the fact that, coming from outside the old aristocracy, and indeed from outside the wider circle of "old" money, they based their political careers on their success in industry. "Industry" for ancient Athens meant capital investment in a slave workforce and the use of that workforce in nontraditional (that is, nonagricultural) commercial pursuits such as silver mining and manufacturing. Agriculture itself remained immune owing to the inalienability of farmland and the resulting impossibility of ever combining numerous small plots into the sorts of plantations that could be worked efficiently by gangs of slaves—as was to happen in Italy only a few hundred years later. Extraction of minerals and factory production were another matter, since as new industries they were not encumbered by limitations imposed by the traditions of the past. Among the known successful such entrepreneurs who entered the political arena were:

Cleon: son of a tanner (tanning is the process for applying tannin, a chemical found in tree bark, in order to produce usable leather)

Cleophon: lyre maker (the lyre, mythically the invention of the god Hermes, who used a tortoise shell as a sound box, was the standard plucked string instrument of Greek antiquity)

Eucrates: flax merchant (flax is a Mediterranean plant from which oil-seed and linen yard and cloth were produced)

Hyperbolus: lampmaker/metalworker/potter (oil lamps; bronze tools, weapons, and utensils; and ceramics constituted the principal durable goods of the ancient Greek world)

Lysicles: sheep dealer/hide stitcher (sheep provided milk, wool, and meat; hides were used for various purposes, including the making of tanned leather garments)

These were not the first Athenian politicians to have accumulated wealth from industrial pursuits. Earlier in the century, Callias and Nicias had been slaveowners on a massive scale, but they were from old aristocratic families and, however lucrative their mining or other nontraditional interests may have been, land ownership remained the core of their fortunes—and reputations. By contrast, our entrepreneurs had risen from social obscurity and, as is usually true of the suddenly wealthy, bore the familiar characteristics of the classic *nouveaux riches,* at least in the estimation of the blue-blood aristocrat: vulgarity, boorishness, in short a general absence of the cultivation that was the birthright of the privileged. As a specific illustration, consider the report of the Aristotelian *Constitution of the Athenians:*

He was the first who shouted on the speaker's platform, who used abusive language, and who spoke with his cloak hitched up around his waist, while all the others used to speak in proper dress and manner.[1]

Establishment types might find such behavior offensive and utterly at odds with their own upbringing and codes of civility, but the fact remains that the aristocrat and the New Rich politician had one important thing in common that united them while setting them apart from all other Athenians: money. Wealth could not replace "good breeding," but it did afford an absolutely necessary ingredient of a political career—leisure. Canvassing, the recruiting of support from citizen voters, was an all-consuming activity that, as today, could occupy much of the candidate's available disposable wealth, time, energy, and other resources. Modern equivalents would be door-to-door visits by the candidates (the author has received several such visits while writing this book in his home office), attendance at popular sporting events, and speeches at rallies—all performed while eating hot dogs and kissing babies. *Dēmokratia* meant just that, "rule by the People," so in any popular election (or referendum), contact had to be made with great numbers of citizens, in the low thousands at least. Unlike the case of the son of the privileged, the ancient Greek New Man did not enjoy the luxury of a ready-made inherited clientele of supporters already in his pocket. At the same time, the necessary demands upon the resources of the entrepreneur-turned-political-candidate are proof that the New Rich politician demeaned by a hostile source as a (mere) tanner or lampmaker was likely in fact the proprietor of a sizable and prosperous factory staffed by a cost-efficient slave labor force. He in all probability did not personally engage in the kinds of onerous manual labor that sapped the spirit and left nothing for political or other non-work-related pursuits.

Cleon

Thanks in large part to the narrative of Thucydides, Cleon's political and military achievements (and final failure), which fall within the first decade of the Peloponnesian War (431–404 B.C.E.), are known, even if details are regrettably lacking. These are:

427: Following the suppression of a revolt by the imperial allied city of Mytilene, on Lesbos, Cleon, as memorialized in the debate recreated in Thucydides' *History*, proposed a decree, eventually passed, calling for the execution of all the citizens, despite the fact that the revolt was the doing of a minority oligarchic anti-Athenian faction. The next day, the Assembly reconsidered and rescinded the decree.

426: Cleon hauled the comic poet Aristophanes into court, charging that his *Babylonians* had slandered the state of Athens (including himself, one of its leaders).

425: After Athenian commanders had surrounded several hundred Spartiate hoplites on the island of Sphakteria, off Pylos, and Sparta had offered terms for peace, Cleon opposed the Spartan terms, assumed command at Pylos, captured the hoplites, and brought them back to Athens as hostages. Thereafter, Cleon remained a hawk committed to total victory over the Spartan adversary.

425: Cleon was probably among the supporters of legislation greatly increasing (by as much as two or three times) the yearly tribute paid to Athens by the imperial allies—thereby enhancing the city's resources for continuing the military operations against Sparta (as well as enriching the city further on the domestic front).

425: Cleon proposed legislation increasing jurors' pay from two to three obols. As discussed in chapter 4, since the jurors seem to have been in large part impecunious older citizens, the measure potentially made for a significant increase in many a household's income. Given the continuing observance of patronal culture even within this urban "democratic" setting, the happy juror "clients" would be expected to discharge their obligation to their "patron" by supporting him in elections. If all went according to plan, Cleon would continue to be successful in his candidacy for the generalship and in the legislature when he wished to initiate decrees.

423: When tiny Skione revolted from the Empire, Cleon proposed the destruction of the town, including execution of its citizens. Unlike the case of Mytilene in 427, in this instance the decree was actually carried out.

422: Two years previously, in 424, a Peloponnesian force under the command of the Spartan general Brasidas had seized the strategically important fortified city of Amphipolis, at the mouth of the Strymon River. The Athenian commander at the time had been none other than the historian Thucydides, at that time serving as an elected general. By now Cleon was at the peak of his success and popularity (and hadn't he, after all, proved his military prowess in the Sphakteria episode?), and the Athenians dispatched an expedition under his command to the Macedonian and Thraceward region with the purpose, among others, of recovering Amphipolis. Brasidas, still on hand, commanded the defensive operations. When the two armies finally met outside the city's fortification walls, the Athenian attacking force was defeated, and Cleon (as well as the victorious Brasidas) was killed in action.

Traditional politics would continue as before after Cleon's death, but the meteoric rise and eventual career (however short) of the tanner's son marked a turning point in the history of the Athenian democracy. Not high birth or inheritance but acquired wealth, personal merit, and spectacular achievement made Cleon the successful leader that he indubitably became—however hostile his cultural, if not political, adversary and witness, Thucydides, might be. Ability and attainment had won out over the principle (to paraphrase a biblical aphorism) that "the virtues of the father are visited on the son." True, Cleon's style was unabashedly populist, but perhaps inevitably so, since, after all, he lacked the "good breeding" of a Pericles. The vulgar public speaking style so savaged by Thucydides probably came naturally to him and for all we know was in keeping with the expectations of the great mass of citizens. But luck as much as ability played a decisive part in Cleon's rise, for how else could a reader of Thucydides' narrative characterize the politician's career-making windfall success at Pylos? However gifted, Cleon was an amateur—an amateur military commander, an amateur speaker, an amateur politician. Things were to change later on.

SPARTANS, THEBANS, AND MACEDONIANS

Sparta: Lycurgus, Founding Father

"About the lawgiver Lycurgus, nothing in general can be said that is not contested, since accounts differ regarding his birth, his travels, his death, and above all of his work as lawmaker and statesman. And least of all do historians agree as to the times in which the man lived." With these uncharacteristically agnostic disavowals, the biographer Plutarch launches his *Life* of the Spartan Lycurgus. "Uncharacteristically" because Plutarch, compiler, popularizer, and belletristic essayist that he was, seldom hesitates to repeat existing traditions and accounts even centuries after the event and even when we think we know that from his vantage point he could not possibly vouch for the truth of what he gives his reader. And if Plutarch, who after all is a Greek writing under the Roman Empire (dates ca. A.D. 50–120) and therefore indisputably an "ancient," admits ignorance, what can *we* dare to say, especially given our inestimably more rigorous standards of historical accuracy?

Well, we can be pretty sure about some very basic propositions. Lycurgus is as good a candidate as any for inclusion among the pivotal figures marking the transition from Sparta the traditional Greek community to Sparta the centralized authoritarian military regime that we have discussed at intervals throughout this book. As we have seen, to judge from the literary and material evidence (especially the fragmentary remains of poetry and painted pottery), early archaic Sparta did not differ in any essential from most other city-states of the period. But, at some point, and in response to the need to maintain control over the enormous enslaved and subject populations (respectively, helots and *perioeci*) that had been the legacy of the city's unprecedented military successes in the Peloponnese, the Spartans brought about a violent reorientation of their ideals and goals—a reorientation that, as we saw, transformed every significant aspect of society and culture. Thus, the emergence in the classical period of the all-pervasive militarism, open marriages, communal parentage, institutionalized male homosexuality, the rise of citizen women to positions of dominance, and so on—all utterly in conflict with the observed custom and practice of contemporary Greek city-states, Athens in particular.

These developments, to judge from the dribs and drabs of reliable dated evidence that have reached us, transpired in stages over a lengthy time. Securely established terminal dates are, at the upper end, the eighth century B.C.E. (at least the seventh-century Spartan poet Tyrtaeus knew of the Great Rhetra) and, at the lower, the time of the Persian invasions (490, 480–479 B.C.E.) when, as recounted by Herodotus, the new "Lycurgan" order was firmly in place and functioning. Besides, the better-known early development of other Greek city-states, the obvious case being Athens, also points to a long process of change (whether gradual or episodic) and to the work of many hands. Why, then, at Sparta, do the ancient sources attribute all to the work of a single Founding Father? Three tendencies typical of ancient Greeks' thinking about their past seem to be at work:

1. Need for a "first finder": The "first finder" is a virtual folklore motif that permeates traditional ancient Greek thinking as evidenced in myths, poetry, and prescientific historiography. Essentially psychological in nature, the positing of a single personage to whom something in the past can be ascribed is typical of ancient Greek protohistory. Institutions, customs, ceremonies and rituals, indeed, all of society and culture could be (and were) traced to these quasi-historical, even legendary or mythical, Founding Fathers (as we are calling them).
2. The process of telescoping. When a lengthy process is reduced to a single point in time (whether attributed to a "first finder" or not), we historians use the metaphor of telescoping (from the collapsing of an old-fashioned handheld telescope, like the "glass" used by the pirates of our own legendary lore). Development, process, evolution, response to environmental forces, underlying causes—these are all concepts characteristic of modern historiography. A Thucydides might approach the standard of modern historiography, but his uncharacteristically elevated thought processes (as he himself would be the first to remind us!) have little to do with how most people were thinking about such matters in antiquity.
3. The process of retrojection. When a long process of development is telescoped, what usually also happens is that the final result of the process, now compressed to a single historical event, is retrojected to a much earlier time, even to the time when the process began—and when the entire process of development still lay in the future. So, in the present case, it is certainly conceivable that a person called Lycurgus initially set in motion a centuries-long transformation of Spartan society and culture. But it is the ancient Greek mind that marks that person out as "first finder," telescopes the transformation to a single point in time, and then retrojects the whole to an unhistorically early setting.

Sparta: Pausanias, the General

When we examined in detail the distinctive social institutions of the Spartans, we suggested the dominating militarism of the Spartan state as an explanation for these isolated and unique departures from the institutions shared by all other Greeks. With the accomplishment of this reorientation of society, militarism dictated that the life of every man, woman, and child, from cradle to grave, be devoted to nurturing the army—the army that was to emerge as Greece's mightiest. Although our discussion was amply illustrated by quotations from ancient writers (especially the Roman-era popularizer Plutarch), no attempt was to made to examine any particular historical Spartans in any detail and therefore to see how the society's militaristic goals were absorbed and expressed in the life stories of real flesh-and-blood people. It is now time that we do so, beginning with the famous—or rather infamous—Pausanias.

Pausanias, son of King Cleombrotus, was the nephew of the martyr of Thermopylae, King Leonidas, the commander at the famous last stand of the 300 Spartiatai. The following year, 479 B.C.E., Pausanias himself played a decisive role in the Persian Wars as commander of the victorious Greek land force at Plataea. But, with an immodesty bordering on hubris, he claimed full personal credit for the great allied triumph. Not only was this excess chastened by the Spartan home government; it was also the target of an admonition to Pausanias by the contemporary Greek epigrammatist Simonides to remember that he was human.[2] To forget one's humanity and the limitations that it imposes is at the heart of the overweening ambition that is hubris.

Arrogance notwithstanding, the next year, 478, found Pausanias again in command of an allied force, this time the fleet operations against Byzantium (now Istanbul, in modern Turkey). After capturing the city, the Spartan king was accused of entering into private dealings with the Persians. Recalled to Sparta, tried, and acquitted, he returned to Byzantium, only to be expelled by the Athenians. Relocating to the nearby Troad region, he was again suspected of dealing with the enemy, recalled to Sparta, and acquitted again. Since the charge of Medism would not stick, opponents at Sparta resorted to the even more serious charge (more serious, at least, to a Spartan) that Pausanias had played a role in the recent uprising of the state-slave helots. Listen to Thucydides' telling of the story, and of its fateful outcome:

Now that Pausanias had turned aggressive, the Greeks were irritated, especially the Ionians and all who had recently been liberated from the Great King. So, approaching the Athenians they asked them in accordance with the alliance to become their leaders and not to give way to Pausanias, should he resort to force in any way. The Athenians accepted the proposals and applied their attention to not enduring any more and to generally arranging things in a way that appeared best to themselves.

Meanwhile, the Lacedaemonians recalled Pausanias in order to question him regarding reports they were getting. Much injustice was been lodged against him by the Greeks when they came to Sparta, and it seemed more an imitation of tyranny than a general's command.... Upon his arrival at Lacedaemon, he was examined regarding any unjust acts against individuals, while on the most serious charges he was absolved of any wrongdoing, for he had been accused not least of collaborating with the Persians—and it seemed to be a particularly straightforward case.... The Lacedaemonians no longer sent Pausanias out as a commander.... They did not dispatch any other commanders later, fearing lest upon their absence from home they would commit acts of misconduct—the very thing that they had seen in Pausanias. They wanted to be through with the war with the Persians and thought that the Athenians were capable of leading the alliance and that they were friendly to themselves at that present time.[3]

With the receipt of the letter [from King Xerxes], Pausanias, despite being already in the high estimation of the Greeks because of his command at Plataea, at that point became even more full of himself and no longer was able to conduct his life in the accustomed manner. Whenever he ventured out of Byzantium he wore Persian clothing and when journeying through Thrace Median and Egyptian spearmen would accompany him. He had his table set in Persian style. He was not able to contain his intentions but by such small actions he forecast what grander things he had in mind to do in the future. He made himself difficult of access and maintained an attitude towards everybody that was so intractable that no one was able to approach. Not the least for this reason the alliance went over to the Athenians.[4]

The first time the Lacedaemonians learned of things of this kind, they recalled him. And when, the second time, he sailed off in the ship of Hermione without orders from them, he appeared to be doing the same sort of thing, . . . at this point they held back no longer but the ephors dispatched a herald with a skatalē-message to the effect that he should not fall behind the returning herald and that, if he did, the Spartiates would declare war against him. And so he, wishing to fall under suspicion as little as possible, returned to Sparta for the second time. At first he was thrown into the brig by the ephors (and, yes, it is permitted to the ephors to do this to the king!), but later he negotiated his release and presented himself for trial to any parties wishing to examine the particulars of his case.[5]

The Spartans . . . had no clear evidence. . . . But he gave rise to many suspicions by his irrationality and imitation of barbarian ways that he did not wish to be on equal terms with the present order of things. And so they scrutinized the rest of his record to see if he had conducted himself in any way outside the bounds of established custom, and especially the incident when he thought fit to have inscribed upon the tripod at Delphi that the Greeks had once dedicated as first fruits from the Persians:

> Commander of the Greeks when he destroyed the army of the Medes, Pausanias has dedicated this memorial to Phoebus Apollo.

Now the Spartans at that time immediately erased this elegiac couplet from the tripod and inscribed name-by-name the cities that had joined together to defeat the barbarian and set up the dedication. . . .

The Lacedaemonians also learned that he was up to something with the helots. And so he was. He was promising them freedom and citizenship if they would all join him in rebellion and in accomplishing all his plans. . . . The story goes that [his conviction and execution] did not happen until Pausanias' lover at the time and most trusted slave turned informer . . . [and when the informer's report was confirmed by trickery in the presence of the ephors] . . . Pausanias, about to be arrested on the street, escaped to safety by running to the temple of the Goddess of the Brass House. . . . The ephors had for the moment fallen behind in their pursuit, but they afterwards ripped the roof off the building and, keeping watch on him while he was inside, removed the doors, walled him in, set up camp before the place, and besieged him out by starvation. When they observed that he was about to die in that condition in the chamber, they removed him from the shrine while he was still breathing. Once so removed, he died immediately. . . . The god at Delphi later commanded the Lacedaemonians to move his tomb to where he had died (and he now lies in the fore-precinct, as stelai declare by their inscriptions) and, since their act had brought a curse upon them, to render up two bodies in place of one to the

Goddess of the Brass House. So they sculpted two bronze statues and dedicated them in the place of Pausanias.[6]

Sparta: Brasidas, the General

Brasidas, put simply, was a war hero, and, given all that we have learned about Sparta, isn't that just what we should expect? Sparta after Lycurgus produced no historians, no poets, no painters, no philosophers—only war heroes. And isn't that precisely what the entire military system that was Spartan society and culture was designed to produce? Yes, but not entirely. Brasidas was indeed a war hero, but if Thucydides' narration of his activity during the Peloponnesian War is to be our guide (and no other independent source of information has survived with which to compare the historian's account), his successes were accomplished *in spite of* the patterns typical of the Spartan military establishment.

The record of achievement is breathtaking. Although Brasidas's authority—whether as ephor, trierarch, or adviser—on campaign certainly originated in appointments from the home government, once in the field he appears to have acted largely as a free agent. Possibly, as with Roman generals on distant campaigns, independence in decision making was a logistical necessity, given the primitive condition of ancient communications and travel. But it is also possible that it was precisely a certain personal flair that set Brasidas apart from the predictable grind of Spartan procedure (and that incidentally made him attractive material for enlivening and adding interest to an otherwise tedious military narrative). Be that as it may, concerning his record of activity there is little room for doubt. Assignments ranged from the defense of Methone to trierarch at Pylos to commander of a force of helots and mercenaries in northern Greece deployed to harry Athenian interests in the region. While in the north, Brasidas executed a midwinter raid on a snowy night against the Athenian stronghold at Amphipolis (at the mouth of the Strymon, on the boundary between Macedonia and Thrace) and managed to capture the town right out from under the nose of the Athenian commander of the squadron defending the position. The year was 424, and that commander (as previously noted) was none other than Thucydides the historian! Two years later, the Athenians dispatched a recovery expedition under the general Cleon (the "New Rich" tanner discussed in the previous chapter), but the undertaking ended in failure, with Cleon falling in combat and Brasidas, too, suffering mortal wounds.

True, Thucydides did not like Cleon, and it is possible that, in an effort to subtly denigrate the man and to poison the memory of his achievements, the historian, already intrigued by Brasidas' so un-Spartan inclination toward independence, further enhanced his Good Guy image as a foil to Cleon's Bad Guy. Absent a competing contemporary account, we shall never know.

Nonetheless, we have in Pausanias and Brasidas two contrasting examples of how individuals fit, or do not fit, into a societal structure—even one inculcated by a cradle-to-grave indoctrination, enforced by a hard-lining authoritarian establishment that permits virtually no self-expression. In both men we find a determined independence, but an independence so different in nature! Pausanias's emerges as a failure of character, a personal ambition out of control. Brasidas's is the equally familiar (to us) example of the person who cuts red tape in order to work around a cumbersome authority structure that cannot respond in timely way to the demands of the moment. So, two very different ways of rebelling against authority. May we then find in these two politicians alternately "bad" and "good," failing and successful individual responses to an intrinsically unworkable and inevitably dysfunctional Spartan "discipline" and militaristic social order?

Sparta: Kings Agis IV and Cleomenes III

When we first introduced Sparta in chapter 4 under the heading "The Mystery of Sparta," we placed great emphasis upon the absence of contemporary evidence, particularly evidence emanating from Sparta itself, that might shed light upon the classical city-state. Thucydides, an Athenian writing during (and shortly after) the Peloponnesian War, 431–404 B.C.E., is an exception, as the preceding paraphrases and quotations concerning Pausanias and Brasidas illustrate. But these vignettes show us eminent military-political leaders in distant theaters far from home—that is, untypical Spartans in untypical settings—and so leave truly shrouded in mystery the Sparta we really want to know and understand better: the unfortified cluster of villages, the bizarre social institutions, and, above all, the ordinary people—female as well as male, slave as well as citizen—who somehow brought this unprepossessing town to military domination and a fleeting leadership of much of ancient Greece.

Nor was the mystique of Sparta simply a problem for a modern age far removed from its subject. Even in antiquity, indeed, among the very classical Athenians contemporary with the Lycurgan city at the zenith of its power, little was (or could be) known. Thucydides seems to have some real information, but his unusual circumstances—a propertied aristocrat with inherited overseas connections, an elected general who had seen military action against the Peloponnesian adversary, and an exile barred from the city of his citizenship and necessarily thrust into association with non-Athenians—may go far toward explaining the anomaly of his access to what was otherwise hidden from view. No wonder, then, that in succeeding centuries the mystique should have continued to play a central, even determining role in the later development of the ancient city. Take, as the principal examples, the next two political biographies, again penned by Plutarch, of the Spartan kings Agis IV and Cleomenes III.

Agis IV

During his short life in the mid-third century (that is, about a century and a half after Sparta's victory in the Peloponnesian War), Agis became in his late teens one of the two kings in the midst of a crisis typical of the prerevolutionary conditions throughout antiquity: grossly unequal distribution of wealth, rampant indebtedness, and (peculiar to Sparta and its unwavering exclusivity) an alarming decline in the number of Spartiate citizens. It is no exaggeration to say that the very survival of Sparta was hanging in the balance. Overcoming opposition by driving out the other king, Leonidas, and deposing the board of ephors, Agis undertook to cure Sparta's ills by reinstituting the ancestral Lycurgan order. The reforms were passed into law, but, before they could be implemented, a countercoup resulted in Agis's execution. The point here is that it was a vision of a return to the city's glory days that had inspired this idealistic, impetuous, and naïve boy—in the event, a boy who proved no match for his more seasoned rivals. Although Agis lived but a short life, his story appealed to the contemporary historian Phylarchus, who wrote it up in sensational romantic style, to survive in the retelling by Plutarch under the Roman Empire.

Cleomenes III

The son of the King Leonidas deposed by Agis but married to Agiatis, widow of Agis, Cleomenes resumed Agis's program of reactionary social reform. Seizing power in the 220s and instituting a Lycurgan-style regime, Cleomenes confronted the same crisis conditions that had brought Agis to power by redistributing the land, canceling debts, and recruiting new citizens from the *perioeci* and foreigners. Additional reforms, some actually true to the Lycurgan Discipline, others not, purported to restore to their pristine condition the all-male barracks and messes, the educational career, and the land army, as well as the more strictly constitutional monarchy (arguably now, however, no longer a functional diarchy), the Gerousia (Senate), and the board of ephors. But the freeing of helots and their recruitment as citizens into the army did not succeed in restoring Spartan military supremacy, and Cleomenes was eventually forced into exile, never to return. No less than his predecessor, Cleomenes was a fit subject for Phylarchus, again to be reworked in characteristic style by Plutarch.

Speaking of Plutarch, it was in Roman times (during which Plutarch lived, though he was a Greek permanently residing in Greece) that Sparta was to see still another, and more determined, reinvention of the mystique (as I continue to refer to the city's lost but hardly forgotten legendary, even mythical, glorious past). Plutarch himself provides an apt parallel for the Spartan case, for, serving as priest at Delphi during the final decades of his life (he died ca. A.D. 120), the antiquarian played a key role in the restoration of the sanctuary under the Roman emperors Trajan and Hadrian. Ever intrigued with things Greek and perhaps desiring a vicarious participation in (and identification with) the greatness that was classical Greece, the Romans were fascinated with the now politically inert historical curiosity and enthusiastically promoted its restoration. But, in contrast with the ambitions of the Spartan Hellenistic kings Agis IV and Cleomenes III, the Roman purpose was not even incidentally directed toward the reemergence of Spartan military and political greatness. Rather, the Romans, like so many of us in modern times, had come under the spell of the mystique, and, being the consummate Mediterranean conquerors themselves, their fascination can only have been mixed with an element of admiration for Sparta's military achievement. Sparta, reasoned the emperors, deserved restoration. But, as they themselves probably sensed, what they restored was the *image* produced out of the familiar combination of curiosity and an almost total lack of information. So, in the end, the Roman antiquarian project produced less the ancient reality (which was beyond recovery in any event) than the physical re-creation of a fantasy. Tourism, as with the historical theme parks of the modern world, inevitably followed, and the reduction of the ancient Greece of this book to pure image was arguably brought to its full fruition, at least in physical (rather than in intellectual) terms.

THEBES

Pelopidas and Epaminondas

Thebes, from the Bronze Age on, was the principal settlement of ancient Boeotia, in central Greece. In classical times, Thebes was an ally of Sparta, but, upon the end of the Peloponnesian War, in 404 B.C.E., it defected from the Peloponnesian alliance. The two cities remained at loggerheads, with Thebes eventually defeating Sparta's forces in the battle of Leuctra, in 371. From that year until 338, when Philip II of Macedon overcame the Theban forces at Chaeroneia, the Boeotian city enjoyed its own rather short-lived hegemony. Thus, the hegemons of the fourth century each ruled for approximately a single generation: Sparta, Thebes, then Macedon (under Philip and, later, under his son, Alexander).

The key political figures of the Theban hegemony were Pelopidas and Epaminondas, whose careers as leaders and generals were roughly contemporary. Specifically, those careers became critically intertwined at the battle of Leuctra, where Pelopidas played a key role in the execution of Epaminondas' strategic designs against the Spartans. Historians of combat have had much to say on this and other Theban military matters, but our present concern is less with names, places, and dates than with the issues of character. Thanks to the survival of Plutarch's *Life* of Pelopidas, we have the biographer's sustained comparison of the two Theban contemporaries:

Pelopidas, son of Hippoclus, was of distinguished family background in Thebes, as was Epaminondas, and having been raised in great wealth and having inherited while still young a splendid estate, he resolved to assist those of the needy who were deserving, in order that he be seen as truly the master of material things and not their slave. For among the masses, Aristotle says, some because of penny-pinching get no use out of their money, while others misuse it because of splurging, and so they live their lives as slaves, the former to financial scrimping, the latter to pleasure-seeking. Now, most of the Thebans, owing a debt of gratitude to Pelopidas, took advantage of his liberality and generosity towards them. Most, accordingly, thankfully profited by the kindness and liberality of Pelopidas towards them. But Epaminondas alone of his friends he could not persuade to share in his wealth. Rather Pelopidas shared in the poverty of Epaminondas, reveling in the simplicity of his clothing, in the meagerness of his table, and in his fearlessness towards hardships and guilelessness on campaign. Like the character Capaneus in Euripides, "a great livelihood was his, but in no way was he haughty on account of wealth," since he thought it shameful to be perceived to be expending more on his own person than on the Theban who owned the least property.

Now Epaminondas, whose poverty was customary and ancestral, made it still more comfortable and bearable by philosophy, and by choosing a life of singleness from the outset. To Pelopidas, by contrast, came a splendid marriage, and children were born as well, but for all that by neglecting his business matters and devoting his whole time to the state, he diminished his substance. And when his friends offered advice, telling him that he was making little of a necessary matter, namely to possess money, he said, "Yes, by Zeus, necessary for Nicodemus here," pointing to some guy who was lame and blind.

The two men were equally suited by nature for the attainment of every excellence, except that Pelopidas delighted more in physical exercise, Epaminondas more in intellectual learning. So the one in his leisure time cultivated interests in athletics and hunting, the other in lectures and philosophizing. While much of worth speaks to the reputation of both men, discerning observers regard nothing to be so great as the good will and friendship that endured uncontested from the beginning through such momentous struggles, military campaigns, and civil administrations. For if you glance at the public careers of Themistocles and Aristides, or of Cimon and Pericles, or of Nicias and Alcibiades, noting how full they were of conflicts, envyings, and jealousies towards each other, and then consider the honor and graciousness that Pelopidas showed Epaminondas, you will rightly and justly label these men co-governors and co-commanders rather than those who continued striving to prevail over one another instead of the enemy.

The true explanation was a striving for excellence on account of which, by not trying to obtain fame or wealth from their efforts (an attitude naturally infested with a harsh and combative enviousness), each of the men, driven from the start by a passion to see the city of Thebes achieve on his watch the highest distinction, regarded each other's successes as his own in the service of this higher end.[7]

What can we make of these centuries-after-the-event characterizations? Do they preserve anything of historical value for the student of ancient Greek politics? Patronage certainly played an important role, for Epaminondas' refusal to take gifts from his wealthy fellow Theban can only be interpreted as a refusal to let the Pelopidas get the upper hand by putting him, the recipient of favor, under obligation to this benefactor. Also in evidence are contrasting approaches to establishing and displaying elite social status in one's personal pursuits. Pelopidas, the man of means, engages in the expensive, time-consuming (and hence, for ordinary people, wasteful) sport of hunting for pleasure. But Epaminondas, lacking inherited wealth, resorts to the poor man's version of cultivated upper-class leisure pursuits by taking refuge in learning and books—in the scholar Plutarch's estimation at least, a mark of good breeding and social superiority. And, while the wealthy Pelopidas made a good marriage, the impecunious Epaminondas remained single. Why we don't know, but lack of financial means might have made him less attractive than his fellow Theban to the families of eligible brides.

For Plutarch, underlying these (for the ancient Greek, all-important) variations was a striving for "excellence" (here translating the Greek *aretē*). For Plutarch, the virtue of excellence seems to be independent of inheritance—of the rule of descent, which in the classical world centuries earlier made or broke a man or woman from cradle to grave. For the classical Greek, but not for Plutarch, one pretty much was what one's parents were, despite all one's personal attainments, strivings, accomplishments—or virtues such as "excellence." And it is for this very reason that we must call into question the historicity of Plutarch's portraits. After all, the essayist did fancy himself a philosopher and indeed quotes Aristotle on the uses of wealth. Granted, Aristotle himself was a rough contemporary of the two Thebans, but it is doubtful whether they, any more than the philosopher's pupil Alexander the Great, ever put into practice the doctrines of this or any other philosopher.

Further compromising the characterizations is the very notion of comparison itself. The pairs that make up the *Parallel Lives* were set up precisely for the sake of comparison, and here, in the final paragraph of our quotation, we can see how Plutarch liked to engage in the polarization of contrasting backgrounds, personalities, and styles. That is to say, the very act of comparing the two personalities may well have resulted in an ahistorical schematization and hence distorted the qualities that made Pelopidas and Epaminondas tick—and that played decisive roles in their political careers and achievements.

MACEDONIA (AND EGYPT)

King Philip of Macedon, Queen Olympias, and Their Son, Alexander the Great

Throughout this book, we have emphasized the personal, as opposed to the ideological, dimensions of political life in ancient Greece. No more startling example could be found than the family—father, mother, and son—whose acts combined to dramatically redirect and irreversibly shape the future course not only of Greece but, indeed, of the whole of ancient Greek civilization.

The seat—and the initial scene of political activity—of the royal family was Macedonia, a region situated to the north and east of Greece proper, extending from its lengthy Aegean coastline into the mountainous interior of the Balkan Peninsula. Strategic position (between coast and interior, between Greece to the west and Asia to the east), tall timber, and precious mineral resources bestowed importance, and earned envy, from an early date. Relations with Greece and Greeks were complicated by the question of the ethnic identity of the Macedonians, a topic of continuing discussion illustrated, for example, by the remaining traces of the Macedonian language. Although seemingly Indo-European, Macedonian is not unambiguously a dialect of the same tongue spoken by Athenians, Spartans, or even the neighboring Thessalians.

Philip II (382–336 B.C.E.), it is no exaggeration to say, literally founded—or, more precise, rescued, reorganized, and redirected—the kingdom of Macedonia. Threatened by the invasions and intrigues of hostile neighbors, Philip, once he had ascended the throne, by overt diplomacy or covert shenanigans secured the kingdom's independence. The military was strengthened by the introduction of new weaponry and of novel infantry tactics (loosely paralleling the advent of hoplite panoply and accompanying battlefield maneuvers in Greece centuries before). New territories were acquired by armed force, with Athens, compelled to surrender Amphipolis, Potaedaea, and Methone, being notable among the victims of Philip's expansionist policies. And, giving hints of a future cosmopolitan vision, the king recruited into a restructured Macedonian nobility prominent influential politicians from throughout Greece—again loosely paralleling, if a parallel is needed, the all-star crew that the mythical Jason, based in nearby Thessaly, to the west, had recruited for his ship Argo before embarking upon his quest to seize the Golden Fleece.

"International" assemblages, whether the crew of Jason's Argo or King Philip II's new "Macedonian" aristocracy, may be characterized as dynastic (from Greek *dunamai,* "be able," "be powerful," hence "dynast"). When the relationship is an asymmetrical one between superior and inferior parties, it may be formalized as a species of patronage, a quasi-institution that has been before us from the beginning. When the relationship is between equals and those equals are significant power-holders, "dynast" and "dynastic" are appropriate terms. Regardless of which model applies in particular cases, there can be little doubt but that Philip adhered to the patterns already familiar in the politics of earlier Greece (and that would, not far into the future, reemerge quite visibly under the Romans). Nor did Philip's dynastic maneuverings end with the recruitment of rising stars from Crete or Mytilene on Lesbos and their installation at Macedonian Amphipolis.

Consider, for example, his relationship with Olympias. She was the daughter of King Neoptolemus of the Molossi, whose tribal state (a form of polity less developed than the classical city-state or federation of city-states) was situated in the mountainous interior of Epirus, to the west. Marrying Philip in the early 350s, Olympias eventually bore him two children, a son, Alexander (later to become "the Great"), and a daughter, Cleopatra (namesake of the Queen of Egypt, to be discussed shortly). When Philip entered into an affair with another Cleopatra (a common female name ancestral among Macedonians), the aggrieved Olympias retired to her native Molossia. At the personal level, such retirement resembles (and, in fact, was the same as) that of the modern wife who, when her husband dallies, returns to her mother's, but, in the terms of international politics, the act also resembled the recall of an ambassador or the breaking off of diplomatic relations. Equally serious, their son, Alexander, was dispatched to exile in Illyria. Eventually, a reconciliation was brought about, although further disruptions and reconciliations were to follow. But our concern here is less with the blow-by-blow details than with the nature of the marital bond and its implications for and impact upon the course of Macedonian political ambitions. Consider, then, from Plutarch's *Life of Alexander*, a portrayal of the Queen in currency centuries later in Roman times:

A serpent was once observed stretched out alongside the body of Olympias as she was sleeping, and this most of all, they say, dulled Philip's ardor and affections for her. As a result, he no longer came often to sleep by her side, either because he feared some spells and charms of the woman against himself or recoiling from contact with her in the belief that she was in cahoots with a superior being. But there is another story about these matters: All the women of this region were from high antiquity addicted to Orphic rites and the orgiastic rituals of Dionysus. . . . Olympias, who pursued these practices and divine inspirations more enthusiastically than other women, and performed them in more barbaric fashion, would provide the revelers with large tame snakes. The snakes would often crawl out from the ivy and the mystic winnowing baskets and wind themselves around the wands and garlands of the women, thus startling the men.[8]

Just another purple patch of rhetorical prose, so typical of these later popularizing writers? Perhaps so, but rhetorical, sensational writing need not imply falsehood. The real question is this: If the behavior described represents anything like the truth (and many a reader, I suspect, can think of parallels among contemporary media celebrities), what were its political dimensions, if any? As pure public relations material, such a story, once in circulation, would certainly have had the effect of magnifying the stature and powers of the Queen and of the monarchy in general. Leaders must be different, must be held in awe, must be feared, and the more divinely godlike (or in her case, demonic) the public image, the better. So understood, Olympias counts as a political figure of the first importance. But there is also the more mundane matter that she was the mother of Alexander, soon to be the most divinely godlike and visionary conqueror the ancient world had seen. Granted, a queen does not necessarily breastfeed, change diapers, and teach the ABCs, but the simple fact of her motherhood can only have influenced enormously, for good or ill, the development of the child, female or male. And this "power behind the throne" had hardly begun to work her influence upon Macedonian politics. But first, what happened to Philip?

As it happened, the couple's (and Macedonia's) dynastic future took an abrupt (and initially negative) turn when the king was assassinated in the year 338 B.C.E. The circumstances of the killing—both the motivation and the act itself—are bizarre in their complexity, and entirely personal. Earlier, the assassin, one Pausanias, had slandered Philip because he had chosen another male, Attalus, rather than Pausanias, as his lover. To retaliate, Attalus's servants had raped Pausanias. When the rape was reported to the king and he chose to ignore it, Pausanias, already rejected and now raped with impunity, decided to take action. By this time, Philip had attempted to buy off the disgruntled Pausanias by appointing him to the highly esteemed post of royal bodyguard, but it was precisely this appointment that played into the assassin's hands. On the occasion of the wedding of the king's daughter, while the wedding party was processing into the theater at Aegae, the bodyguard

Pausanias sprang from his position and stabbed Philip to death before the stunned onlookers.

The outcome of the murder was the ascent of Alexander to the throne, and, more crucial, as we know in retrospect, to the command of the Macedonian expeditionary force against Persia. We can always play the "what if?" game, although we'll never know for sure whether the assassination actually changed the course of ancient (and later) history. But it is the purely personal, and accidental and unpredictable, nature of the event that needs to be emphasized. For an ancient Greek parallel, one could instance the murder of the tyrant's son Hipparchus at Athens nearly two centuries before. That act arose from uncannily similar sexual origins and yet, for all its personal motivation, resulted in setting in motion a chain of events that eventually issued in the fall of the tyranny and the institution of the democracy. Purely inborn human impulses, along with politics and ideology, must be included among the factors that made for the unfolding of epochal historical events in ancient Greece.

While Alexander was on campaign, the widowed queen virtually ran the Macedonian empire. "Virtually" because a nominal viceroy (literally, "in place of the king"), Antipater, had been appointed by Alexander. But, as history teaches us, formally appointed position and actual controlling influence, especially when a wife and mother and her son, as in this case, are at issue, do not always coincide. Yes, Olympias was never a formally appointed officer of the state; indeed, she did not even attain the truly powerful position of a dowager Queen (as did, in modern times, Victoria of England). Nonetheless, her ability to influence the course of events, were the full facts (including those surrounding the assassination of Philip!) known to us, may have been decisive.

Cleopatra VII, Queen of Egypt

Egypt, once conquered by Alexander the Great, was ruled by Macedonians continuously from Alexander's death, in 323 B.C.E., until the defeat of Queen Cleopatra VII (the subject of the present discussion) and her lover the Roman dynast Marc Antony by Octavian in the battle of Actium in 31 B.C.E. From 304 B.C.E., the monarch was a descendant of Alexander's general, Ptolemy son of Lagus, and all the kings bore the name (or title) Ptolemy. Ethnically Macedonian Greek-style monarchs, the rulers were also Egyptian pharaohs, and the combination of ethnicities was reflected in the administration, culture, and language distribution of the Ptolemaic regime. Foreign "Greek" kings and queens, a museum and library designed along classical lines at the capital in Alexandria, and the use of Greek in administration exemplify the veneer of Hellenism imposed upon the land and people of the Pharaohs. The first Cleopatra, wife of Ptolemy V Epiphanes, early in the second century B.C.E., stood at the head of a long line of namesakes culminating in the seventh, daughter of Ptolemy XII Auletes. Upon Auletes' death, our Cleopatra ruled as queen jointly with her younger brothers, Ptolemy XIII and Ptolemy XIV, later with Ptolemy XV Caesar—supposedly her son by the Roman dynast Gaius Julius Caesar. With Marc Antony, who succeeded Caesar as her lover, Cleopatra VII bore twins, Antony and Cleopatra, and a second son, Ptolemy Philadelphus. When, finally, "Antony and Cleopatra" were driven to flight from Actium in Greece and repaired with their navy to Egypt, the two lovers chose suicide over the humiliation of surrender. Thereby, with the queen's demise, Macedonian rule came to an end, and Egypt was annexed as a province by the Romans.

What, to cut to the chase, is the place of Cleopatra in a book about politics and society in ancient Greece? As a person of Macedonian descent and cultural identity, she manifestly belongs in any book that also includes Philip II and Alexander the Great. But what are we to make of her official position as monarch, of her romantic (but not necessarily only or merely romantic) liaisons with the Roman political leaders Julius Caesar and Marc Antony, and of her sustained (indeed, lifelong) efforts on behalf of the interests of the kingdom of Egypt? If the classical Greece of Athens and Sparta is to be our standard, no woman could normally aspire successfully to such a position of title, leadership, or influence. So, an initial question that has to be answered is this: How was a Cleopatra possible? If we can answer this question, then we may also be able to understand how a Cleopatra did *not* exist, indeed *could not* have existed, in the most successful political (and societal and cultural) regime of the ancient Greek world, classical Athens.

Ancient Mediterranean antecedents may make Cleopatra's case less anomalous than it appears when set against a classical Athenian background. For one example, Mycenaean Bronze Age Greece, peopled by the same Hellenic stock whose descendants were to become classical Athenians, was certainly ruled by monarchs, and the queens of King Agamemnon at Mycenae, of King Menelaus at Sparta, and even of King Aegeus at Athens—namely Clytemnestra, Helen, and (admittedly a foreign woman) Medea—left their marks in myth as women of enterprise, determination, and impact. For another, postclassical Hellenistic Greece witnessed the emergence of a powerful female presence in the royal courts, with the Macedonian Olympias, just discussed, representing only the example most relevant to Cleopatra's case. For still another, the upper-class matrons of Rome had already, by the time of Caesar and Antony, because of complex local and institutional preconditions that cannot be examined here, come to wield a major influence in matters public and political, as well as private and domestic. Within this broader setting, it is the virtually invisible and largely inconsequential status of free citizen females in the Golden Age of Athens that may more legitimately be regarded as anomalous. Why, then all the fuss at Rome? Why the monstrous, wicked woman of the contemporary Roman poets?

The fundamental reason is political, and that reason speaks to the essentially political nature of Cleopatra's dealings with the Romans, notwithstanding their erotic and romantic context. Cleopatra's child by Caesar, Caesarion, could lay claim to leadership of the Roman state should a certain course of events transpire (e.g., the ascendant Roman dynast be defeated; the capital be removed from Rome to Alexandria; the son of Julius Caesar, dictator at Rome until his assassination, in 44 B.C.E., be placed on the throne). No one, on the eve of the battle of Actium, in 31 B.C.E., could be certain that things would work out differently should the winds of chance blow against Roman interests. Fears, rumors, gossip concerning the foreign woman, reflecting by now well-founded apprehensions regarding her ability to control the emotions and actions of the love-smitten Antony, filled the air and eventually were recalled in the literary persons of Rome's destined founder, Aeneas, and his foreign Carthaginian lover, Dido, in Virgil's state-sponsored foundation epic, the *Aeneid*. And, if this were not enough, Cleopatra represented to the Roman mind monarchy, the rule by king (in Latin, *rex*), an idea that had been anathema since the overthrow of the last of Rome's kings, the hated Tarquin the Proud. And a half-millennium later, the specter of monarchy had once again been reawakened by the personal ascendancy of the dictator Julius Caesar (whose pretensions to monarchy, it seems, were the ultimate cause of his assassination). That is, it was precisely the political dimension of Cleopatra's actions that posed a threat to the Roman establishment and even to the ordinary Roman on the street. The alternately admiring and demonizing images of the women eventually found their way into such later ancient writings as Plutarch's *Life of Antony*. Take, for example:

Although she received many letters from Antony and his friends summoning her, she so despised and ridiculed the man as to sail up the river Cydnus in a barge with a gilded stern, with purple sails unfurled, pulled by silver oars keeping time to the oboe accompanied by pipes and lyres. She herself lay under a gold-embroidered umbrella, adorned like Aphrodite in a painting, and slaves costumed as Cupids in a painting stationed to either side were working their fans. In like manner the prettiest of her attendants, dressed as Nereids and Graces, were at the rudders and the ropes. Wondrous aromas from burning incense offerings overwhelmed the river's banks. Some people followed along from the start on both sides of the river, while others came down from the city to behold the spectacle. When at last the entire crowd in the marketplace had dispersed, Antony was left sitting on the tribunal by himself. And the story made the rounds that Aphrodite was leading a band of revelers to Dionysus for the good of Asia.

... [P]erceiving the soldier and blue collar in Antony's jokes, Cleopatra now used the same towards him in a relaxed and self-assured manner. For, as they say, her beauty in itself was not so striking, nor of the sort to stun people when they saw her. But getting to know her inescapably kindled a fire, and her looks in combination with her persuasiveness in speech and with the mood that somehow enveloped her company stimulated a reaction in people. Delight attended the sound of her voice as she spoke. And her tongue, like an instrument with many strings, she deftly turned to whatever language she wished and so dealt with only a very few foreigners through an interpreter, but to most she gave her replies on her own, whether they were Ethiopians, Troglodytes, Hebrews, Arabs, Syrians, Medes, or Parthians. ...

At all events, she took such hold over Antony, that while his wife Fulvia was waging war in Rome against Caesar (Octavian) in service of his interests, and a Parthian army was being mobilized in Mesopotamia..., Antony was whisked away by Cleopatra to

Alexandria, and amused himself there with the pastimes and games of a boy on vacation, and spent and frittered away that ... most precious of commodities, as Antiphon put it, time.[9]

In the light of these brief selections from Plutarch, it is not surprising that the author of the article on Cleopatra VII in the most recent edition of the *Oxford Classical Dictionary* writes: "The legend of Cleopatra has proved even more powerful than her historical record." As an instance, the article goes on to observe that in later antiquity Cleopatra was named as the author of treatises on hairdressing and cosmetics. Obviously, she was not the actual author of such writings but rather, in conformity with the tendency in antiquity to ascribe writings of unknown or obscure authorship to Big Names (famous examples are Aeschylus, Plato, and Hippocrates), the treatises could plausibly be passed off to the unsuspecting as the writings of a woman famed for her beauty. That is to say, what counted in most people's minds were not the facts but the reputation, the popular conception, the image. And, in Cleopatra's case, if Plutarch can be believed, we can observe the queen's own image-producing efforts in action: My translations "Aphrodite in a painting," "Cupids in a painting" render, respectively, the Greek *graphikōs* and *tois graphikois*, an adverb and a plural noun that refer literally to painters and their activity. The Queen had become the creator of her own legend in the image of contemporary depictions of the goddess of love.

Our study of politics and society, among its other concerns, has maintained that image operates as a force in history alongside, and even overriding and dominating, the facts about the particular person, event, or idea. Plutarch has given us the stuff of Cleopatra's public image, and whether his account is ultimately true to the facts or not is beside the point. What counts in the final analysis is what people at Rome believed, since in the end it was beliefs that brought about Cleopatra's destruction and the incorporation of Egypt into the Roman Empire. So, let Cleopatra stand as our final political biography and as a fitting illustration of the personal, celebrity-driven, and essentially imaginary forces that seemed to have played so crucial a role in shaping the politics of ancient Greece in their societal context.

Appendix: Texts, Visuals, and Web Sites

All books such as this one are based, directly or indirectly, upon source materials. Throughout, the reader's attention has been drawn to the ancient Greek sources from which the discussions ultimately derive, and the Further Readings relate specifically to the topics under review in the specified chapter. Here my purpose is to make a broader sweep over the whole of Greek (and, where relevant, Roman) antiquity and to identify the accessible source materials that will help my readers in their own investigations into the subjects and issues addressed by this book.

HISTORIES OF GREECE

Standard in English is the second edition of the *Cambridge Ancient History*, 14 vols., Cambridge 1970–2000, with vols. 1 and 2 in their third edition. J. B. Bury and R. Meiggs's *A History of Greece to the Death of Alexander the Great*, 4th ed. (New York: St. Martin's Press, 1975) and N.G.L. Hammond's *A History of Greece to 322 B.C.*, 3rd ed. (Oxford: Oxford University Press, 1986), though still useful, lack attention to the social and cultural themes that have driven the study of ancient history in recent decades. Nicholas F. Jones's *Ancient Greece: State and Society* (Upper Saddle, N.J.: Prentice-Hall, 1997) concentrates on societal questions. Sarah Pomeroy, Stanley Burstein, Walter Donlan, and Jennifer Roberts are the joint authors of *Ancient Greece: A Political, Social, and Cultural History* (New York and Oxford: Oxford University Press, 1999). Perhaps the best single book in English on the theme of the present book is W. Robert Connor's *The New Politicians of Fifth-Century Athens* (Princeton, N.J.: Princeton University Press, 1971). Wider in range is Raphael Sealey's *A History of the Greek City States ca. 700–338 B.C.* (Berkeley and Los Angeles: University of California Press, 1976). A good companion to the earlier centuries of these narratives is G. R. Stanton's *Athenian Politics c. 800–500 B.C.: A Sourcebook* (London and New York: Routledge, 1990).

TEXTS OF GREEK AUTHORS IN ENGLISH TRANSLATION

Nearly all of the ancient Greek authors referenced in this book are available in readable, up-to-date English translations in the Penguin Classics series. Besides readability, a very attractive feature of the Penguins is their use of the same book and chapter numbers, and of book and line numbers for poetry, that are used in the scholarly ancient Greek (and Latin) editions and in all classical commentaries, dictionaries, encyclopedias, and other professional academic publications. This feature makes it easy for the reader to go back and forth between translation and relevant academic materials. Additionally, some of the Penguins are provided with introductions, brief commentaries, glossaries, and so on. Not a few represent the expert authoritative opinion of seasoned veteran scholars in the author or subject in question.

For readers, classicist as well as nonclassicist, with an interest in the original Greek or Latin text (as well as needing an English translation), the Loeb Classical Library is without peer. A century in the making, the LCL has now reached 500 volumes, and virtually every major author is represented, including all referenced in the present book. Fragmentary authors are usually collected by genre under titles such as Greek Lyric Poetry, Greek Epigrams, and so on. Many are equipped with scholarly notations on the manuscripts, interpretive footnotes, authoritative introductions, and the occasional Appendix. As classical scholarship progresses, the publisher, Harvard University Press, continues to reissue some of the older versions with fresh translations and supporting materials. As with the Penguins, many of the Loebs represent the work of leading classicists, and they are held in high regard by professional academics.

GENERAL REFERENCE WORKS

Among reference works in English, the *Oxford Classical Dictionary,* now in its third edition (1996), does the best job of combining authoritative opinion with accessibility for the nonprofessional; at 1,640 pages, it covers nearly every subject touched upon in the present volume. Although the prior editions still possess value, the third introduces many new topics reflecting the experience and interests of today's world. Differing in its arrangement in 32 topical chapters is the *Oxford History of the Classical World* (1986), like the OCD the work of many of leading scholars of the Anglo-American classical community. For those in search of exhaustive collections of ancient sources, with references to the scholarly secondary literature, the Pauly-Wissowa *Real-Encyclopaedie der klassischen Alterturmswissenschaft,* begun late in the nineteenth century, is now available in an abridged English-language edition under the title *Brill's New Pauly: Encylopaedia of the Ancient World* (Amsterdam various dates). Unlike the two Oxford publications, however, even the abridged *Pauly* is massive in bulk and unlikely to be found outside a major academic or public library.

ATLASES

Many atlases of the classical world, of varying design, are available. Standard (as well as recent) is R.J.A. Talbert, *Barrington Atlas of the Greek and Roman World* (Princeton, N.J.: Princeton University Press, 2000). Also recommended are Robert Morkot's *Penguin Historical Atlas of Ancient Greece* (London and New York: Penguin, 1996); Michael Grant's *Atlas of Classical History* (New York: Oxford University Press, 1994) and *Routledge Atlas of Classical History* (London: Routledge, 1994); and Richard Talbert's *Atlas of Classical History* (New York: Macmillan, 1985).

CITIES OF ANCIENT GREECE

For an authoritative encyclopedic gazetteer of the ancient Greek city, every academic library should have Mogens H. Hansen and Thomas H. Nielsen's *An Inventory of Archaic and Classical Poleis* (Oxford: Oxford University Press, 2004). Running to 1,396 large, densely packed pages, the *Inventory* is arranged by region and catalogues a total of 1,035 city-states (out of an original estimated 1,500). Each entry is equipped with references to ancient sources and to the scholarly secondary literature. Hansen's Introduction covers preliminarily matters of definition, typology, and source materials and, at 150 pages, constitutes a major book in itself. Supporting the *Inventory* are the many monographs on the Greek city-state previously issued by The Copenhagen Polis Centre, which conducted the project under Hansen and Nielsen's direction. Any reader pursuing an interest in a particular city-state could hardly do better than to begin with the entry in the *Inventory.*

Athens, inevitably the primary focus of attention in virtually any topical study of ancient Greece, has been very well covered in English-language publications that are at once authoritative and accessible. Again, a good place to begin is the entry in the *Inventory,* in this case written by Hansen himself under the heading "Attika," pp. 624–642. For an overview of the archaeology of the city, a good choice would be R. E. Wycherley's *The Stones of Athens* (Princeton, N.J.: Princeton University Press, 1978). The technical reports, written by archaeologists, on the American excavation of the Agora can be found in the periodical *Hesperia*, the journal of the American School of Classical Studies in Athens. Ancient references to the Agora are collected and translated by Wycherley in *The Athenian Agora: Literary and Epigraphical Testimonia*, vol. 3 (Princeton, N.J.: Princeton University Press, 1957), while other volumes in the Agora series present the results of the excavations (architecture, pottery, inscriptions, coins, and so on) for use by the specialist. Wycherley and Homer A. Thompson's *The Agora of Athens*, vol. 14, summarizes the excavations up to the time of its publication date, in 1972. More recent is John M. Camp's *The Athenian Agora: Excavations in the Heart of Classical Athens* (New York: Thames and Hudson, 1986). For a readable, yet detailed, discussion of the classical port city, the standard treatment in English is R. Garland's *The Piraeus: From the Fifth to the First Century B.C.* (Ithaca, N.Y.: Cornell University Press, 1987).

For Sparta, Graham Shipley's article "Lakedaimon" in the *Inventory*, pp. 569–598, covers the region with Sparta itself, no. 345, at pp. 587–594. Authoritative and accessible are W. G. Forrest, *A History of Sparta 950–192 B.C.*, 2nd ed. (London: Hutchinson, 1968); P. Cartledge, *Sparta and Lakonia: A Regional History 1300–362 B.C.*, 2nd ed. (London and New York: Routledge, 2002), and Cartledge, with Anthony Spawforth, *Hellenistic and Roman Sparta: A Tale of Two Cities* (London and New York: Routledge, 1989). Valuable are the relevant chapters in Anton Powell's *Athens and Sparta: Constructing Greek Political and Social History from 478 B.C.* (London and New York: Routledge, 1988).

For Macedonia, Miltiades Hatzopoulos and Paschalis Paschidis treat "Makedonia" at pp. 794–809 in the *Inventory*. Free-standing histories include N.G.L. Hammond's detailed and scholarly *A History of Macedonia*, vol. 1 (Oxford: Oxford University Press, 1972) and R. M. Errington, *History of Macedonia* (Berkeley and Los Angeles: University of California Press, 1990). More accessible are Eugene Borza's *In the Shadow of Olympus: The Emergence of Macedon* (Princeton, N.J.: Princeton University Press, 1990); Borza, with Beryl Barr-Sharrar, *Macedonia and Greece in Late Classical and Early Hellenistic Times* (Washington, DC: National Gallery of Art, 1982); and Borza, with W. Lindsay Adams, *Philip II, Alexander the Great, and the Macedonia Heritage* (Washington, DC: University Press of America, 1982).

"From Syria to the Pillars of Herakles," pp. 1233–1249 in the *Inventory,* treats Egypt at pp. 1234–1235. The Ptolemaic period is the subject of P. M. Fraser's *Ptolemaic Alexandria* (Oxford: Oxford University Press, 1972) and R. S. Bianchi's *Cleopatra's Egypt* (Brooklyn, N.Y.: Brooklyn Museum, 1988). Among many treatments of Cleopatra, notable are Stanley M. Burstein, *Reign of Cleopatra* (Westport, Conn.: Greenwood, 2004); Michael Grant, *Cleopatra* (New York: Dorset, 1992); Susan Walker and Sally-Ann Ashton, *Cleopatra* (London: Bristol Classical Press, 2006); Diana E. E. Kleiner, *Cleopatra and Rome* (Cambridge, Mass.: Harvard University Press, 2005); and Prudence J. Jones, *Cleopatra: A Sourcebook* (Norman: University of Oklahoma Press, 2006).

TELEVISION PROGRAMS, DOCUMENTARIES, EDUCATIONAL FILMS

Many productions relevant to our subject have aired on cable stations and are in many cases available in VHS or DVD format from commercial online outlets. Particularly germane here are:

In the Footsteps of Alexander the Great (PBS 1997)
Foot Soldiers: The Greeks (A&E 1998)
The Greeks: Crucible of Civilization (PBS 1999 and 2000)
Athens and Ancient Greece (Questar Video 2000)
Rise and Fall of the Spartans (History Channel 2000)

ELECTRONIC SOURCES

Classics and ancient Greek history are no less blessed than other academic fields with an abundance of electronic online sources—textual, archival, and pictorial. Fortunately for the user of this book, a very handy and easy-to-use collection of sites has already been assembled by the American Philological Association at its own Web site under the title "Electronic Resources for Classicists: The Second Generation." A professional classicist or other academic will easily find his or her way around this well-organized collection, but for the benefit of the reader new to my discipline and unfamiliar with its terminology I offer here a brief list of the sites most relevant to politics and society in ancient Greece. (For creators of the various sites and other details, please visit the APA register.)

Overviews, Meta-sites, Gateways

Ancient Near East
Classics and Mediterranean Archaeology
Kirke
The On-Line Survey of Audio-Visual Resources for Classics

The Library of Congress Classics Resources Home Page

Atrium: includes updates of TV programs on the ancient world
Canon of Greek Authors and Works
Classical Drama Sites
Databases, Web Projects, and Information Servers

Diotima: resources for study of women and gender in the ancient world
The Perseus Project: various classical subjects, including ancient Greek history

Bibliographies, Indexes, Reviews

Bryn Mawr Classical Review
Bryn Mawr Electronic Resources Review
Classics Search Engines
Database of Classical Bibliography
Greek Sites on the Internet
Histos: A journal of ancient historiography
Internet Resources
UCLA Library Collections and Internet Resources in Classical and Byzantine Studies

Classical Journals: Home Pages

Arethusa
Arion
Classical Antiquity
Classical Journal
Classical Review
Histos
New England Classical Journal
Phoenix

Pictorials, Images, Visuals

The Beazley Archive
Diotima Images
Dr. J's Illustrated Greek Sites and Lectures: created by Dr. Janice Siegel
The Getty Museum
Greek Language and Archaeology at the University of Indiana
The Kelsey Museum of Archaeology
Literacy and Orality
Maecenas: Images of Ancient Greece and Rome
Mythological Images

Schools, Centers, Projects, Initiatives: Home Pages

American School of Classical Studies at Athens
Center for Hellenic Studies
Corinth Computer Project

Notes

CHAPTER ONE

1. Mogens Herman Hansen and Thomas Heine Nielsen, *An Inventory of Archaic and Classical* Poleis (New York: Oxford University Press, 2004).

2. John S. Traill, *Persons of Ancient Athens* (Toronto: Athenians, 1992).

3. For a more complete discussion, see Nicholas F. Jones, *Rural Athens under the Democracy* (Philadelphia: University of Pennsylvania Press, 2004), pp. 240–245.

4. *Phaedo,* 230d.

CHAPTER THREE

1. Thucydides, 1.10.2.

2. Plutarch, *Life of Lycurgus,* 6.1–2.

3. Thucydides, 4.80.3–4.

4. Plutarch, *Life of Lycurgus,* 28.1–4.

5. Plutarch, *Life of Lycurgus,* 8.1–4.

6. Plutarch, *Life of Lycurgus,* 9.1–2.

7. Plutarch, *Life of Lycurgus,* 13.1; 19,1; 20.1–4; 21.1.

8. Plutarch, *Life of Lycurgus,* 16.1–2.

9. Plutarch, *Life of Lycurgus,* 16.2.

10. Plutarch, *Life of Lycurgus,* 16.4.

11. Plutarch, *Life of Lycurgus,* 15.1–2.

12. Plutarch, *Life of Lycurgus,* 17.1–4.

13. Plutarch, *Life of Lycurgus,* 18.1.

14. Plutarch, *Life of Lycurgus,* 10.1–2, 12.2.

15. Plutarch, *Life of Lycurgus,* 18.4.

16. Plutarch, *Life of Lycurgus,* 22.1–2.

17. Plutarch, *Life of Lycurgus,* 14.2.

18. Plutarch, *Sayings of Spartan Women,* 240F.

19. Plutarch, *Sayings of Spartan Women,* 241A.

20. Plutarch, *Sayings of Spartan Women,* 241B.

21. Plutarch, *Sayings of Spartan Women,* 241C.

22. Plutarch, *Sayings of Spartan Women,* 241F.

23. Plutarch, *Sayings of Spartan Women,* 241F.

24. Plutarch, *Sayings of Spartan Women,* 242C.
25. Plutarch, *Sayings of Spartan Women,* 242C.
26. Plutarch, *Sayings of Spartan Women,* 242D.
27. Aristotle, *Politics,* 2.6.7–11, esp. 11.
28. Plutarch, *Life of Lycurgus,* 14.1.

CHAPTER FOUR

1. *Constitution of the Athenians,* chapters 63–65.

CHAPTER FIVE

1. *FGrH* 115 F 89.
2. 27.3.
3. *Life of Cimon,* 10.1–6.
4. *Characters,* 4.
5. *Acharnians,* 27–39.
6. Herodotus, 5.71.1.
7. Thucycides, 8.54.4.
8. *Against Konon,* 54 (see esp. ch. 4).

CHAPTER SIX

1. Herodotus, 5.72.3–4.
2. Herodotus, 8.41.1–3.
3. *Lysistrata,* 506–514.
4. *Lysistrata,* 516–521.
5. *Lysistrata,* 521–522.
6. *Lysistrata,* 571–586.
7. *Women at the Thesmophoria,* 1160–1169.
8. *Women at the Thesmophoria,* 276–278, 279–281, 292–294.
9. *Women at the Thesmophoria,* 331–341, 349–351.
10. *Women at the Thesmophoria,* 383–394, 428–432.
11. Plutarch, *Life of Pericles,* 24.3–6.

CHAPTER SEVEN

1. *Life of Solon,* 1.1–4.
2. *Merriam Webster's Collegiate Dictionary,* 10th ed. (Springfield, Mass.: Merriam-Webster, 1994), p. 670.
3. *Life of Themistocles,* 1.1–2.
4. *Life of Themistocles,* 3.1–4.
5. *Life of Pericles,* 7.1–5.
6. Thucydides, 6.16–18, especially 16.1–3.

CHAPTER EIGHT

1. *Constitution of the Athenians,* 28.3.
2. Plut. *Cons. Apoll.* 6.105a.
3. Thucydides, 1.95.
4. Thucydides, 1.130.
5. Thucydides, 1.131.
6. Thucydides, 1.132–134.
7. *Life of Pelopidas,* 3–4.
8. *Life of Alexander,* 2.4–5.
9. *Life of Antony,* 26.1–28.1.

Further Readings

CHAPTER 2

An excellent translation of Aristotle's *The Athenian Constitution,* with introduction, notes, and other aids, is by P. J. Rhodes in the Penguin Classics series (1984). Aristotle's *Politics* is widely available in English, but it is largely concerned with theory and its more specific content frequently relates to Greek cities other than Athens. The thousands of Athenian inscriptions underlying much of the discussion are generally not available in English (the exceptions being a few major laws or decrees of mostly historical significance) and require advanced reading knowledge of ancient Greek. For the Agora, in and around which the organs of the Athenian democracy were physically seated, see R. E. Wycherley's *The Athenian Agora: Literary and Epigraphical Testimonia* (Princeton, N.J.: Princeton University Press, 1957) and his and Homer A. Thompson's *The Agora of Athens* (Princeton, N.J.: Princeton University Press, 1972). More narrowly archaeological is John M. Camp's *The Athenian Agora: Excavations in the Heart of Classical Athens* (New York: Thames and Hudson, 1986).

Interpretations of the Athenian constitution and of Athenian politics are available in abundance. A keyword search will produce dozens of recent titles in accessible, readable English. This chapter (and much that follows) draws in part upon the author's own book publications: *Public Organization in Ancient Greece* (Philadelphia: American Philosophical Society, 1987), a comprehensive study of the internal constitutional segmentations of Athens and the other 200 city-states for which we have evidence; *Ancient Greece: State and Society* (Upper Saddle River, N.J.: Prentice-Hall, 1997); *The Associations of Classical Athens. The Response to Democracy* (New York: Oxford University Press, 1999); and *Rural Athens Under the Democracy* (Philadelphia: University of Pennsylvania Press, 2004).

CHAPTER 3

For Plutarch's *Life of Lycurgus,* see vol. 1 in the Loeb edition of the *Parallel Lives* (Cambridge, Mass.: Harvard University Press, 1959); for his essays "Sayings of Spartans," "The Ancient Customs of the Spartans," and "Sayings of Spartan Women," see vol. III of the Loeb edition of the *Moralia* (Cambridge,

Mass.: Harvard University Press, 1961). For more recent translations of the same writings, see "Plutarch on Sparta" in the Penguin Classics series (2005). Among the voluminous secondary literature, especially pertinent to the presentation here is E. N. Tigerstedt's *The Legend of Sparta in Classical Antiquity,* 3 vols. (Stockholm: Almqvist and Wilksell, 1965–1978). Among traditional historical (and political) narratives, notable are W. G. Forrest, *A History of Sparta 950–192 B.C.,* 2nd ed. (London: Hutchinson, 1968); P. Cartledge, *Sparta and Lakonia: A Regional History, 1300–362 B.C.,* 2nd ed. (London and New York: Routledge, 2002); and A. Powell, *Athens and Sparta: Constructing Greek Political and Social History from 478 B.C.* (London and New York: Routledge, 1988). Sarah B. Pomeroy's *Spartan Women* (Oxford and New York: Oxford University Press, 2002) is the definitive study of its subject.

CHAPTER 4

The principal ancient source for the subjects of this chapter is Aristotle's *The Athenian Constitution,* available in English translation with introduction and notes by P. J. Rhodes in the Penguin Classics series (London: Penguin, 1984). Many translations of Plato's *Apology* are also available. The Penguin *The Last Days of Socrates,* translated by Hugh Tredennick (1954, revised 1969), includes as well the other dialogues concerning the trial, *Euthyphro, Crito,* and *Phaedo.* D. M. MacDowell's *The Law in Classical Athens* (Ithaca, N.Y.: Cornell University Press, 1978) has a chapter on courtroom procedure. More densely documented is A.R.W. Harrison, *The Law of Athens,* two vols. (Oxford: Oxford University Press, 1968, 1971). Physical remains are collected and interpreted in the *Athenian Agora* series of volumes, especially *Ostraka* (edited by Mabel Lang; Princeton, N.J.: Princeton University Press, 1990), *The Lawcourts at Athens* (edited by Alan L. Boegehold; Princeton, N.J.: Princeton University Press, 1995), and, covering all the relevant material from the square, R. E. Wycherley and Homer A. Thompson, *The Agora of Athens* (Princeton, N.J.: Princeton University Press, 1972).

CHAPTER 5

Since, as we have seen from the beginning, public life was dominated entirely by males, almost any account of, say, politics in classical Athens, is ipso facto an account of the politics of "the world of men." For some of the specific topics covered in this chapter, the following can be recommended: David Whitehead, *The Demes of Attica 508/7-ca. 250 B.C.: A Political and Social Study* (Princeton, N.J.: Princeton University Press, 1986); Nicholas F. Jones, *The Associations of Classical Athens: The Response to Democracy* (New York: Oxford University Press, 1999); *Rural Athens under the Democracy* (Philadelphia: University of Pennsylvania Press, 2004); and, on the symposium, Oswyn Murray, ed., *Sympotica* (New York: Oxford University Press, 1990).

CHAPTER 6

Ancient sources are conveniently collected in Mary R. Lefkowitz and Maureen B. Fant, *Women's Life in Greece and Rome,* 3rd ed. (Baltimore: Johns Hopkins

University Press, 2005). Among several standard accounts, still useful is Sarah B. Pomeroy's *Goddesses, Whores, Wives, and Slaves: Women in Classical Antiquity* (New York: Schocken, [1975] 1995). Statements made here about women in the rural villages summarize scholarly presentation in Nicholas F. Jones, *The Associations of Classical Athens: The Response to Democracy* (New York: Oxford University Press, 1999), and Jones, *Rural Athens under the Democracy* (Philadelphia: University of Pennsylvania Press, 2004).

CHAPTER 7

The *Lives* of Plutarch are available in Greek with facing English translation in the Loeb Classical Library series (*Parallel Lives*) and in contemporary English only in the Penguin Classics. Library or Internet searches by politician's name will yield references to many modern (and accessible) scholarly or popular biographical accounts.

CHAPTER 8

The *Lives* of Plutarch are available in Greek with facing English translation in the Loeb Classical Library series (*Parallel Lives*) and in contemporary English only in the Penguin Classics. Library or Internet searches by name of political figure will yield references to many modern (and accessible) scholarly or popular biographical accounts.

Index

ABOUT THE AUTHOR

NICHOLAS F. JONES is Professor of Classics, University of Pittsburgh. He is the author of four books on Greek social and political history.